Education with Characte

The establishment of citizenship education as a compulsory subject has recently been accompanied by the government's policy of 'promoting education with character'. Schools are identified as having a crucial role to play in helping to shape and reinforce basic character traits that will ultimately lead to a better society. This radical new policy is explicitly linked to raising academic standards and to the needs of the emerging new economy.

This book provides an introduction to character education within the British context by exploring its meanings, understandings and rationale, through the perspective of a number of academic disciplines. The author examines character education from a philosophical, religious, psychological, political, social and economic perspective to offer a more detailed understanding of character education and what it can offer. He also considers how British schools can implement character education successfully and what lessons we can draw from the American experience.

This book will be of interest to academics, researchers, policymakers and teachers with responsibility for citizenship education in their schools.

James Arthur is Professor of Education and Head of Educational Research at Canterbury Christ Church University College. His publications include *Social Literacy, Citizenship Education and the National Curriculum* (RoutledgeFalmer, 2001) and *Schools and Community* (RoutledgeFalmer, 1999).

Education with Character
The moral economy of schooling

James Arthur

RoutledgeFalmer
Taylor & Francis Group

LONDON AND NEW YORK

First published 2003 by RoutledgeFalmer
11 New Fetter Lane, London EC4P 4EE

Simultaneously published in the USA and Canada
by RoutledgeFalmer
29 West 35th Street, New York, NY 10001

RoutledgeFalmer is an imprint of the Taylor and Francis Group

© 2003 James Arthur

Typeset in Goudy by GreenGate Publishing Services, Tonbridge, Kent

British Library Cataloguing in Publication Data
A catalogue record for this book is available from the British Library

Library of Congress Cataloging in Publication Data
A catalog record for this book has been requested

ISBN 0–415–27779–5 (pbk)
ISBN 0–415–27778–7 (hbk)

In Memoriam
Rose Margaret Arthur
27th June 1932–30th May 2001

Contents

Acknowledgements

In the course of writing this book I have been assisted by a number of friends and colleagues both in Britain and the USA. I would like to offer my sincere thanks to Professor Karen Bohlin, director of Boston University's Centre for the Advancement of Ethics and Character who allowed me access to the applications of the winners of the National Character Award for 1999–2001 together with the use of the Kevin Ryan Library in Boston. She was also kind enough to read through the final manuscript and offer useful comments and suggestions. I would like to thank the Department for Education and Skills for providing me with access to some of the responses to the consultations on the Green Paper, *Schools: Building on Success* (February 2001).

I wish to record my appreciation to Dr Richard Bailey, Professor Jon Davison, Dr Simon Gaine, Dr Lynn Revell and John Spencer for reading parts of the early drafts of this book and offering suggestions. I would particularly like to thank John Upton for assisting me with the final editing of the text. I would also like to thank Professor Gerald Grace and Professor Karen Bohlin for writing the forewords to this book. All those who have offered suggestions or comments are of course not responsible for any of the opinions expressed here or for any of the book's flaws, for which I alone am responsible.

Preface

My interest in character education extends back to my preparation for teaching and continues with my current role in the education of future teachers. However, it became more focused when I was involved as a member of the National Forum for Values in Education and the Community in 1996. As a participant in the discussions which led to the Statement of Values which the Forum issued in 1997, I grew increasingly interested in how character and citizenship education could provide schools with a 'new' way of thinking about moral education. In 1998 I was invited by Professor Amitai Etzioni to give an address to the fifth annual White House/Congressional Conference on Character Building in Washington DC. I found myself on the same platform as Nick Tate, the then director of the Qualifications and Curriculum Authority (QCA). It was clear then that Tate was also interested in character education, principally from a virtues perspective. On my return to Britain I participated in various consultations with QCA about spiritual and moral education, became a member of the History Task Group in 1999 to revise the History National Curriculum, and have since been a member of a sub-group of the Citizenship Working Party as well as a member of groups on citizenship in the Department for Education and Skills and the Teacher Training Agency. As a result of my involvement in policy development I had access to discussions and information that helped me in 2000 to write parts of *Schools and Community: The Communitarian Agenda in Education* (RoutledgeFalmer) in which I suggested that character education was part of the educational agenda of New Labour. It was therefore no surprise to me that in the following year the government published its Green and White Papers which detail how it seeks to promote 'education with character'. Of course, no one will say that they do not believe in education with character, but what educational meaning do they give this phrase? This book has been written as an introduction to this important development in educational policy and aims to explore the imprecise meanings often attributed to character education from different perspectives.

James Arthur
Canterbury, April 2002

British foreword

It is ironic that 'education with character', which is the subject of this book, has a history and a cultural lineage which causes many people to react negatively to the very idea. For these critics, 'education with character' is simply a modern recontextualization of an older and flawed concept of character education about which they are deeply sceptical. From this perspective the project of character education is compromized by its historical associations with various forms of religious and moral indoctrination of the young. Others have a sharp awareness that character education (or more correctly 'schooling') was the defining feature of a class-based cultural system in England in which 'public-school character' was constructed for a leadership class and 'respectable character' was used as a social control device for the working class. These negative, in modern times by the obvious appropriation of character education in political ideologies such as Fascism and Communism in imperialist projects for the building of new social orders.

However, as James Arthur argues in this scholarly, lucid and balanced text, we can hardly abandon the quest for a defensible and liberal form of education with character simply because of these historical and political distortions. What we (parents, teachers and students) have to try to do is to construct an education with character which promotes the formation of 'good persons' and 'good citizens' (with the widest consensus possible in a pluralist society) while at the same time respecting the personal integrity of young people. If character education is not to become a person-dominating strategy of State, Church, community or ideological group, then a complex and sensitive matrix of educational principles and practices, relevant to a pluralist and democratic society, has to be evolved. This is a major challenge involving as it does some attempted integration of the educational cultures of home, community and school, and some necessary dialogue with powerful external agents of cultural formation such as the mass media. The great value of Professor Arthur's book is not that he gives us the answer to this major challenge of 'what sort of character education is needed?' but that he provides the critical materials for all of us to try to construct an education with character that will enhance virtue while eschewing moral conditioning.

Of all the definitions of character given in this book the one that speaks to me most powerfully is that of Ernest Hull SJ: 'Character is life dominated by principles, as distinguished from life dominated by mere impulses from within and mere circumstances from without.' But, as James Arthur points out in this comprehensive and thoughtful study, such an insight is only the starting point for the education with character project. What we still have to do in contemporary conditions, by dialogue and by practice, is to seek answers to the crucial questions raised here. What are the principles which characterize the good life in a pluralist and democratic society, and how, through liberal projects of education with character, can we encourage their formation?

This book will assist all those who recognize that such questions are fundamental for the future of education and for the emergence of the good society.

Professor Gerald Grace
Institute of Education, University of London, May 2002

American foreword

A comprehensive and unrivaled interdisciplinary review of character education, James Arthur's *Education with Character: The Moral Economy of Schooling* offers instructive insights for educators and policymakers not only in Britain but in the United States as well. All readers will benefit from Arthur's challenge to consider the moral and intellectual principles that inform various conceptions of character and its formation. *Education with Character* is a timely and important book worthy of serious engagement.

Considering that the American people have been clamoring for a return to a focus on character and ethics in public schools for over a decade, the relevance of Professor Arthur's work is undeniable. Moreover, the depth of insight that *Education with Character* offers may be precisely what is lacking in American discourse on the subject. While there is general agreement about the need for character education, there is little consensus – and arguably understanding – regarding the various theories and principles that give shape to character education in American public schools.

In the United States as in Britain, it has been traditionally understood that individuals need to possess certain virtues to be capable of self-government. Laws and institutions can sanction and control human action, but they cannot make a person virtuous. Fear of sanction does not engender loyalty or honesty. Nor does functioning well politically – savvy with respect to democratic processes – constitute civic virtue. Virtuous individuals are not charlatans or performers, politically astute and socially savvy but morally bankrupt. Schooling within a democracy has to embrace on some level both an intellectual and moral vision of education. As James Arthur suggests: 'The quality of political life in a democracy is largely determined by the quality and character of its people.'

This link was well understood in early American education, which was viewed primarily as a moral endeavor. The development of intellect and character was central to the enterprise of learning. Because virtue was considered a means to sustain 'the body politic', a direct approach to moral instruction prevailed. Students were taught Scripture and moral adages. By 1836 the *McGuffey Reader*, a more secular resource, became the mainstay of the American curriculum. Rich in moral tales, selected Bible stories, exhortations and moving accounts of heroism and patriotism, this reader presented students with images of a virtuous life on a daily basis.

Twentieth-century social Darwinism and the increasing emphasis on the scientific method gradually led to a break with earlier moral and philosophical traditions. Morals and values, formerly a staple in the American public-school curriculum, were drawn into the private realm. And virtue, both in the classical and Christian sense, began losing ground in public education.

The anti-establishment movement and the sexual revolution of the 1960s intensified the segregation of objective moral values from schooling. Morality and traditional ideals were questioned, and perhaps rightly so. Growing consciousness of racism, segregation and unequal opportunity for women, followed by spirited disagreement over the war in Vietnam, gave rise to the gradual erosion of what had previously been regarded as a consensus on traditional and shared American ideals.

Moral authority, once vested firmly in both schools and teachers, receded dramatically. Teachers distanced themselves from students' moral development and attempted to become neutral facilitators, leaving students free to arrive at their own values and to figure out some of life's toughest questions without guidance. They were encouraged to view society's traditions of civility and ideals with skepticism and even scorn. As a result, civic and moral education were severed from one another – a severance that largely continues to the present day.

Yet perhaps general dissatisfaction with this approach indicates the astuteness of Arthur's insistence on the need to reconnect civic and moral education in a pluralistic society. James Arthur's *Education with Character* reminds educational leaders that a child's character is inevitably influenced by the ethical standards implicitly or explicitly taught in schools and challenges them to think more consciously about the values they seek to promote. Arthur's book aptly focuses on the contribution of virtue ethics, not merely as a philosophical perspective but as a point of entry into the question of what it means to live well in public and private life. Arthur penetrates the classical and modern notions of virtue and draws from a wide range of disciplines to provide a more complete vision of how character is formed. *Education with Character* offers a fresh and nuanced perspective for educators, who believe with him that 'family and school are at the heart of the moral economy for they, especially when operating together, hold out the best possibility of nurturing in the child the ability to transcend self-interest and to regard the interests of others as in some way their own' (pp. 146–7).

This book will stimulate both American and British policymakers to bring intellectual dialogue on character education to a new level. As Arthur suggests, 'education with character' should not be reduced to a widely popularized movement or a narrow political agenda. Character education – the result of home, school, and community working together – should seek to cultivate the practical intelligence and moral insight students need to author their own choices. To act in ways consistent with the ideals of democracy, students need an ability to make informed decisions based on thoughtful deliberation and to engage in dialogue that addresses the underlying principles that inform political arguments. Schools must teach students to pursue the truth, not simply the lowest common denominator. Such an education will enable students to judge and critique those customs, social institutions and laws that hinder both their own and others' civic or moral development, and to support laws and institutions that sustain a healthy moral economy.

Professor Karen E. Bohlin
Executive Director, Center for the Advancement of Ethics and Character, Boston University

1   Character and the litany of alarm

Character is simply habit long continued.

Plutarch

To emphasise the idea of character is to recognise that our actions are also acts of self-determination; in them we not only reaffirm what we have been but also determine what we will be in the future. By our actions we not only shape a particular situation, we also form ourselves to meet future situations in a particular way. Thus the concept of character implies that moral goodness is primarily a prediction of persons and not acts, and that this goodness of persons is not automatic but must be acquired and cultivated.

Stanley Hauerwas (1981: 49)

One of the most significant ethical developments during the past two decades has been a deepening concern for character. We are rediscovering the link between private character and public life. We are coming to see that our societal problems reflect, in no small measure, our personal vices. Scholarly discussion, media analysis, and everyday conversation have all focused attention on the character of our elected leaders, our fellow citizens, and our children.

Thomas Lickona (1991: 49)

To enter on a discussion about character and, even more, about character education is to enter a minefield of conflicting definition and ideology. It is rare indeed to find an educational topic about which there is so much fundamental disagreement. The only generally agreed position seems to be acknowledgement of its importance.

There is, first, the question of how to define character: can there be said to exist such a thing as a regular and fixed set of habitual actions in a person that constitutes his or her character? A Marxist might regard character as a fluid entity determined by the power structure of the existing society; a Calvinist as an unvarying orientation decided by God. Various shades of psychological and psychiatric opinion would point to early socialization or lack of it as being responsible. Secular liberalism, long predominant in educational theory, looks to modification and reinforcement through discussion and persuasion. Character education is inherently a multidisciplinary endeavour, which requires its adherents and critics to ask divergent questions and employ disparate methods in approaching the subject.

Given the multifarious positions taken in respect of character, it follows that the discussion about character education, and whether it is possible, is equally discordant. The variety of approaches results in a bewildering variety of educational schemes and curricula. This may be seen as a positive phenomenon potentially resulting in concrete classroom solutions, or perhaps as a wasteful overlapping of character education resources. James Leming (1993a) believes that this diversity of academic opinion hampers effective development of character education as a school subject. He says that: 'the current research in the field consists of disparate bits and pieces of sociology, philosophy, child development research, socio-political analysis, and a variety of different programmes of evaluation'. It has proved a difficult task for teachers and academics to arrive at a clear and workable definition of character, and more particularly, character education.

Why, then, enter this minefield? In short, because it is important. 'Character education' is a rapidly growing movement. In the USA there has been a proliferation of organizations, courses, literature and curriculum materials seeking to promote character education. The New Labour government in the UK, with its heavily moralistic ethos, has taken up the baton. The establishment of citizenship education as a compulsory subject has been accompanied by the Green Paper, *Schools: Building on Success* (February 2001) and the White Paper, *Schools: Achieving Success* (September 2001). The latter speaks at length of 'education with character'. The goal of this 'education with character' appears to be to instil certain virtues so that they become internal principles guiding both the pupil's behaviour and decision-making for operation within a democracy. It is intimately connected with citizenship.

Given the generally agreed importance of the topic, it is the aim of this book to review some of the existing work and its underlying assumptions in order to clarify the confusion of programmes currently in our schools. Such a task should not be approached without an honest statement of one's own position. First, that there is such a thing as character, an interlocked set of personal values which normally guide conduct. Character is about who we are and who we become, good and bad. Second, that this is not a fixed set easily measured or incapable of modification. Third, that choices about conduct are choices about 'right' or 'wrong' actions and thoughts. I believe that we can be active in shaping character in ourselves and in others. Character education is normally viewed as a specific approach to moral education. The argument is, that character education is not simply about the acquisition of social skills: it is ultimately about what kind of person a pupil will grow up to be. Whilst recognising the wide range of factors involved in the formation and expression of character, I intend this book to concentrate on moral aspects of the concept of character. The moral economy of schooling refers to how schools teach and develop character and how they establish norms to evaluate character. At the very least it is about organizing the school around a vision and ethos that links the ethical to the demands of public life.

The litany of alarm

Those who have advocated character education in America and Britain often present it as a response to a list of ills facing society which originate in the behaviour of juveniles. This list would normally include the following, which have all shown a stubborn increase despite many attempts by government, schools and welfare agencies to address their causes: suicides, especially of young males; teenage pregnancy and abortion; the crime rate, particularly theft by minors; alcohol and drug abuse; sexual activity and sexual abuse; teenage truancy and mental health problems. This teenage dysfunction has to be contextualized and set against a backdrop of family breakdown, domestic violence, poverty and the media's provision of an endless diet of violence and sex. Perhaps as a result of this, increasing numbers of children are arriving in early schooling showing symptoms of anxiety, emotional insecurity and aggressive behaviour. They seem devoid of many social skills and suffer low self-esteem. There are many reasons for the existence of these symptoms but they have a common effect in significantly reducing the ability of the school to develop positive character traits.

Thomas Lickona (1996) lists a further set of indicators of youth problems: dishonesty; peer cruelty; disrespect for adults and parents; self-centredness; self-destructive behaviour, and ethical illiteracy. Altruism often appears as the exception whilst self-interest has become the rule. The general moral relativism of society is also routinely blamed by character educators for this litany of social and moral breakdown, which is often referred to as a 'crisis in moral education' (see Kilpatrick 1992: 13f.). This moral relativism, it is claimed, has replaced the belief in personal responsibility with the notion of social causation. All of the social indicators above have increased rapidly since the 1960s and there is clear evidence, from a brief reading of *British Social Trends*, that the problems are increasing with greater rapidity. Gertrude Himmelfarb (1995: 222) details how the statistics concerning social ills (crime, drunkenness, illegitimacy, pauperism, vagrancy etc.) in England in the nineteenth century and early twentieth century were all recording some decline, but fails to mention that other problems such as divorce, drugs, teenage prostitution and suicide were not recorded at all. Whilst Himmelfarb praises Victorian virtues, she does not suggest a return to them.

Social statistics today are often claimed to be far worse than those of the Victorian era and, according to character educators, show how our situation is deteriorating. They point to the social statistics to be found in *British Social Trends* (2002), which indicate that schoolchildren and young people in the age range 14–24 commit the greatest number of crimes in Britain. This category has the highest abortion rate, together with being the largest user of illegal drugs. It is also the category (from age 18) that has the lowest participation rate in local and general elections. Some of the statistics for this group exceed the rates for abortion, teenage pregnancy and crime in most countries in Europe and in the USA. The virtual irrelevance of the central tenets of the Judeo–Christian moral tradition to the lives of most British young people is often considered another significant factor in the perceived decline in moral standards. Schoolchildren are also regularly exposed to explicit images in the media with the implicit message that sexual activity is the norm, while many parents and teachers are silent on the matter.

A criticism levelled at promoters of character education by certain commentators is that they do not examine sufficiently the complex issues that underlie many of the social statistics they detail. David Purpel (1997: 147) makes the point that 'Even if there has been a significant increase in teenage pregnancies there is still a question of why it is considered a moral transgression.' He asks which framework character educators use to criticize the degeneration they see around them. For Purpel, teenage pregnancy and divorce are not problems at all. Others would strongly argue that there never was a 'golden age', with every generation for the past two hundred years producing its own 'litany of alarm' and harking back to the good old days. Harry McKown (1935: 18–34), writing in America in the 1930s, provides his own litany. He bemoans the social break-up of the family (caused by economic pressures as opposed to marital difficulties); he decries the excessive individualism of the age; notes the decline in citizen participation in elections; abhors the 'tremendous increase in crime'; is saddened by fewer young people attending Church; is concerned by the negative effect of advertising on the young; and sees the implications for morality in everything from public dancing and smoking to the wearing by young people of 'types of close-to-nature clothing and bathing suits'.

Timothy Rusnak (1998: 1) believes that fear is the justification for many character education programmes in the USA. The same sense of 'fear' is perhaps justification for the Social Affairs Unit's publication in 1992 of *Loss of Virtue: moral confusion and social disorder in Britain and America* (Anderson 1992). Hyperbolic reaction to events often expresses itself as society-wide moral panic. The murder of James Bulger in 1993 was an example of this in Britain. The case involved two 10-year-old boys who captured, tortured and murdered a toddler in Liverpool. Their crime inspired a public debate about morality and character which was stimulated by the sensationalist tabloid press. Teachers at the boys' school were criticized for failing to instil a sense of morality in their pupils. The Church of England was also blamed for not enunciating moral principles clearly enough. The trial judge in his summing-up referred to a horror film called *Child's Play 3*, about a malevolent doll. The judge was struck by the similarities in the film to the method of the attack used by the boys on their victim. It was clear that someone, or something, had to be blamed – a scapegoat was needed. Although many found it difficult to accept that children could have been wholly responsible for this murder, the boys were found guilty and given long custodial sentences. But events such as these are not exclusive to our time. There are many such cases in the past. In 1954, for example, a 16-year-old British Boy Scout stabbed a 72-year-old woman to death with 29 blows because he was afraid she would discover his forgery of some Scouting certificates.

It is unlikely that an adequate working definition of character education for schools can be found by analysing extreme examples of child behaviour. Nor should efforts to control a child's destructive or extreme behaviour be held out as character education. The truly valuable function of the litany of alarm is to help us fix our attention on how effectively to address the social and moral problems of individuals and society.

The rediscovery of character education

Terry McLaughlin and Mark Halstead (1999: 136) take issue with contemporary approaches to character education in the USA, alongside two major critics of the movement in America – David Purpel (1997) and Robert Nash (1997). They claim, rightly, that American character educators generally begin with detailing the social ills of society and then offer character education as a remedy; that these character educators also believe that core values can be identified, justified and taught. In addition, they claim that character educators seek explicit teaching in the public schools of moral virtues, dispositions, traits and habits, to be inculcated through lesson content and the example of teachers, together with the ethos of the school and direct teaching, and measure the success of character education programmes by the changes in the behaviour of pupils. Character educators also, they claim, leave explaining difficult moral concepts until later in the pupil's development. McLaughlin and Halstead then criticize these views, arguing that character education is narrowly concerned with certain virtues, that it is restricted, limited and focuses on traditional methods of teaching; also, that there is a limited rationale given for the aims and purposes of character education by those who propose it in schools and that there is a restricted emphasis on the use of critical faculties in pupils. They observe the character education movement: 'lacks a common theoretical perspective and core of practice' (1999: 139).

Whilst McLaughlin and Halstead are reasonably sympathetic to character education, they paint a bleak picture of current practices in the USA. Above all, they fail to deal with Nash, whose language can often be extreme. Nash (1997) believes that most models of character education are deeply and seriously flawed, authoritarian in approach, too nostalgic, pre-modern in understanding of the virtues, aligned to reactionary politics, anti-intellectual, anti-democratic and above all dangerous. He seeks to replace this tradition of character education with one that is not based on any moral authority and lacks a common moral standard by which to evaluate competing moral vocabularies. McLaughlin and Halstead might have pointed out that he cannot condemn other competing moral vocabularies as he so obviously does from his own post-modern position. It appears that Nash refuses to acknowledge that all education rests on assumptions and beliefs and that a plurality of positions, including character education, can co-exist. Nash's main contribution to the debate is to emphasize the importance of intellectual enquiry in educating for character.

In the case of Purpel, McLaughlin and Halstead, they do not answer his claim (1997: 140) that character educators are 'disingenuous' in their debates about character education and that they are effectively a conservative political movement with a hidden agenda. In any event, there is no necessary connection between a conservative political outlook and character education. Many have believed in the possibility of perfecting man through the alteration of his environment, as this book illustrates and as can be demonstrated by the experiments in character education in nineteenth-century Britain (see chapter 2). The real issue for character education lies in rationale and justification and in finding an answer to the question of why some character educators associate the concept with virtue ethics.

David Brooks and Frank Goble (1997) in *The Case for Character Education* follow a standard structure of argument used by many who advocate school-based character education. As previously mentioned, Harry McKown (1935) was one of the first to develop a model of writing about character within the context of schooling, a framework which has since been adopted by many others. McKown's book defines character education, presents a 1930s litany of alarm, explains why we should have character education in schools, describes the objectives of such a programme, suggests how it should be in the curriculum, through the curriculum and as an extracurricular activity, how it should be in the home and community and how it might be assessed.

Brooks and Goble follow the same pattern. They first ask: what is wrong with kids? Their answer: 'They just don't seem to know the difference between right and wrong' (1997: 1). They then focus on pupil rates of crime, etc., detailing a litany of alarm. This leads to the conclusion that something needs to be done. They cite a lack of standards as the reason for the problem and offer character education as the solution. They attack all the other methods of moral education, ranging from values clarification to cognitive theories of development, and this is followed by the outlining of a number of teaching methods for character education. A virtue ethics approach to character education is suggested, but what this would entail for teaching in schools is never explained.

The book has a Foreword by the retired chief executive of the McDonnell Douglas Corporation (acting as chair of the Board of the Character Education Partnership) in which he emphasizes the idea of crisis in American society: 'Today in America we have far too many twelve-year-olds pushing drugs, four-teen-year-olds having babies, sixteen-year-olds killing in epidemic numbers. We have crime and violence everywhere, and unethical behaviour in business, the professions and in government.' The book appears to be an inadequate explanation of why schools should adopt character education programmes. Brooks and Goble ignore the effects of poverty, the lack of educational resources, particularly the absence of good teachers in some schools, and the effects of increased ethnic and religious diversity in school and society.

A more educationally relevant and realistic approach to character education is provided by Edward DeRoche and Mary Williams (2001: 165). They present a range of practical suggestions for designing and implementing a character education programme in school. They acknowledge that research into the effectiveness of character education is extremely limited and that what research there is does not provide much proof of any effectiveness at all. They draw on the review of character education research by James Leming (1993a) and agree with him that didactic teaching methods have no significant effect on character development and that the development of reason does not necessarily result in a related change of behaviour. DeRoche and Williams argue strongly in favour of individualized school-based character education programmes that are designed by the whole school community within a context of guiding pupils to pursue what is worthwhile and good in life. To the question of whose values or virtues should be taught they answer that they must have consensual allegiance in the community. They give emphasis to community, particularly the powerful influence of the ethos of a school on character development. They are not alone in emphasizing this area since others, such as Kevin Ryan and Karen Bohlin in their excellent text (1999), give very serious attention to character building in community, to which we will return in chapter 9. All of these books, whether consciously or not, follow a model which has its origins in McKown's 1935 seminal work and which was revived by Thomas Lickona's publication of *Educating for Character* in 1991.

It is important to stress that few in America or Britain would consider the school the most important location for character education, even if it remains the main public institution for the formal moral education of children. The mass media, religious communities, youth culture, peer groups, voluntary organizations, and above all parents and siblings, exert significant influences on character formation. It cannot be easily assumed that the school makes more of a difference than any of these. However, it would be reasonable to suggest that certain positive features of the school will contribute to character development. It is common in society to hold pupils responsible, not only for their behaviour, but also for their own character. Yet the burden of character education has inevitably been falling principally on the school. Obviously, some schools have the potential to be more effective than others at influencing character development. Some would argue that the ordinary state school has a more limited role and would need to open longer and for many more days in the year to have a greater effect on character formation. The 35 state boarding schools in Britain, in which children board near the school supervised by teachers, are perhaps more likely or have the potential to influence children's character development on the basis of increased time spent together. Private schools have traditionally made a virtue of this very point, but it does not necessarily follow that boarding school arrangements will influence character for the good. These schools, like any other, undoubtedly produce characters, but that they build ethical character is not ensured. Whilst there is no common definition of character education, it can be seen that its promoters believe that much of our current ethical relativism is unacceptable and that you can, through education, influence a child's character for the good. Character education promoters generally seek a stronger emphasis on a positive school ethos, increased academic work, viewing the teacher as moral authority and strengthening the role of parents in partnership with schools and teachers. Whilst some private schools may still attempt to promote a character-building ethos, parents may not necessarily share the values of this ethos in their family life. As parents increasingly consider their relationship with private schools as one of contractual service there is always the danger that the real influence on character formation within these schools may be peer group pressure. It is also significant that government policies on 'character education' and citizenship education do not apply to private schools.

In reviewing the diverse views of character educators in America A.T. Lockwood (1997: 179) develops a 'tentative' definition of character education, which is rather useful for this book. He defines character education as a school-based activity that seeks to systematically shape the behaviour of pupils – as he says: 'Character education is defined as any school-instituted program, designed in cooperation with other community institutions, to shape directly and systematically the behaviour of young people by influencing explicitly the non-relativistic values believed directly to bring about that behaviour.' He details three central propositions: first, that the goals of moral education can be pursued, not simply left to an uncontrolled hidden curriculum and that these goals should have a fair degree of public support and consensus; second, that behavioural goals are part of character education, and third, that antisocial behaviour on the part of children is a result of an absence of values. There is of course a presumed relationship here between values and behaviour.

I would add a fourth proposition: that many character educators not only seek to change behaviour, but actually seek to produce certain kinds of character. This is not to suggest a passive involvement on the part of the individual, but rather involves the individual's active and conscious participation in their own formation. Character education holds out the hope of what a person can be as opposed to what they are naturally. Character education is not the same as behaviour control, discipline, training or indoctrination; it is much broader and has much more ambitious goals. Whilst good character and good behaviour are similar, the former is broader in scope. Character is an inclusive term for the individual as a whole. Consequently, for many character educators 'character education' has much more to do with formation and the transformation of a person and includes education in schools and families, and through the individual's participation in social networks. A greater understanding of the relationship between parenting and character development is urgently needed. In the end it may well be impossible to provide a definition of character that captures all its meanings and its various uses in schooling and education.

Despite this the British government has effectively rediscovered character education. There seems to be a growing awareness in New Labour that effective policies for the many problems in education and in society can only be developed through a knowledge of the defects in character formation in families and schools. Recognizing that there is a broad-based and growing public support for 'moral education' in schools, the government aims to heighten national awareness of the importance of character education and encourage its development.

Schools are identified as having a crucial role to play in helping shape and reinforce basic character traits. This represents a new and radical government education policy and is a notion of character education that is explicitly linked to both raising pupil school performance and meeting the needs of the emerging new economy or information age. Character is above all about what people do. In this respect the government has moved the debate on to a much more explicitly behavioural dimension in education since character is often observable in one's conduct. The introduction of citizenship education is also identified as having a major role to play in reinforcing 'education with character' in schools. New Labour clearly have an ethical agenda for the reform of schooling in Britain.

The aim of this book is to provide an introduction to character education within the British context by exploring its meanings, understandings and rationale through the perspective of a number of academic disciplines. This descriptive exercise includes conceptual analysis and builds a more comprehensive picture of character education to allow for a more informed debate. It allows for the identification and cross-fertilisation of appropriate theories and theoretical frameworks arising out of the humanities and social sciences that relate to character education. The book asks what can be done in British schools and what lessons we can draw from the American experience. The book's focus is educational, but it also moves through some of the difficulties and possibilities for character education from within each of the disciplinary perspectives discussed. Each chapter will examine how a discipline uses character in its literature and how it differs from the uses of character in other disciplines.

In chapter 2 an overview of the history of character education in Britain is presented. Chapter 3 outlines one of the main philosophical rationales for character education by describing the virtue ethics approach. In chapter 4 the relationship between character and certain key theological concepts in the Judeo–Christian tradition is explored and reviewed, whilst in chapter 5 the uses and limitations of the cognitive development approach to character education are discussed in the context of a number of development theories. In chapter 6 the political context from left and right perspectives is examined and chapter 7 investigates the sociological basis or foundation for character education. Chapter 8 considers the relationship between the economy and character education and chapter 9 discusses some of the current educational practices in character education. Chapter 10 considers what makes a successful character programme in school and, by way of illustration, reviews some award-winning programmes in American schools. Finally, chapter 11 summarizes the recurrent themes in each chapter and offers some conclusions about the future of character education in Britain.

2 An historical perspective on character formation

To put the necessity of properly educating the children of the working classes on its lowest footing, it is loudly called for as a matter of police, to prevent a multitude of immoral and vicious beings, the offspring of ignorance, from growing up around us, to be a pest and a nuisance to society; it is necessary in order to render the great body of the working class governable by reason.

Leonard Horner, factory inspector, 1837
(quoted in Green 1990: 251)

Character is destiny.

George Eliot (1819–1880)

There were many eighteenth-century thinkers who advocated training in character and believed that the moral rather than the intellectual aims of education were the most important. James Barclay, for instance, urged that teachers should only be selected for the role if they had strong characters as he considered their example to be crucial. As he said: 'Example is allowed to be stronger than precept, and children especially are much readier to copy what they see than what they hear' (Hutchison 1976). Barclay was a member of the movement now known as the Scottish Enlightenment and many of his ideas were strikingly modern, including his opposition to rote learning and the importance he placed on the consideration of the influence of a child's home on his or her educational progress. Another Scot, David Fordyce, spoke of developing the child's imagination in moral matters and wrote that 'dull, formal lectures on several virtues and vices' were of no use in the formation of good character. Francis Hutcheson, professor of moral philosophy at the University of Glasgow in 1747, advocated greater study of character. He sought to 'search accurately into the constitution of our nature to see what sort of creatures we are' (*ibid*). What was needed, he argued, was an objective study of human nature, particularly a study of motives and behaviour. John Locke also believed that character formation was more important than intellectual attainment. There were those, however, who took a negative view of human character and doubted whether it could be developed for the good. Hannah More, a leading Protestant moralist of the eighteenth century, believed that infants were 'beings who bring into the world a corrupt nature, and evil disposition, which it should be the great end of education to rectify' (see Jones 1952). Attempts at this type of rectification manifested themselves in schools through strict discipline, punishments and rote learning and were misapplied, particularly to the poor as a form of social control rather than character development.

Character education at New Lanark

The formation of character could be said to be the aim that all general education has historically set out to achieve. It is an aim that has often not been explicitly stated: it has simply been assumed. This has been the prevailing story of British education. There have been early exceptions, one being the Institution for the Formation of Character established by Robert Owen in 1816. Robert Owen was an industrialist, social theorist and educational pioneer. Beside his factory in New Lanark, Scotland, he built a 'school', which opened on 1 January 1816 with the title 'Institution for the Formation of Character'. The Institution taught school-aged children during the day and adults by night. It had public halls, community rooms and the first ever nursery school, which Owen called a 'playground'. Owen was also the first to argue that teachers should be trained, by the State if necessary explicitly to promote character education. It is therefore worthwhile reviewing his educational ideas on the subject.

Owen was a utilitarian and believed that the best possible training was required for people to live the good life. He sought the formation of a good community. This required the formation of good characters. As he said in his *Essays on the Formation of Character* in 1813, three years before the Institution was opened: 'the essence of national training and education is to impress on the young ideas and habits which shall contribute to the future happiness of the individual and the State; and this can be accomplished only by instructing them to become rational beings'. Owen, believing in the importance of early education, not by ignorant parents but by trained professionals, sought the removal of children from the 'untaught' and 'untrained'. He wished to 'train children from their earliest infancy in good habits of every description', and only afterwards must they be 'rationally educated'. This sounds very Aristotelian (see chapter 3), but Owen was much more influenced by Rousseau. The parents who worked in his factory left their children in the nursery from the age of one. Owen prescribed that the children's experience in the Institute should be natural and spontaneous – that they should enjoy themselves. He anticipated much contemporary psychology by suggesting that the idea of good and evil is acquired by children before the age of two and that these durable impressions can result in damage to the subsequent formation of their characters. His son, also called Robert, wrote *An Outline of the System of Education at New Lanark* in 1824, in which he was very conscious of the influence of parents on the habits of the children. The aim of the Institute was to 'improve the habits, dispositions and general character' of the children. Owen senior did not believe that children should read books until the age of twelve – the older children in the Institute attended lectures and participated in discussions rather than read. Rewards and punishments were banned in the Institute, particularly violence as a form of punishment. Owen himself was an atheist and only permitted religious instruction because the parents desired it. He saw education as the instrument for formation of social character and he sought, through this attempt at improving character, to reduce class differences in society.

Many visitors came to New Lanark to see this experiment in education and were impressed. Three Poor Law guardians from Leeds wrote a report on the Institution in 1819 that included the following paragraph:

> In the education of the children the thing that is most remarkable is the general spirit of kindliness and affection which is shown towards them, and the entire absence of everything that is likely to give them bad habits, with the presence of whatever is calculated to inspire them with good ones; the consequence is, that they appear like one well-regulated family, united together by the ties of the closest affection. We heard no quarrels from the youngest to the eldest; and so strongly impressed are they with the conviction that their interest and duty are the same, and that to be happy themselves it is necessary to make those happy by whom they are surrounded.
>
> (Cole 1953: 89)

The eventual demise of the Institute was as a direct result of Owen's disavowal of religion which was not acceptable to many local Church of Scotland clergymen.

His educational followers were many, but they sometimes produced crude social experiments in schools. Teacher Edward Craig, for example, invented what he called the 'Charactrograph', a machine with numbers representing each pupil in a class together with four coloured counters by each number. The white counter represented freedom from reproach; red, excellent conduct; blue, a minor fault, and black, a serious offence. The machine was displayed each morning on the teacher's desk and registered white for each child. By the end of the day the members of the class would know what state they and others were in. Some teachers went as far as placing a counter around the child's neck indicating the immediate state of their character (see Stewart and McCann 1967: 162–3). Nevertheless, it seems clear that after Owen many nineteenth-century intellectual theorists accepted the romantic ideal of growth and personality development. Writers such as Coleridge, Ruskin, Arnold, Carlyle and Mill 'grasped hold of the idea of development of character, both as a solution to the social problems of the age and as an educational ideal worthy of pursuit on its own terms' (Miller and Kim 1988).

Victorian moral education

Victorian education had conscious moral purposes, particularly in the economic and religious domain. The production of characters suited to the needs of work was one of the principal goals of nineteenth-century elementary schools for the poor. Children in these schools were taught the 'habits of industry' for they were destined for either the factories or domestic service. Character training formed the core of their schooling and included a form of moral development firmly based on the Ten Commandments and stories from the Bible. Moral conduct was taught in the context of religious doctrine and Sunday schools, in the absence of an elementary school, taught the basic skills of literacy whilst extolling the virtues of Christian living. The teacher's role in these schools was to inculcate specific social roles typified by a pattern of behaviour in children. Children accepted without question the moral training provided and expected to be pun-ished for bad habits. The emphasis was on obedience and duty to all forms of authority in society and absolute conformity to predetermined social roles. The teachers themselves were often not well educated and were selected for their ability to exhibit virtues in and outside of school. The overwhelming majority were women. They held a restricted outlook on educational matters, which resulted in crude and mechanistic methods of teaching. The catechetical approach to teaching religion influenced their approach to education in general.

> A Circular letter of the school HMIs in 1849 (quoted in Hunt 1976) made clear that teachers of the poor were to improve their [pupils'] habits and manners, to promote a sense of order and decorum, a respectful obedience to their parents, teachers and superiors, to cultivate an intelligent disposition to fulfil the duties of their station in life, and to enable them to see how their interests and happiness are inseparable from the well being of other classes in society.

In 1862 Samuel Smiles published his *Self-Help: With Illustrations of Character and Conduct*, which sold 20,000 copies in its first year and achieved sales of 250,000 by the end of the century. Whilst we should not underplay the influence of Calvinism on Smiles' thought, the underlying philosophy of the book promoted a kind of sec-ular ethic. Smiles appears to have adopted an Aristotelian approach to character formation (1862: 331) for as he says: 'Knowledge must be allied to goodness and wisdom, and embodied in upright character, else it is nought .... The acquisition of knowledge may, it is true, protect a man against the meaner felonies of life; but not in any degree against its selfish vices, unless fortified by sound principles and habits.' Smiles preached a gospel of self-improvement through diligence, thrift and good character and in his sequel, entitled *Character*, published in 1871, he attempted to divorce the idea of a 'gentleman' from its upper-class connotations so that the virtues he recommended could count as constitutive of the moral worthy person no matter what their class. He advocated the establishment of a national education system in order to teach his virtues of character.

Quentin Bell (1968: 28) sums up this whole secular movement:

> Thus, in Victorian England, we find that the apostles of progress, having swept their churches clean of sacraments, altars, priests and pulpits, leaving nothing save a bare structure of ethical assertions, returned to curtained,

cushioned, upholstered homes in which every sort of buried sexual supersti-
tion, traditionalist tyranny and emotional cant served as covering for dirty
unswept corners and nameless secular filth.

Initiatives to promote Christian character education continued with the establishment of the Young Men's Christian Association (YMCA) in London in 1844 with
the explicitly stated aim: 'the winning of young men to Jesus Christ, and the building in them of Christian character'. Many of the lectures given at the YMCA were
nationalistic and evangelical rants which dwelt on the inferiority of the Catholic
characters in Europe as compared to those in England (see Bardsley 1861).

Society in nineteenth-century Britain was acutely class-conscious and children were viewed as miniature adults to be inducted into the ways of social
convention. Character was viewed as a class-based concept which contained
within it a judgement regarding an individual's status as much as their good conduct. The growing middle-classes realised that money alone would not secure
them the coveted status of the 'character of a gentleman'. Increasingly they sent
their sons to the rapidly expanding number of independent schools. There was a
marked revival of interest in character formation for middle class children in the
1820s, beginning in some reformed public schools (Rothblatt 1976: 133–4). The
formative influence of teachers replaced the wider societal influences on pupils
to become the main facilitators for this shaping of character. It was considered
important that pupils developed strong characters from which they could take a
principled stand, usually in favour of the established virtues of society. Stefan
Collini (1985) identifies these Victorian virtues as including: bravery, loyalty,
diligence, application and manners. Thomas Arnold, the headmaster of Rugby,
gave voice to middle-class aspirations by emphasizing that the educational ideal
should be the production of the 'noble character', the 'man of character' or more
precisely the Christian manly spirit, better known as 'muscular Christianity'.

Arnold's aim was no less than the formation of the Christian character in the
young through 'godliness and good learning'. As David Newsome (1961) notes,
it was a movement to reunite religion and morality. There is no doubting
Arnold's religious fervour – he would frequently break down in tears in front of
the school on hearing the story of the Passion. He was obsessed by sin, particularly the urge to sin which he believed boys especially feel, and he used corporal
punishment in an attempt to eradicate it. The school as a place to explicitly train
character was what came to distinguish the English public school from all other
Western school systems. Thomas Hughes, in *Tom Brown's Schooldays* (1957 edition: 65), describes how after dropping Tom off at Rugby, his father reflects on his
hopes for the outcomes of Tom's education: 'If he'll only turn out a brave, helpful,
truth-telling Englishman, and a gentleman, and a Christian, that's all I want.'
The novel follows how Tom defeats the bully Flashman, later the subject of a
number of books by George McDonald Fraser, and gradually demonstrates the
strength of character that wins him true friendship among his peers. Many
Victorian novels provided a common and influential frame of morality that effectively set ideals and standards of conduct for boys.

Supporters of Arnold were strong adherents of character formation. As well as instituting stern disciplinary regimes in their schools, they encouraged reading of selected great authors to discern the essential core of 'common' values. The Revd G. G. Bradley, headmaster of Marlborough School, in evidence to the Taunton Commission, which considered the endowed secondary schools (*Schools Enquiry Commission* 1868: 420), wrote: 'I would give unusual weight to the teaching of English language, literature, and history, to attempt to humanise and refine a boy's mind by trying to familiarise him with English poetry, and to inspire him with the best authors whom I could place before him.' The Clarendon Commission (1864: 56ff.), which reported on the nine principal public schools, found that among other virtues it was partially 'their love of healthy sport and exercise' that helped 'in moulding the character of the English gentleman'. There was a strong belief that games developed manliness and inspired, *inter alia*, the virtues of fairness, loyalty, moral and physical courage and co-operation. Games in the private schools were thus constituted as a course in ethics.

The public schools also socialized young men into the habit of good manners. In this regard character was a form of social and moral capital and the function of the school was to provide the right environment in which the 'right' people could, at an early stage, get to know one another. The upright stance of the Victorian gentleman seemed to provide outward confirmation of an acquired well-formed character. It often amounted to little more than the appearance of conformity to a set of public virtues, revealing nothing of any inner moral qualities. For many, character was not an ideal, but a display of the required manners solely towards those they considered their elders and betters. This was an education designed for the social elite and generally for men. Sheldon Rothblatt (1976: 135 and 102) reminds us that it was in the 1860s that character formation made a forceful appearance in Oxford and Cambridge Universities, but it often resulted in conduct that was 'self-consciously painful', on the part of undergraduates and dons alike. This class-bound society was changing rapidly and it remained impossible to develop workable notions of character for all.

Nevertheless, it is important to remember that British society was relatively homogeneous in religious outlook at this time. There was a common set of values derived from scripture and Protestantism. Morality was not a controversial issue for most schoolteachers since the generalized Protestantism which pervaded culture was implicitly accepted by teachers and by those who wrote the school textbooks of the period (Arthur *et al.*, 2001: 61f). The distinct moralistic strain in Protestantism strengthened the general assumption that moral instruction was synonymous with religious instruction and if this was not always the case, then religion could certainly be relied upon to aid moral instruction. Protestantism in late nineteenth and early-twentieth century Britain consisted of a spectrum ranging from strict evangelicals who battled the forces of evil at one end to liberal Protestants for whom religion was more cultural than theological at the other. Character education at these two extremes was clearly very different. It was also a time when the heroes of society were religious-based exemplars such as Dr Livingston and General Gordon. Even when a Victorian abandoned religious belief this did not necessarily mean a lowering of ethical standards. Instead, agnostics pursued the moral life as a good in itself. For them, the motivation was not the promise of eternal reward or eternal punishment. Their enthusiasm for instilling moral character in the masses was often greater than that displayed by some evangelicals. In many ways they continued to live on the moral capital of their Christian inheritance.

As the religious basis for morality began to decline – for some the latter became the surrogate of the former – there developed a heightened awareness of the need to uphold moral standards in society and individuals. Gertrude Himmelfarb (1995: 27) reviews a number of prominent Victorians who, whilst abandoning a revealed religion, nevertheless gave their full support to the task of transmitting 'duty' and moral behaviour to the young. This was the secular ethic, which profoundly influenced the progress of character education in schools. Secular character training became an alternative to the moral lessons derived from Bible teaching, and those who used the term 'character training' were often the progressives in education. They adopted this language to avoid conflict with religious-based moral education, but it remained an ethic firmly based on puritan foundations. Until 1870 the Church of England and other Protestant denominations dominated the provision of schooling, but their constant disagreements pushed the supervision of education increasingly into the hands of the government. The Education Act of 1870 in England did not establish free state education for all, it merely supplemented the provision of schools already undertaken by the Christian denominations. Because of the deep divisions within Protestantism the religious teaching in these new schools could not be based on any one denominational creed; instead a morality free from any denominational influence was taught. This led to the separation of morality from religion, despite the retention of compulsory Christian worship and religious instruction in state schools. Many Anglican schools converted to state school status as it was felt that the general moral ethos was compatible with Anglican ideas. The secularization of state schools and many church schools grew throughout the early part of the twentieth century, encouraged by the campaigns of the National Secular Society, founded in 1866, for secular and compulsory education for all.

The perceived need for some form of character education in schools was evident from the alarm that many eminent Victorians showed when discovering the social and moral conditions of the poor in the industrial cities. Disturbing statistics began to be produced. These spurred on some to promote 'self-help' policies whilst others sought to improve social conditions. Educational progressives such as Charlotte Mason organized systems of character training through the Parents National Educational Union, founded in 1887. Arthur Ackland (1980: 206), chairman of the Cooperative Society and a fellow of Christ Church College, Oxford, gave a series of lectures in 1883 to groups of workers advocating improved training for teachers so that they could develop critical thinking in their charges rather than continue to teach by rote. He believed that the examples of the great men in English history would help develop the character of young and old alike and make them better Englishmen. He divorced Christianity from this character training and retained this view even when appointed vice-president of the Committee of Council on Education in Gladstone's last Ministry.

Secular morality and character

In 1886 the Ethical Union was established by a group of agnostics with the primary objective of seeking a secular basis for morality. They became interested in the education of character and formed the Moral Instruction League in 1897, which campaigned for anti-religious policies and the promotion of moral reform through legislation. The Moral Instruction League was opposed to Bible-reading in schools and encouraged parents to withdraw their children from religious lessons. Members of the organization sought election to school boards and to influence the course of political debate by lobbying Ministers such as Ackland, who was more than willing to listen to them. It appeared that the government's view of character training was very similar to the League's. In the *Introduction to the Education Code* of 1904 and 1905 (and subsequent Codes), it was stated that: 'The purpose of the public elementary school is to form and strengthen the character and to develop intelligence, of the children entrusted to it.' The Code had a clear moral tone and advocated that children should learn about the heroes of England's past through the medium of story-telling by the teacher. Sir Robert Morant, who compiled the Code for the Ministry, also produced in 1905 a *Handbook of Suggestions for Consideration of Teachers and others concerned in the work of the Public Elementary Schools*. This has a section on the Formation of Character in which teachers are encouraged to try and improve manners in pupils along with punctuality, neatness, cleanliness, truthfulness, respect for others and a 'cheerful obedience to duty'. The language and the notion of character here are more Greek than Christian in origin and the kind of Christianity that was encouraged in schools was more ethical than religious. The Moral Instruction League was having some influence on government policy, but perhaps only because there was a degree of convergence with liberal Protestant thought. Most politicians concerned in administering schooling were devout Christians who despised the Ethical Union.

The Moral Instruction League comprised many of the leading educational thinkers and philosophers of the time. It aimed 'to substitute systematic non-theological moral instruction for the present religious teaching in all State schools, and to make character the chief aim of school life' (see Hilliard 1961). It further stated:

> The aim of moral instruction is to form the character of the child. With this object in view, the scholar's intellect should be regarded mainly as the channel through which to influence his feelings, purposes, and acts. The teacher must constantly bear this in mind, since knowledge about morality has missed its aim when no moral response is awakened in the child. A moral instruction lesson ought to appeal to the scholar's feelings, and also to affect his habits and his will.

This was a good definition of character education in its day and whilst the League did not recommend any specific teaching methods it did produce a syllabus for use in schools in 1901, which was known as the Graduated Syllabus of Moral Instruction for Elementary Schools. This was published as part of a Moral Education Series, commissioned by members of the League and practising schoolteachers. A total of seven books were published between 1904 and 1913. Other authors, such as James Reid (1906) and F. H. Ellis (1907), produced character manuals based on the syllabus. J. H. Wicksteed (1913) wrote *Conduct and Character*, and W. H. Baldwin and W. Robson, in the same year, produced another in the series with the title *Lessons in Character Building*. Whilst the League did not use the term 'character education' in its name, it was nevertheless clear from its aims, its syllabus and its many publications that this was exactly what it was about.

It is worth examining the content of these two books. Wicksteed produced a scheme of lessons which had already been tried and tested in schools with 5–14 year olds. The lessons were all based on a series of what may be called 'virtues', each lesson dealing with a particular virtue. Under-sevens looked at cleanliness, tidiness, manners, kindness, fairness, truthfulness and courage. It is not difficult to see why cleanliness and tidiness were on the agenda, as children in elementary schools often lived in the most appalling conditions. These seven 'virtues' were then generally repeated in every year up to the age of fourteen, but in each subsequent year from the age of seven new 'virtues' were added: at seven to eight, gratitude; eight to nine, honesty, justice, self-control, work; nine to ten, humanity, obedience, order, perseverance; ten to eleven, honour and prudence; eleven to twelve, habits, patriotism, zeal, thrift; twelve to thirteen, peace and war, ownership, conscience; and thirteen to fourteen, cooperation, the will, self-respect and ideals. Baldwin and Robson (1913) followed the same syllabus but concentrated more on the latter years of schooling and particularly on the 'habits of industry'. Pride in one's work was emphasized. All of these lessons could be taught separately or integrated into the school's general curriculum. The Board of Education in *Circular 753* (1910: para. 2) made explicit this connection with school subjects. For example, it said: '... English is not merely an accomplishment, but an index to and a formative influence over character'.

Religion was of course excluded from this syllabus and W. Archer, addressing the League's annual meeting in 1914, made an explicit attack on religion as the basis for morality. The secular ethic was very much part of the League's activities and it never attempted to validate morality by reference to religion. As well as there being a high number of agnostics, many of its members were actively anti-religious. Consequently, there was a crisis for the authority of morality since the question needed to be asked: on what was it now based? In rejecting a correspondence to an eternal order, the League was unable to give an adequate explanation of the basis of its morality. There was also increasing confusion at the end of the nineteenth century as to where the proper location of character education should be. Mason (1906) produced a book to help parents develop the character of their children and many thought character training should remain chiefly in the home, particularly as schoolteachers were always viewed as *in loco parentis* – they supplemented, not supplanted, the character training received in the home. The movement for secular character training appeared to dominate educational thought but not practice in most schools and character education became intrinsically associated with the progressives in education. A number of local education authorities, such as Cheshire County Council, produced schemes of instruction on character for use in their schools. This movement was certainly influenced by developments in the USA, particularly the Character Education League, which produced many curriculum materials with the explicit aim of teaching and developing in children 31 virtues that would result in an integral virtue called 'character' (see McClelland, 1992). These virtues were almost identical to the Moral Instruction League's syllabus so there must have been some cross-fertilization of ideas.

A number of Christians produced books that linked character training with the Christian religion, such as Watkinson in 1904 and Lord in 1926. After all, the majority of schools in this period were still operated by the churches. The Sunday School Movement was also eager to instil virtuous character in pupils, but Dorothy Entwistle (in Wood 1994: 410) indicates that even from this Christian approach there was a surprisingly secular outlook. The virtues promoted by the Sunday School Movement, such as 'good temper', 'self-sacrifice', 'helping others', etc., could have been accepted by the Moral Instruction League for they were common human values. The Roman Catholic Church placed great store by the character of the teacher in the classroom and sought teachers 'who combine a love of and sympathy with children' (Wenham 1892: 198). Teachers were encouraged to mix with children in the playground to influence them through example, showing them the virtues of a good Christian life. In response to the activities of the League a number of books were written for parents and teachers. Ernest Hull, an English Jesuit, wrote *The Formation of Character* in 1910 to help guide the young to form a character based on principles. He provided the following definition (1910: 117): 'Character is life dominated by principles, as distinguished from life dominated by mere impulses from within and mere circumstances from without.' The Roman Catholic Church also had the work of the French Dominican Martin Gillet which was translated in 1914 under the title *The Education of Character*, and which gave a good response to emerging secular alternatives. The Catholic tradition of Thomism had always accepted that basic morality was available to all men without necessity of religion. In Catholic schools morality was still firmly rooted in notions of faith. The Anglican and Nonconformist Churches increasingly focused much of their attention on extracurricular activities in forming character and they established or allied themselves with the Boys' Brigade in 1883, Boy Scouts in 1908 and Girl Guides in 1910.

The government and character education

The League had begun to moderate its anti-religious campaigns after 1900, and also began to campaign for compulsory moral education in schools. It failed in this endeavour, and by 1909 it had changed its name to the Moral Education League. The Moral Education League's work, based on the production of manuals for moral teaching, did not survive long after the First World War. In 1919 it changed its name again to the Civic and Moral Education League and a year later the word Moral was dropped. The organization now meshed itself with the cause of citizenship education. Citizenship education at the time was seen as a continuation of earlier character training (Batho 1990). Hughes (1915) in *Citizens to Be*, speaks of the moral formation of citizens and says that service to neighbour should be a moral habit. Professor MacCunn at Glasgow University produced a book in 1919 entitled *The Making of Character*, which also emphasized public service and duty to neighbour. After the 1920s there were fewer books that dealt specifically with character training in the school, training in character often being incorporated into ideas and discussion about citizenship. Nevertheless, the *Report of the Consultative Committee on the Primary School* (1926: 93) recognized that: 'The schools ... have broadened their aims until it might be said that they have to teach children how to live', and E. A. Mountford provided a textbook on teaching the virtues for schoolteachers in 1933 entitled *The Education of Character*.

The Board of Education's Handbook for 1937 continued to make explicit that: 'The purpose of the Public Elementary School is to form and strengthen character.' The Handbook emphasized that the corporate life of the school should avoid anything that undermines character formation and listed the habits of industry, self-control, duty, respect for others, good manners, fair play and loyalty as the kind of virtues that should be cultivated. In the same year the Church of England held a conference in Oxford on education and condemned the promotion of individualism within education circles, especially the concept of what it called 'free personality', by which children were being encouraged to do as they pleased. The Conference warned about the role and development of the State in areas like character education, with Fred Clarke (1938: 2) claiming that the increasing role of the State in schooling would mean that it would eventually be 'committed to a particular philosophy of life and seeking to organise the whole of life in accordance with a particular doctrine of the end of man's existence, and in an all-embracing community life which claims to be at once the source and the end of all human activity; a State, that is to say, which aims at being also a Church'. In the same year the Spens Report on secondary education spoke of education as 'fostering the free growth of individuality'. The Education Act 1944 saw the duty of schools as being 'to contribute towards ... moral development in the community': it did not ask schools to wholly provide it. Three years later the Ministry of Education's Advisory Council for Education produced a report entitled *School and Life* (1947: 97ff.) that expressed concern about the danger of a moral vacuum and strongly advised schools to provide some kind of moral code for their pupils. The report, whilst recognizing that schools should help build 'strong characters', noted that for many people the division between right and wrong was no longer a strictly moral one thus causing 'increased moral perplexity and confusion' in society and schools.

In 1949 the Ministry of Education published a paper entitled *Citizens Growing Up: At Home, At School and After* in which it is stated that 'good citizens must first be good men'. The document has a section on character which briefly details why and how it must be improved and there is an appeal to 'public virtues' and an exhortation to develop an improved moral tone in schools. The Ministry's yearbook (1949: 11) also advocated the introduction of 'social activities' in schools in order to develop character. The Scottish Education Department produced *Young Citizens at School* the year after, the result of a government-organized conference of teachers that addressed the issue of training character in schools. The document concluded that: 'Direct moral teaching, in the sense of precept dealing with virtues in the abstract, evidently found little place in the thought of the great body of teachers. But stress was laid on the focus of example on the formation of good habits' (1950: 13). After 1950 it is difficult to find any references to character in government education publications until 2001. It also becomes rare to see Protestant accounts of character formation for pupils in state schools – one of the last being W. H. Backhouse's *Religion and Adolescent Character* in 1947. In 1951 the editors of *The Yearbook of Education* at the Institute of Education in London produced a volume that sought to examine 'the ways in which ... the school contributes to the formation of moral character, sentiments, attitudes, ideals and ethical standards' (see Lauwerys and Hans 1951). In one of the edited papers, T. H. Pear (1951: 313) claimed that it was still generally assumed by most teachers in England that they were involved in the training of their pupils' characters. Pear proceeded to attack the kind of character training extant in English private schools as narrow and class-based.

Character education also has a long association with activities outside the school. The Outward Bound movement, which Kenneth Roberts *et al.* (1974: 12) called the 'character training movement', avoided using the term 'character training' because of its connotations with fascist youth organisations. However, character formation was an explicit aim of courses such as the Duke of Edinburgh Awards, which were extremely popular among Britain's youth between the 1950s and the 1970s. These out-of-school field courses were run by voluntary bodies and involved hill-walking, rock-climbing, sailing, lectures and discussions. The idea was to build character through living together and taking responsibility for one's actions. Community service and duty to one's neighbour were emphasized. It was character education by doing, through experiences in common. Opportunities for these types of character building activities declined after the 1970s in response to a fall in demand, but they were and still are key elements in any attempt at character building.

The idea of character training in schools did not die off completely within the English context as it was still promoted by people such as Sir Richard Livingstone (1954:5), head of an Oxford College. In a lecture at Doncaster Grammar School in 1954 he explained that we must form good habits in children together with appropriate virtues in order to build character. He did not believe that teachers or teacher educators gave sufficient attention to character formation and he produced

his own litany of alarm. Independent and Church schools continued to give attention to character formation. John Dancey (1963: 90), writing on public schools,
emphasized the continued interest of private schools in character education. The
development of self-confidence, capacity for leadership, loyalty and social skills
were all part of the rhetoric of a private education. Boarding schools, of course,
have unique opportunities to help build character, above all through the fact that
pupils live in the school separated from their parents. Greater influence can thus
be exerted on the formation of the pupil's character. Sport was still seen as an
excellent tool for character training, but a private education by itself provided no
guarantee of a good or well-formed character.

Church schools also emphasized character education and Grech's book on
Educating Christians, published in 1960, concerning the formation of the
Christian character, was used by many teachers in Catholic schools. In 1979
Professor Alan McClelland, newly appointed professor of education at the
University of Hull, gave his inaugural lecture on the subject of general character
education. There was obviously still some interest in discussing character educa-
tion within mainstream education.

The progress of the movement for character education appeared to mirror the
times. Whilst the majority of schools in 1900 were still church schools, there was
a drift away from Christianity as the basis for character education in schools. The
volume of writing about character in the British context had declined by the
1920s and 1930s: there were a number of reasons for this. During these decades
character training became associated with the youth policies and practices of
totalitarian regimes in the Soviet Union, in fascist Italy and finally in Nazi
Germany. For some the term character training had become tainted by association, however loose, with organizations like the Hitler Youth Movement. In spite
of this, virtually every school in Britain was responding in some implicit way to
the educational goal of developing character.

It is debatable whether the negative findings of the Character Education
Enquiry conducted by Hugh Hartshorne and Mark May (1928–1939) in America
adversely affected the very strong character movement in the USA or had any
influence in Britain. This enquiry denied that there was anything that could be
called character, which it defined as the persistent disposition to act according to
moral principle in a variety of situations. The research methodology employed
was limited and we should treat the conclusions with a degree of circumspection.
They took the profile of a morally mature person as their model and asked a series
of questions of young people about stealing, cheating and lying. The conclusions
were: first, that there is no correlation between character training and actual
behaviour; second, that moral behaviour is not consistent in one person from one
situation to another; third, that there is no relationship between what people say
about morality and the way that they act; and finally, that cheating is distributed
– in other words that we all cheat a little. This could have dealt a major blow to
traditional character education for it was a research claim that character education was not effectively producing behaviour that conformed to the principles
being taught by modelling, lecturing and use of rewards and punishments.

However, the report was not widely distributed and James Leming (1997: 35) indicates that books on character education continued to appear, at least in America.

Ethical relativism also had an influence on the character education movement and most definitely on Hartshorne and May. They shared with many of their contemporaries certain presuppositions about human behaviour that made their methods and their conclusions likely to be confirmed. Johnson (1987: 67) believes that they thought in crudely naturalistic terms and he explains:

> Any particular behaviour was thought to be learned in specific situations, as it produced results satisfying to the individual, and it would be repeated only in response to situations sufficiently alike to call for that behaviour. Learning thus becomes essentially atomistic, situation-specific, and little if at all related to any general form of reasoning. Hence it will do no good to teach moral principles – if there are any, … or to hope that such principles, if taught, will produce any general form of recurring behaviour we could call general conduct or character.

Whilst British education was certainly influenced by developments in the USA it is extremely doubtful that this American research is the reason for the decline in publishing about character education in Britain. The provision of moral education continued on the British school curriculum throughout the 1930s and 1940s with very little in the way of intellectual discussion or analysis of what actually went on.

By the 1950s and 1960s cognitive psychology became a discipline and gave great emphasis to Lawrence Kohlberg's theories, helping to make them popular in education. The success of Jean Piaget, Lawrence Kohlberg and Eric Erikson was due to their themes of development which indicated progress. These themes satisfied the demands of culture at the time. British culture and society had become more pluralistic and therefore schooling became more sensitive to the increasing heterogeneity of children in many schools. These cognitive approaches to moral education – character education – were also more compatible with the liberal traditions of critical thinking rather than a didactic, virtues-based approach: with no substantive content for character education, it was believed by many in education to be less susceptible to criticism from ethnic and religious groups in society. Many of those who still explicitly talked about character had to use the term 'moral education' to describe their character goals.

In the 1960s there was increasing discussion about the development of character and the *British Journal of Psychology of Education* held a number of symposia on the theme in the early 1960s (see Peters 1960). The Newsom Report (*Half Our Future*, 1963: 52–59) devoted a chapter of its discussion to moral and spiritual education, but saw a restricted role for schools: 'Theirs is a limited, though a vital role and they are neither the community nor the church. Society must not look to schools to solve its moral problems, but it expects and gets from them an important contribution towards their solution.' Even the Plowden Report

(*Children and their Primary Schools*, 1969: 572), which gave such emphasis to child-centred learning, was still able to recommend that pupils 'should be brought to know and love God and to practise in the school community the virtues appropriate to their age and environment'. Here the promotion of virtue and the link between religion and morality are firmly asserted. Still, child-centred learning and the promotion of stage theories of development appeared to remove some degree of responsibility from teachers for the education of their pupils. The new disciplines of educational psychology and sociology seemed to indicate that much in education and schooling was essentially predetermined and that ideas such as character education were of limited value to teachers.

The important work in the USA of Peck and Havighurst (1960) on character education helped to revive explicit thinking in the area, even though they concluded that each generation tended to perpetuate its strengths and weaknesses of character and that character formation in the early years was relatively unmodifiable. The 1960s and 1970s were concerned with values clarification and procedural neutrality in the classroom and there was a widespread presumption in favour of moral relativity. It was the reaction against this relativistic thought that has seen the re-emergence of more traditional approaches to character education. In Britain, people such as John White (1990) have explicitly called for the return of character education in schools despite the fact there has been little in the way of empirical research or major evaluation of character education programmes in the USA or Britain.

Conclusion

There is a long history of ill-conceived and ineffective efforts at character education in Britain. The kinds of character that teachers and educational thinkers espoused and the training methods they used also varied enormously. Liberal Protestantism sought the reduction of religion to morality in the nineteenth century and the early part of the twentieth century: in this mission it was more effective than the small number of vocal secularists in Victorian society. Basil Mitchell (1980: 161) aptly comments: 'This is why the Victorian Age, although possessing much that we are in process of losing, cannot be cited as a paradigm of Christian morality. The Victorians idolised morality, giving it that supreme importance which they were increasingly unable to accord God. Hence the morality they believed in and practised was in constant danger of becoming legalistic and joyless.'

The Victorian period was certainly a high point in character education, or perhaps more accurately in the use of the language of character. The Victorians meant many things by character and many of these meanings did not apply to schooling. They were far more concerned with the idea of the will and the power of the will to do the right thing – for it was generally assumed that people did know the difference between right and wrong and it was only weakness of will that caused them to err. The theory of character formation they operated led to much ambiguity and contradiction in behaviour. Robert Owen's experiment in the social reconstruction of character through integrating character with society was an example of a utopian theory of character formation. Much more general was the view that character equalled a socialization in good manners and in a particular form of social conduct. Whilst there was a recognition that human nature could be directly shaped by education, the notion of character was largely embodied in laws, institutions and social expectations. The school as a place to train character was not a totally new concept, but it came to distinguish the English private school.

The progressives at the beginning of the twentieth century were reacting against educational practices such as rote learning and the enforcement in schools of patterns of traditional formal behaviour. However, they did not provide many viable alternatives to the various pedagogical methods used for teaching character education at the time. There was great interest in character formation in the early 1900s. Michael Sadler (1908: v) conducted a major international enquiry into moral instruction to ascertain whether or not British schools could learn how to strengthen the character of the young. This was a major study on the influence of education upon character that has never been repeated since. It is interesting that the study found that many British teachers were uneasy with moral education in schools and disliked the moral syllabuses on offer, whilst at the same time agreeing that character building was part of their role. Little appears to have changed. The 1910 Board of Education Circular 753 (para. 36) envisages its own literary canon: a body of great literary works to which pupils need to be introduced. It made clear that pupils 'should be taught to understand, not to criticise or judge' the great works. Moral education continued to be taught in schools in a fairly conventional and non-critical way.

The 1960s marked a turning point. Psychology became the dominant discipline in moral and character education and few philosophical, sociological, and theological accounts were advanced. Progressive theories in education increasingly put an emphasis on individual rights and child-centred learning. The focus was on the needs of the child. Moral education had to be inclusive and uncontroversial. Some, like Gilbert Ryle (1975), wrote about the possibility of teaching virtues in the mid 1970s, but this was rare. By the 1980s and 1990s we see a growing interest in the virtues and their rediscovery for character education. The recent Green and White Papers in education (2001) are really a furtherance of pre-1950s government thinking on character education, which explicitly attempted to promote certain specified virtues through providing opportunities for 'social activities' in schools. There are striking similarities between government policy on character in 1949 with that of 2001.

3   The virtues of character

> What the morality of the virtues articulated in and defended by the moral rhetoric of our political culture provides is, it turns out, not an education in the virtues but, rather, an education in how to seem virtuous, without actually being so.
>
> Alasdair McIntyre (1999: 131)

> If virtue can be taught, as I believe it can be, it is not through books so much as by example. In that case what would be the point of a treatise on virtues? Perhaps this: to try to understand what we should do, what we should be, and how we should live, and thereby gauge, at least intellectually, the distance that separates us from these ideals.
>
> Andre Comte-Sponville (2002: 1)

In reading the works of moral philosophers it is immediately noticeable that few commit themselves to any substantive moral conclusions concerning character and most ignore reflection on the period of childhood and the formation of character. They prefer to analyse and clarify general moral concepts. A great many educational philosophers have viewed morality as being primarily the process of making decisions. They have been concerned about rationality and autonomy in moral education, particularly the outcomes of moral reasoning rather than the ends or application of moral judgements. This has led to an emphasis on what Paul Hirst (1974) calls 'forms of thought' or the methodology of reaching a moral decision. This is the modern liberal position on moral education which aims to encourage critical thinking upon the values encountered in life – to form the person who can make autonomous, critical and rational moral judgements. This is what Ruth Jonathan (1999: 64) calls the 'morally self-defining individual'.

John Rawls (1971) is perhaps the best exponent of this position, since for him education is essentially about designing a system of ethical codes or rules *ab initio*. His argument is that we construct our own morality, since ethical development is a constant process in which nothing is ultimately fixed. Therefore we must continually re-examine our ethical and moral assumptions to see whether they make sense. The individual, in Rawl's theory, is the unit of analysis and he constructs a quasi-legal system designed to maximize self-interest and minimize damage to others. In this framework there is a tendency to see society as a collection of atomized individuals with absolute rights that are enforced in the courts, courts which adjudicate on conflict in such a way as to preserve the rights of individuals. This liberal theory has often been criticized for being too abstract and individualistic, ignoring the social nature of human beings. The theory Rawls has developed, like any theory that elevates rational autonomy and accords centrality to justice, tends to neglect areas of human experience such as the central place of family and school, in which the moral formation of agents and citizens actually takes place. Contemporary liberal morality emphasizes process over content and critical autonomy over social interdependence. It is why Alasdair McIntyre claims that the modern vision of morality is an endless series of new dilemmas. It is also why he claims (1985: 2) that 'the language of morality' is in 'grave disorder'. Increasingly, he and others believe that there is something fundamentally wrong with conceptions of morality in liberal society.

McIntyre (1967, 1985, 1987) describes how this 'disorder' and destruction of moral understanding and conduct occurred because of the Enlightenment. He argues that up until this point it was a matter of common knowledge that morality was tied clearly to the virtues. Virtue was widely believed to be a force that had a good effect – the disposition to do what was good. The virtuous individual was understood to be someone who perceived and acted upon situationally unique moral requirements. Virtue was a way of being. This knowledge was lost in the Enlightenment, which promoted a prevailing instrumentalization of social relations. In *A Short History of Ethics* (1967) McIntyre reviews the contributions of Hume, Kant, Bentham and Mill to moral philosophy and dismisses their theories of reason, passion, choice and utility in moral thinking and action. Three dominant groups of moral theories were left in the post-Second World War period: Kantian ethics, utilitarianism and meta-ethics – the last having no interest in guiding behaviour or improving character. Modern society had abandoned many of the virtues and, for McIntyre, this society was now fragmented and defined by three archetypical characters: the bureaucratic manager who manipulates all in the pursuit of profit; the rich aesthete who seeks pleasure and experience above all else; and the therapist who helps the others through each day. Teachers participate in this general culture of fragmentation, fitting within the archetype of the therapist. McIntyre (1999: 128–9) believes that in regard to education, modern society has too indeterminate a conception of the virtues, which leaves the individual morally resourceless. He says:

> Education that purports to teach a morality neutral between rival controversial standpoints concerning the virtues will end up in teaching a largely indeterminate morality. This morality, that of the rhetoric of commonplace usage, lacks determinate answers to those questions in terms of which any substantive and determinate account of the virtues has to state its positions.

For McIntyre, we are left with a choice between the isolation of individuals or membership of a community which helps to give us an identity and purpose in life. The small community provides a framework for our self-understanding through the narrative we tell and share with each other and ultimately live. Within this framework the virtues can once more thrive, for a moral tradition is a necessary backdrop for the development of character.

Against this theoretical background there is increasing emphasis among those concerned with character education on the relationship between thinking and doing, between decision-making and actions and between beliefs and conduct. Some have suggested that it is merely a case of teaching children the difference between right and wrong and that children should be coerced by teachers into doing what is right. This is a simplistic view of character education. For one thing, it is extremely unlikely, in our day, that one could easily return to telling people what to believe or how to act. Roger Straughan (1999: 260) helps us by focusing on the twin concepts of education and morality. He comments:

> Morality is basically about what it is right to do and not to do and about what reasons may be given why something ought or ought not to be done. Education is primarily concerned with offering ways of thinking and under-standing which again provide reasons why certain things ought to be believed and certain procedures followed. Both morality and education, then, contain a 'theoretical', reasoning element and a 'practical', doing ele-ment, so it would be surprising if the double-barrelled concept of moral education did not exhibit these features to an even more marked degree.

Straughan rightly places emphasis both on doing and thinking, but we also need to take into account the fact that moral education is not conducted within a social vacuum. It is why Ruth Jonathan (1999: 64) argues that the challenge arises from the fact that:

> to develop in the young the capacity for critical reflection on values cannot in and of itself provide an adequate framework either for the development of individual commitments or for the shared social understandings that both shape and reflect commitments. Indeed, the rationale for such reflection in individuals presupposes the exercise of a surrounding framework of value that both supports and sustains, and against which personal values are elab-orated and modified.

Jonathan argues for the existence of a well-grounded social framework of sub-stantive values from which character education can extend. It is from this social framework that those concerned with character education have recognized they must start.

It is not surprising that philosophy has begun to dominate much of the most recent debate on character education. Character education is a diffuse and emotive topic and the arguments for and against often run to extremes. We need to remem-ber that character education is not identical to moral education since character development involves the emergence of certain enduring traits, only some of which can be classed as moral. Certainly in the formation of character all of the constituent parts of education – physical, intellectual, and moral – make a contribution. Character can be said to be the sum total of a person's characteristics, affective, cognitive and physical. I believe that children are born with the promise and potential for rich characters, which they can only develop over time as they are nurtured and mature into adults. But they are born with certain biological and temperamental dispositions which determine, along with how they are nurtured in the home and the wider contact with the social environment they experience, the way in which they will learn the process of making choices. It is part of human nature to develop a character and formal education makes a contribution.

Christine McKinnon (1999: 62) views character as a function of experiences, memories, natural inclinations, genetic make-up, temperament and the judgements an individual makes. Character in this view is more all-inclusive than virtues. Virtues are chosen and acquired because they have the capacity to help us become the person we ought to become, but we remain unique individuals and characters even if we acquire exactly the same virtues as others. The importance of motivation, and especially the will, cannot be underplayed as these will vary in children with exactly the same virtues, which explains the emergence of different kinds of character in children. Joel Kupperman (1988, 1991: 143) argues that the advantage of a 'character ethics' over a virtue ethics is the holistic approach it adopts: character is more than the acquisition of moral virtues. McKinnon (1999: 72) maintains that many qualities other than virtues go towards making a good character. She asserts that a virtue theory that stresses the importance of character requires that individuals be actively involved in self-consciously constructing a character. She concludes that developing such a character is constitutive of leading a good life. Both Kupperman and McKinnon recognize that the notion of character encompasses something broader than education in virtue, yet they maintain that virtue theory best captures the richness and complexity of an ethical life. Perhaps this is because virtue ethics gives first place to human flourishing as opposed to mere human functioning.

In contemporary philosophy of education there has been a growing emphasis on 'virtue ethics' (Carr and Steutal 1999; Halstead and McLaughlin 1999) as an answer to the question: To what extent are we justified in influencing the character of the young? Virtue here is seen as an admirable character trait and virtue ethics a form of moral reflection which gives a central place to such traits of character. Some academics and teachers are advocating the restoration of virtue-centred character education in schools. This is happening at a time when the philosophy of Aristotle is having something of a revival, championed by the likes of Elizabeth Anscombe (1958), Alasdair McIntyre (1985) and Owen Flanagan and Amelie Rorty (1990).

Ancient virtue ethics

Plato's *Republic* was the first work on the philosophy of education. It is concerned with educating people so that a just society is achieved. To have or to form a good character is also to become fully human. Socrates, the tutor of Plato, taught that virtue is knowledge of the good. Socrates made a sharp distinction between those who are good and those who are not: to be perfectly good needs a perfect knowledge of the good – so can a child who has no knowledge of moral principles be good? In *The Republic* Plato answers that only the philosopher who knows the form of the good can be the completely good man. Plato did accept that there was a lesser goodness which was attainable on the way to the ideal of the good and could be produced by the right training. Plato realized that goodness depends on habit together with intellectual apprehension of what the good is. Aristotle, who was in turn Plato's pupil, agreed with him on many of the fundamentals of his theory of education, but developed the principles further.

Both *The Republic* and Aristotle's *Ethics* and *Politics* concern themselves with the question of how a good person should live. They are also about how society should structure itself to make this type of life attainable. Both construe education as being related to the activities of the State and also conceive education as part of the art of politics. Plato's *Republic* outlines how each individual is destined to play a specific role in a society which aims at the good. These books were addressed to an audience that today would be considered undergraduate: mainly aristocratic young men who had already developed a degree of maturity, self-control and order in their lives. They had already developed habits of action based on experience, formed early in their childhood. What they received from Plato and Aristotle was the final stages of the process of moral education. For the Greeks the attainment of the good life was the goal of human existence and the virtues were the qualities that made a life excellent, particularly the virtues of courage, generosity, honesty and loyalty. The person who possessed the virtues led the best life.

In modern discussions about character, most writers tend to polarize this ancient debate. They argue that, in Plato's case, if a person knows the good he will do it. In contrast, Aristotle says we become good by practising good actions. From Plato there is the idea that character education is about improving thinking skills, whilst in Aristotle it is primarily about practising right behaviour. In one there is an emphasis on moral reasoning without moral action, in the other, conformity without inner conviction. This is to overstate their differences. Both believed that character must be actively cultivated in the young. Both were concerned about whether ethical behaviour could be taught. They debated mainly in terms of virtue and the virtuous, and morality for them was not about rules or principles but the cultivation of character. Conformity to a set of moral rules was not their aim in the development of this character: character development involved *being* a certain kind of person and not merely *doing* certain kinds of things.

In Aristotle's case, right moral conduct was not a matter for explicit teaching. For him, there is rationality in every moral choice and this cannot be omitted from the process through which virtue is formed. The child requires direction as well as knowledge. Whilst children must eventually decide voluntarily how to act in a certain way, this is achieved gradually as they become freer to make their own decisions. According to Aristotle, virtues are developed by an individual over time and signify a specific excellence in them of some kind. He describes two kinds of virtues: moral virtues – which are qualities of character, and intellectual virtues – which are qualities of mind. Aristotle lists a total of twelve moral virtues, together with a number of intellectual virtues including wisdom, intelligence and scientific knowledge. He recognized that a person may have the ability to think about the good without having the disposition to implement it. In contrast, it appears that Plato did not think that anyone willingly acted immorally, and explained that if they did so act then it was through ignorance of the knowledge of the good. Applied to education this would suggest that all the teacher needs to do is point out the error in behaviour and the child will act accordingly. Many of those who advocate character education, such as Edward Wynne and Kevin Ryan (1993), justify their position by appeals to virtue ethics. To understand their arguments we need to know what virtue is, why it is necessary to be virtuous and what these virtues are today.

Modern virtue ethics

Aristotle gave more specific attention to the process of education than did Plato. He suggested that there are clear developmental stages in education. The first stage is the training of the body; the second is the training of character; and lastly comes the training of the intellect. He observed that intellect appears later in the child. Only after children have built certain good habits within the second stage can they reasonably move to the stage of comprehension. In the words of Gerald Hughes (2001: 19) Aristotle offered the young men he taught 'the theoretical backing to a process of moral training which had already been largely completed'. There is a paradox here: students who already have virtuous characters through their actions are to be taught how to think about moral decisions. And yet Aristotle says that unless you already have skills to think correctly about moral decisions, then you cannot be virtuous. In his *Ethics* (II 6, 15) Aristotle defines virtue in the following way: 'A virtue is a deliberated and permanent disposition, based on a standard applied to ourselves and defined by the reason displayed by the man of good sense.' Virtue is thus seen as a standard which is based on reason and which is conducive to the good, and with it we have a human capacity to deliberately seek the good for itself.

   Thomas Lickona (1991) would argue that there is a synthesis developing out of the competing approaches to character education within the framework that virtue must be practised not merely taught. He acknowledges that having a character is not equivalent to having a moral vocabulary. David Carr and Jan Steutal (1999: 187) explain that human beings exhibit both negative characteristics which need to be restrained and positive ones which need to be cultivated. This is why it is important to form a clearer understanding of the role of the virtues in moral education. The meaning of character traits, dispositions and habits is essential for understanding the role of virtue ethics in character education. A detailed understanding of virtues can be obtained by consulting, among others, Philippa Foot (1981), Alasdair McIntyre (1985), Nancy Sherman (1989), David Carr (1991), Robert Sandin (1992), David Carr and Jan Steutal (1999), and Gerald Hughes (2001).

Elizabeth Anscombe (1958) recommends the replacement of discussion about moral rights and wrongs with discussion about virtues. As she put it:

> It would be a great improvement if, instead of 'morally wrong', one always named a genus such as 'untruthful', 'unchaste', 'unjust'. We would no longer ask whether doing something was 'wrong', passing directly from some description of an action to this notion; we should ask whether; e.g., it was unjust; and the answer would sometimes be clear at once.

Anscombe called into question modern moral philosophy, which she claimed merely analyzed the language and meaning of morality and was in no way concerned with helping to guide human behaviour. She claimed that it was misconceived and did not understand ethical reasoning, that it in fact had no real understanding of the psychology of human reasoning (mental concepts such as will, desire, intention and the rest), lacked a range of moral psychological concepts with which to describe and evaluate moral behaviour, and was in fact a narrow rationalism. Since the publication of Anscombe's article 'Modern Moral Philosophy' in 1958, a new and important strand has emerged in moral theory, placing greater emphasis on the nature of moral character and the virtues.

It could be said that modern moral philosophy, for Anscombe, did not say enough about the complex relationship between character, identity and conduct. Therefore it had little to say about character education. Virtue ethics, she argued, provided a better foundation for reasoning about moral problems and about character development. It can even be argued, with Anscombe, that our current confusion about the nature and force of moral obligation makes it very undesirable to direct pupils to make decisions completely for themselves about what ought morally to be done or avoided. Focusing on kinds of behaviour as exemplifying a particular virtue or vice is much more likely to encourage a concrete and reflective grasp of what it is good to do and to be. Specifically, if a school identifies and promotes habituation in virtue as providing sustenance for the school community, its pupils will find it easier to reflect upon and modify their thinking and behaviour, rather than merely emphasizing (even self-chosen) rules to which individual actions must conform.

McIntyre (1967: 64) succinctly summarizes the position:

> We therefore exhibit rationality in two kinds of activity: in thinking, where reasoning is what constitutes the activity itself; and in such activities other than thinking where we may succeed or fail in obeying the precepts of reason. The excellences of the former Aristotle calls the intellectual virtues; of the latter, the moral virtues ... intellectual virtue is the consequence usually of explicit instruction, moral, of habit. Virtue is not inborn, but a consequence of training.

McIntyre (1985: 105) believes that the virtues of tolerance, obeying good rules, cooperation and the like are practices that enable the realization of good for ourselves and for others. Schools establish practices through their policies on discipline, safety, etc. to realize this good for individuals. The virtues contained within these practices sustain the practices that in turn sustain the virtues. Virtue ethics focuses on the individual character and not on rules or the isolated actions of an individual. It is as natural for a child to judge and choose as it is for them to begin questioning their life, and the life of others, and through this thinking process to make changes to their own behaviour and way of thinking. This is not a neutral process carried out within a vacuum, but is conducted and evaluated against and within the standards of the community, which is the context for any decisions made.

In Susan Meyer's (1993: 125) reading of Aristotle's *Ethics*, children are deemed to lack reason and therefore cannot act according to it. Since virtuous activity must involve rational decision-making, in the face of daily life, children are only, she concludes, morally responsible to a diminished degree. Children are not in control of the development of their character for they are under the control of parents and, to a much lesser extent, teachers. They need to move from what Aristotle calls 'nurture and care' to adulthood before they can be considered fully responsible for all their actions and, above all, their character. Nancy Sherman (1989: 7) describes how Aristotle's theory is practical in this respect since he emphasizes the role of parents in transmitting the virtues. Parents act as both role model and judge for the child's actions whilst they grow. Sherman (1989: 152f.) details how through the stable bonds of love and trust with parents this transmission of virtue takes place. But even with the best moral education, there is still no certainty that the child will perform the right actions. The adult stage of human growth is clearly considered important for character development. The young need to be prepared for life by being brought into contact with a world of exemplary characters in literature and in culture.

David Carr (1991: 16) recognizes that educating individuals to become virtuous is a complex matter. He believes that character traits must be deliberately and systematically formed in the young. Gerald Hughes (2001: 73) makes the important comment that:

> Moral training is not merely a quasi-Pavlovian conditioning of knee-jerk responses; it involves the young also in learning to use the concepts of morality with increasing sophistication, to esteem morally admirable behaviour, and to feel shame when they fail to live up to the standards proposed to them. Their more nuanced moral vocabulary goes hand in hand with more discriminating affective responses to situations, and together these add up to a gradually improving ability to make good moral judgements.

As Joel Kupperman (1991: 16–17) says:

> If character is formed along with, or somewhat in advance of, the ability for rational reflection, then moral education cannot merely be a series of rational appeals. It must affect the formation of character in children who are not

yet in a position to go very far in making rational choices about the people they want to be.

In a contemporary education setting, Brian Wilcox (1997: 259) reminds us that virtues

> ... have been displaced from their former central position. In their stead are rules which aspire to universality. Attacks on virtues have usually been attacks on the teaching methods employed to teach them and in this there has been much to be concerned about. Virtues in so far as the term is used at all, are seen simply as dispositions necessary to produce obedience to rules.

Concern about teaching methods in virtue approaches is longstanding, but Wilcox advocates a return to virtue approaches. For him character is understood in terms of virtues which give the person a 'moral sense', by which they may not only reason that things are good or bad but feel them to be so. The individual can then act when confronted by unique moral situations. Being virtuous is not a matter of following a set of prescribed rules, but rather of expressing one's moral character in attitudes, feelings and deeds. Virtuous people are disposed not simply to do the right thing, but to become the right sort of person. For the Aristotelian, teaching the virtues means developing certain human excellences in the child. Aristotle believed that there were two main reasons why a child found it difficult to understand why they should behave in certain ways: the child's inexperience of life and its lack of rationality. The teacher's role is to describe to children what the ideal virtues are as expressed in action, as well as providing the positive environment which will help lead the child to acquire the traits of character necessary for the formation of good character.

There is one direct and popular method used in schools for the formation of virtue in children, that of telling stories. Teachers know that children are often fascinated by the fictional characters they find in books – especially those characters that misbehave. Authors use characters to teach a moral story – for example, Pinocchio disobeyed his father and ended up in serious trouble. The same moral story is found in *The Tale of Peter Rabbit*. This is a virtue ethics approach to education: it helps shape and train character. Stories, poems and songs all contribute to moral education and it is why the use of story is advocated by many who promote virtue ethics as a basis for character education (Bennet 1993; Coles 1997). Kilpatrick (1992) outlines the relationship between imagination, desire and action in these stories and describes how they need to be used in order to help build character. Using the clear moral lessons inherent in history and fiction, teaching becomes a lesson in applied ethics. This leads to a debate about which stories should be told in the class, as there are those who are unhappy with the ethical messages in some children's literature. The debate over whether books are useful in conveying moral messages or virtues and vices is longstanding. In 1783 the Edinburgh Pantheon Society debated the motion 'Does reading novels tend more to promote or injure the cause of virtue?'. Some believed that there was a dangerous tendency to elevate private passion over public duty in works of fiction (see Porter 2000: 287).

Virtues have corresponding vices, but a person who is considered good would be one who had virtues and lacked vices. Virtues are also partly constitutive of a person and need to include a motivational element – you need to choose, to want, to prefer to be virtuous. Virtues are not competences and one is not virtuous because one obeys the rules. Some virtue ethics approaches to character education are almost completely associated with duty and not the wider promotion of human excellences. There appear to be two main approaches to teaching character education. First, the teaching of relevant habits of action in which moral virtue is generally a mean position between an excess and a deficiency: for example, courage is a mean between the excess of rashness and the deficiency of cowardice. Teaching seeks to establish a balance between these two polarities. The second approach involves the teaching of a conception of the good character and virtue in which everything is explained in the light of this conception. We teach what a person ought to do in a situation by reference to what a good person would do.

The first of the approaches is that which Aristotle taught. He believed that the 'mean' acted to help regulate our emotions and feelings to people and situations so that we would eventually be able to conduct ourselves with dignity. The vices of excess and deficiency therefore must be avoided. If we take Aristotle's example of the virtue of modesty, the excess to be avoided is shyness whilst the deficiency to be avoided is shamelessness. His virtue of truthfulness has an excess of boastfulness and a deficiency of understatement, and so on. The implications for character education are clear. If a child becomes angry at a rebuke given by a teacher for their bad behaviour, then it is the duty of the teacher to try and help the child to accept their feelings of anger for what they are: a natural emotional response. The child can either review the situation and correct their behaviour or continue to act in a way which will attract further rebukes and lead to further anger and frustration. The teacher seeks to help the child by explaining why it is right to behave in an appropriate manner, but is also teaching the child, consciously or not, how to feel in the right way. This requires the child's understanding, so the child needs to know why it is important to feel and act in particular ways. Feelings are not to override reason, but should conform to it. The child learns to control its feelings as well as to display the appropriate behaviour. The development of the child's good character can lead to good actions. The principal criticism of this process is that there is no simple way to determine good actions, but it is also its principal strength in that it allows us to deal with the real complexity of living.

Those who advocate character education should not endorse Aristotle's theory completely. They need to be aware of some of the pitfalls in deploying his arguments. First, Aristotle identified virtue with a particular class of people, as Thomas Arnold did in Victorian Britain. In Aristotle's time this class was the aristocracy and it is why Peter Simpson (1992) believes that Aristotle's theory is inseparable from the opinions of the aristocracy and their politics. Aristotle's virtues only fully existed for the elite of society. Second, despite Aristotle's emphasis on good parenting as being essential for the transmission of the virtues and the building of character, he believed that mothers had inferior characters to those of fathers. Third, Christopher Cordner (1994) notes that Aristotle would not have recognized the virtues extolled by character educators, such as kindness, compassion, forgiveness, apology, repentance, remorse and humility, since many of these are Christian-inspired. Fourth, do not some virtues conflict with each other? Can the virtues of honesty and loyalty co-exist? Aristotle was not clear about how the virtues are bound together. The system of Aristotelian virtue and character formation is not the same as modern virtue ethics or character education. In chapter 2 we saw how the Victorians emphasized certain virtues and how in the early twentieth century a different set of virtues was extolled, but most of these were intrinsically linked to the idea of social class. In the next chapter we will see how Christianity added further virtues to Aristotle's list and how, in our own day, virtues such as tolerance and openness continue to be added to the roll.

Virtues and education

The National Forum for Values in Education and the Community, established by the School Curriculum and Assessment Authority (1996–1997), sought, in describing the core values which it believed society would agree upon, some kind of agreement on the principles for developing virtuous conduct. The Forum, which was made up of a group of 150 people from diverse backgrounds, agreed that to assert that there were no shared values in a pluralist society was false. The Forum produced a set of core values which, it claimed, were applicable to all, irrespective of class, sex, gender, race or religion. These included: friendship, justice, truth, self-respect, freedom and respect for the environment. A poll of 1500 adults commissioned by the government found that 95 per cent agreed with these core values. These were 'consensus ideals' – values presented as ideals. Other societies have tried exactly the same process of identifying commonly held positions. McClelland (1992: 80) describes how the Educational Policies Commission of the National Educational Association and the American Association of School Administrators also identified 'a generally accepted body of values' in 1951, which included many that were subsequently identified by the National Forum: truth, respect for persons, commitment to brotherhood, acceptance of individual moral responsibility, etc. These 'essential' values, the Commission said, should be transmitted in the nation's schools, the school having the right and responsibility to teach them. Like the National Forum, the Commission claimed no universal or transcendent source of meaning for its values; its basis for validity was the consensus among those who were consulted in their production. It seems that the search for inclusiveness in moral matters results in removing or reducing potential conflict to the minimum. This results in moral values being taught in school in such a way that it is restricted to the principles about which there is essentially no disagreement in society.

Some argue that virtue education is no more than a morally and educationally dubious training in the unreasoned following of rules. The opponents of character education and virtue ethics have often overstated the fears of indoctrination. There are several responses to this. Allegations are often levelled against character educators who adopt virtue ethics approaches that they are concerned with indoctrination, blind rules for behaviour, discipline, rewards and punishments, control and didactic methods of teaching. To indoctrinate is defined as to teach something that is true or universally accepted, regardless of evidence to the contrary or in the absence of evidence at all. It is a pejorative term, as it originally referred to the teaching of Church doctrine in a more intolerant age. Indoctrination became associated with educational methods of totalitarian regimes and is now viewed as an unjust practice in Western democracies. And yet every teacher indoctrinates to some extent, as children do not always understand the reasons why they should believe and act in certain ways even whilst teachers insist that they should do so. Much is accepted on authority and it could be argued that children grow into virtue, the rational basis for which they learn as they develop but have no hope of learning unless the underlying dispositions are already there.

Today many argue that ethical decision-making is a free process without any predetermined outcomes – everything can be disputed and in any case children should make up their own minds. This approach is not followed in schools as teachers adopt committed lines on a range of issues including the elimination of bullying and racism. Avoiding moral training does not mean the avoidance of influencing the pupil morally. If there is a refusal to teach the child the rules of behaviour in school, then it could be argued that the child is free from imposed custom, the counter-argument being that to deny a child the necessary skills for social living could inhibit rather than promote their freedom. Training and education should be combined in schools, since not only are pupils being trained in certain social skills which are functional and predetermined and which match certain operations, but they are also having their minds opened. Training and education are interwoven in the early stages of schooling and it is through them that the practice of virtues is formed alongside the development of rational and self-critical capacities. Virtuous behaviour without thinking is a philosophical and ethical impossibility. Virtues require reflection. Spangler (1983: 80) notes: 'Character formation is training in moral virtue in order that the higher rational life of the human being may be pursued without emotional or external disturbance.' One can still accept that there is a latent rationality in every child and seek to cultivate decision-making and develop this through practice – this is exactly what Aristotle suggested.

M. D. A. Freeman uses the term 'liberal paternalism' (1983: 53) to describe the responsibility parents have to ensure that their child receives an education that will best equip them for eventual autonomy and fulfilment. This may involve subjecting the child to disciplines and rigours against their will, and may involve curbing their freedom. This is justified if it leads to the child's eventual 'rational independence' as an autonomous adult. However, in a fuller reading of Freeman it is clear that whilst he believes that every child has the right to the best possible upbringing, he denies that parents have any significant rights over their children, particularly the right to restrict the child's decision-making.

John Stuart Mill, in his essay *On Liberty* in 1859, emphasized that: 'To bring a child into existence without a fair prospect of being able, not only to provide food for its body, but instruction and training for its mind, is a moral crime, both against the unfortunate offspring and against society.' Mill was also concerned with the question of whether or not one person can legitimately exercise power over another. He believed that each person had the right to pursue their own interests in their own way so long as they did not interfere with anyone else pursuing their interests, the so-called 'harm' principle. Mill justifies the making of an exception in the case of the immature person, on the grounds that A can interfere in the affairs of B if it helps B to develop into a mature person capable of equal and free discussion. This could be called Mill's theory of character cultivation. In liberal accounts of moral education, where there is an emphasis on the desirability of free decision-making, the concession is still made that exerting moral influence upon pupils will sometimes be necessary – in order to eliminate bullying, for example. If such antisocial vices are not challenged, it can be argued, a child's freedom to participate in civil society is seriously undermined. It is on this basis that 'liberal paternalism' has sought to justify coercion and restraint in moral education.

Thus, formation of human character is not straightforward, falling as it does into many philosophical categories. A character trait, for example, is a way of behaving that is not always accompanied by a rational motive or intention. Traits are also concerned with the manner in which goals are pursued – not the goals themselves. Dispositions are natural but can also be developed in a person. Consequently, we have to decide which dispositions should be cultivated in which environment and by what methods. Dispositions can be skills or virtues. Habituation is repeated experiences and/or actions of the same type which give rise to habit in a person – that is, a permanent mental disposition for a certain type of behaviour. Virtues are learned personal traits and are of different psychological types. They are linked to and understood through a particular tradition. Some rely on behaviour, like hospitality, which could be viewed as a manifestation of certain underlying virtues such as generosity; others on emotions, like gratitude, and yet others are about thought, such as wisdom, understood as reflection on experience. Ultimately, as Julia Annas (1993: 55) says: 'having a virtue is having one's character developed in such a way that one not only grasps what the right thing to do is but takes pleasure in doing it; one is repelled by the thought of wrong acting'.

In the first stage of the virtue approach to moral education, habits are formed. As Norman Bull (1969: 123) says:

> The value of habits is threefold. First, they do away with the necessity for making endless moral judgements. By becoming habitual, second nature, and more or less automatic, they by-pass many areas that would involve constant decision-making. Secondly, they build up recognisable attitudes. Many habits concern relationships with others, and so play a real part in moral conduct. Habits of kindness and courtesy, for example, shape and express attitudes

towards others. Thirdly, by coping with less important and more peripheral concerns, habits leave the individual free to concentrate upon crucial moral areas, where judgement must be conscious, deliberate and concerned.

The formation of habits is not unreflective. Nancy Sherman (1989: 30) says: 'Aristotle insists as a requirement of virtue that we be open to inquiry and a reflective grasp of our ends. This indicates reflection on our ends, conceived not abstractly but embodied and clothed in concrete circumstances. Only in this way do we actually reflect on our selves and our lives.' Jerome Kaplan (1995) also argues that young people should be active and responsible in their education and says that: 'if education focuses on the interplay of intellectual and moral virtues, then character ceases to be a collection of predetermined behaviours'.

Robert Sandin (1992: 168) reminds us that the exercise of virtue 'is for Aristotle the exercise of reflective and responsible choice in the actions out of which the virtuous disposition or trait is formed'. Carr and Steutal (1999: 252) say: 'Virtuous conduct requires the kind of sensitive independent judgement which cannot be secured by mechanical adherence to general rules or precepts.' Burnyeat (1980: 73) adds that habituation of virtues must involve a 'cognitive slant'. McIntyre (1985: 155–6) notes that for Aristotle, 'excellence of character and intelligence cannot be separated' and 'genuine practical intelligence in turn requires knowledge of the good, indeed itself requires goodness of a kind in its possessor'. John White (1990) also adopts a virtue ethics approach to education and points out that as long as children flexibly and intelligently learn virtues then it is fine to teach them basic morality. Indeed, he describes early education as 'the formation of dispositions', with the purpose being 'to shape the tendencies and propensities with which children are born into settled dispositions of certain sorts'. Habituation as understood by Aristotle is not the mere mechanical repro- duction of an action type. Sherman (1989: 29) emphasizes that one has to think about one's actions and calls the process 'critical habitation'. However, she also believes that Aristotle's view is that the purpose of ethical enquiry is a deepened commitment and improved ability to lead the good life by those who already 'care about virtue' (1989: 71).

Hughes (2001: 80) sums up how he thinks Aristotle might have responded to these allegations of indoctrination and unreflective obedience:

> I think Aristotle's best line of reply to this difficulty is to say that *any* way of educating the young is, like it or not, inevitably going to inculcate some morally significant beliefs and traits of character. The idea that one can maintain a complete moral neutrality in the upbringing of the young is sim- ply an illusion, and a potentially dangerous one at that. But if the moral code in which the young are educated includes teaching the distinction between what is basic and what is less obvious in ethics, and includes the outlines of a method of assessing moral beliefs, one can justifiably claim that no alter- native training can be shown to be less indoctrinatory.

By this method children are not forced to adopt a particular moral outlook or stance through a non-rational means of teaching and learning. The cultivation of virtue does not mean the abandonment of rationality – it simply provides a moral setting for the exercise of reasoning. The neo-Aristotelian position understands the development of good character in terms of fostering knowledge of moral principles, applying the principles to particular cases and developing a disposition to act as the principles require. Good and right action are not simply a question of epistemology, but must result from being a particular kind of person for whom virtuous conduct is part of one's very being. Becoming a different kind of person through learning requires a justification. For schools, the question of why we learn certain virtues must be capable of answer.

Freeman's (1983: 59) 'liberal paternalism' potentially provides parents and teachers with the power to intervene in children's lives with the justification that it will make them better people, but it is an extremely limited kind of power, based on what Freeman calls 'intervention directed at conduct that is irrational judged by a neutral theory of the good'. Freeman asks whether or not adolescents should require parental permission to use contraceptives or have an abortion. His answer is that parents and teachers may intervene to discourage sexual activity and experimentation whilst encouraging the practice of contraception and he gives the girl, rather than her parents, the final say in abortion decisions – no matter what her age. He argues that this combines protection with autonomy and concludes:

> Protection can be justified because sexual maturity is not necessarily intellectual maturity. An adolescent may find it difficult to defer gratification. This is a defect in practical rationality. It is incumbent on us to supply the rationality that is missing. This can best be done within a framework of education and counselling, rather than compulsion. The age of consent has no real meaning and I would abolish the concept totally.

Sex between children is not considered morally wrong and far from allowing intervention to 'curb' the child's freedom, Freeman advocates counselling with advice on contraception. Freeman adopts the same conclusions on the rights of children as David Archard (1993), including denying that parents have the right to intervene in the sexual lives of their children.

Richard Peters (1962) in a lecture on character development at Harvard University argued that: 'moral education is a matter of initiating others into traditions and into procedures for revising and applying them; these come to be gradually taken in as habits of mind'. He also says that moral education must 'bite on behaviour'. He outlines the tension in much character education: that the child will not understand rules for behaviour in the early years and that they will need to have their impulses regulated. At some stage we need to understand the reasons for doing things – but which rules to pass on and how to do it? Peters never accepted the totality of Aristotelean virtue ethics in character education, preferring instead to offer character education as a supplement to Lawrence Kohlberg's approach to moral education.

Carr (1984a) categorizes his three theories of moral education. The first he calls the 'adaptation theory', which he associates with theories of relativism and utilitarianism found in the work of Durkheim. In this model, moral education consists of the ways in which people are initiated into the moral ideology of the culture. The difficulty is caused by having to distinguish between moral elements and the socialization process. The second he calls the 'autonomy theory', which he associates mainly with Kant and moral development: moral education is deciding for oneself freely and consciously. The main problem here is the overemphasis on process rather than content. The third model he terms 'virtue theory' and it is to this theory that he gives his approval. The model cultivates the moral virtues through imitation and the guided practice of moral conduct. The main concern to be addressed is what virtues should be taught and how one secures the teachers to model them.

Teaching and schooling are moral practices and are two of the vehicles by which young people are enabled to explore seriously what it is to be human. For Jacques Maritain (Gallagher 1967: 104–8) the responsibility of the school is intellectual not moral: to teach children how to think, not how to act. He emphasizes the family role in developing virtues but agrees that knowledge is a general precondition for virtue. He also asserts that the atmosphere of the school is crucial and makes the distinction between inner formation and external observance. Maritain believes that both situation ethics and code ethics are inadequate for character education: love of one's neighbour, for him, is the basis of character development.

Others like Mortimer Adler (1990: 54) believe in 'absolute and universal principles', that the proximate ends of education are the moral and intellectual virtues whilst the ultimate end is a good human life. Mary Warnock (1977: 143) thinks that moral education is not a subject for the school curriculum. She believes instead that the example of teachers and a positive school ethos are better moral educators. What needs to be recognized is that there are numerous approaches to character education and much disagreement between proponents and opponents.

Conclusion

The roots of virtue theory are in Plato and Aristotle. They concur in acknowledging the importance of training or education in the virtues as essential to achieving personal excellence and living the best kind of life. Given their concurrence, we should beware modern discussions that polarize their differences. True, Plato emphasizes cognition, Aristotle habituation. But they fundamentally agree that ethical behaviour can be taught and that reason alone is not sufficient to make a person morally good: action is also required. Virtues are necessary and these virtues represent the tendencies, attitudes and capacities in all of us that make it easier to behave in certain ways. Virtue is the power to realize moral good, to act in the face of inner and outer obstacles, altruistically if need be. A person of character derives this character from the decisions and actions he or she makes. As these decisions and actions are repeated they become habits which further evolve into character. The educational ideal of rational autonomy is limited. We do not think about every decision and every action that we take in life. The child needs to have some trust of authorities, whether they be parents, teachers or other significant people. Some uncritical obedience is necessary, particularly in the early years of childhood. Too much current discussion on the virtues of character is unhelpfully polarized.

Genetic make-up, the influence of parents, adults, peer group and teachers, even chance – all play a part in the decisions that we make in life. The extent to which all our decisions can be rational is necessarily limited. A morally mature person is one who has first learnt to relate to others in positive ways. Character education must be about respect for others as unique human beings. Character education must inculcate the acknowledgement that, despite superficial differences, all are worthy of respect. The pupil needs to learn to balance self-interest against the needs of others and develop a capacity to show generosity, extend friendship and express a sense of sympathy for others. This will involve behaviour, attitudes, feelings and rationality. O'Leary (1983) sums this up:

> Moral education is concerned with the development of reason and of a person's ability to act in morally appropriate ways. These, however, are not two separate enterprises but rather linked by way of traits of character. In developing those traits of character known as virtues, moral education enables a person to act for good reasons.

We should remember that moral education cannot be taught in schools in the way that other subjects are taught. Understanding truthfulness provides no guarantee that the child will practise honesty in his or her dealings with others. We also need to remember that all are not born equal in their capacity to build a character of virtue. Some children find the acquisition and practice of virtue painless whilst others find it easier to acquire vices. In this respect, the circumstances in which our characters are formed are crucial since virtue is, for the most part, acquired.

Virtue ethics begins by posing the question: what kind of person should I be? It answers that I should be a person who possesses the virtues. Robert Louder (1987: 66f.) notes that the possession of these virtues is not always observable in actions and so the idea of abandoning rules is utopian. He believes that virtue ethics is an inadequate basis for character development and that those who advocate it are overly optimistic about the power of virtues. Gilbert Harman (1999) goes so far as to suggest that the idea of a virtuous character is an illusion. He claims that contemporary social psychology shows that there is no such thing as character traits. Kupperman (2001) responds to Harman by defending virtuous character as an ideal in moral education. Virtue ethics has some clear advantages over a rules- or principles-based morality and Michael Slote (1992) believes that it might even possibly ground our ethical thinking. However, as Robert Audi (1997) notes, there is a need to move from explaining virtue ethics to what constitutes acting from it. We need to be able to identify when we act from virtue.

Audi (1997: 189) also makes it clear that: 'Virtue need not be acquired, moreover, from studying moral values as such; it is normally acquired by imitation and socialisation, and it probably cannot be taught without models.'

One problem associated with a virtues approach to character formation is that there is often an untidiness about the virtues to be acquired. It is impossible to provide an exhaustive list of the virtues that are necessary for character, for their existence appears arbitrary. Virtues may also be lost or weakened as well as strengthened. Character educators need to give reasons why certain virtues are necessary for character development. Character development in the virtues occurs over a whole lifetime. Different virtues are suitable for responding to different types of educational problems. Virtues incorporate cognitive as well as affective dimensions. The aim of education for many character educators is the production of virtues through an initiation into an entire pattern of life that reinforces good reasons with virtuous practices. Good conduct is conduct that displays a virtue and these virtues are human excellences that enable one to live in accordance with one's nature as a human being. Some believe that we have lost the traditional framework of practices and beliefs that sustained a life of virtue.

So we return to Aristotle, who desires to know what it means to lead a good life. In attempting to answer, it is he who provides us with the foundation for a commonality of purposes in education. Ronald Beiner (1992: 149) summarizes the basic Aristotelean theory thus: 'Its basic conception is that moral reason consists not in a set of moral principles, apprehended and defined through procedures of detached rationality, but in the concrete embodiment of certain human capacities to be constitutive of a consummately desirable life.' As we have seen in chapter 2, the aim of teaching virtue was very common in elementary schools in England, but it was often a faulty and class-bound idea of the virtues. Robert Hutchins (1938), as president of the University of Chicago, expounded a philosophical view of the person that defined: 'The object of education is the production of virtue, for virtue is that which makes a man good.' After endorsing a virtue ethics approach to education he stresses the connection between the intellectual and moral virtues: 'The great and specific contribution that a college or university can make to the development of virtue is in supplying the rational basis for it, that is, developing the intellectual virtues.' Aristotle would have agreed, for this stage of education provides the reasons why we have learnt the virtues in the first place. Questions of how teaching and learning have occurred previously, whilst important, are secondary to the reasons for learning. The learning of virtues cannot be conducted in isolation from the social context or cultural tradition in which they exist. Virtues not only help us achieve our life goals, but are educationally worthwhile in themselves.

4 Theological insights into character

His divine power has granted to us all things that pertain to life and godliness, through the knowledge of him who called us to his own glory and excellence, by which he has granted to us his precious and very great promises, that through these you may escape from the corruption that is in the world because of passion, and become partakers of the divine nature. For this very reason make every effort to supplement your faith with virtue, and virtue with knowledge, and knowledge with self-control, and self-control with steadfastness, and steadfastness with godliness, and godliness with brotherly affection, and brotherly affection with love.

2 Peter 3–7

Deep within his conscience man discovers a law which he has not laid upon himself but which he must obey. The voice of the law, ever calling him to love and to do what is good and to avoid evil, tells him inwardly at the right moment, do this, shun that. For man has in his heart a law written by God. His dignity lies in observing this law and by it he will be judged.

Gaudium et Spes (para. 16), Second Vatican Council, 1966

In Britain today we live in a pluralistic society in which our values appear to be constantly changing and in which children are presented with all kinds of models and exposed to all kinds of opinions about right and wrong. As part of this pluralism there are a number of different faith communities with their own schools and their own understanding of the formation of human character, particularly its expression as part of the moral education provided in their schools. These faith schools explicitly recognize moral obligations and incorporate these into their religious traditions and practices. For them, there is a clear and intimate relationship between the character of a person and the religious faith they practise. This belief in God affects the choices they make, the relationships that they forge, the lifestyles they adopt and the attitudes and behaviour they exhibit. In Britain, the main source of these moral practices has been Christianity. Christianity has its own view of the end of human life and its own particular theological categories for filling out the nature of human character. In chapter 2 we saw the historical influence of this tradition in the example of Thomas Arnold and the evangelicals. More recently, as described in chapter 3, Christians and others have been engaged in the revival of virtue ethics as a possible basis for the moral education of the young.

There are clear lines of division separating the secular and religious ideas of character. The ancient virtues of Socrates, Plato and Aristotle included prudence, justice, fortitude and temperance. In addition to recognizing these 'cardinal virtues' Christianity gives first place to the 'theological virtues' of faith, hope and love. The latter directs the human being to God whilst the former are concerned with neighbour and self. To love God and one's neighbour as one's self is the general moral aim for a Christian. The question for the Christian is not 'How ought we to live?' but rather 'How ought we, who have been gifted by God, to live?' Christians are obliged to love and cannot easily adopt the secular language of morals without losing what is distinctive about their belief system. In contrast to secular theories of human development, Christianity seeks to explain aspects of human development and human character differences by reference to God. For the secular theorist, some children are different because they have not developed as fully or as far in their characters as others. The task is one of providing the right environment for them to flourish. In contrast, the Christian view of character begins with God. What is considered right or wrong is defined by reference to God. God's teaching about what is good for human beings is considered to be revealed in the life of Jesus Christ and transmitted through the Bible and Christian doctrine. This may be viewed as the practice of a variety of command ethics since distinctions between right and wrong are linked to the commands of God. Above all else, Christianity proposes an ultimate world-view from which all lesser concerns are judged.

The Christian believes that God is holy and we, being created in the image of God, must attempt to reflect that holiness in our lives. Human behaviour is not only judged by other humans – it is judged by God. We are unique moral agents, according to Christian teaching, able to know and do what is good. We are also free rational beings who are called to an eternal destiny with God. Christians are fulfilled through embarking upon a journey to their final end – eternal life with God. They are concerned in this life with how to form character in order to facilitate progress to this end. Christians seek the best sources of moral knowledge and how best to convey these to the young. For the Christian, revelation from a perfect Creator must be the major source of guidance.

In Christian teaching, each person has the capacity to choose freely. It is only through the exercise of this free choice that a person can be held responsible for his actions. A freedom to choose makes the person what he is. A choice is not merely a decision between different actions in a particular situation, it is a fundamental decision about the character that one desires oneself to be. Our actions give us a moral identity. Character, as the Catholic moral theologian Germain Grisez (1983: 41) says, 'is the integral existential identity of the person – the entire person in all his or her dimensions as shaped by morally good and bad choices – considered as a disposition to further choices'. We shape our character by the choices we make and by what we freely choose to do. In Catholic teaching, true freedom is a capacity to do not simply what we wish, but the good we ought.

Character in Christian ethics

There has been a renewed interest in character education and virtue ethics among theologians, both Protestant and Catholic, perhaps because of their concern for a stronger conception of moral agency in theological ethics. In developing a Christian view of the virtues, Stanley Hauerwas and Charles Pinches (1997: 114), both Protestants, believe that forgiveness is at the very heart of the Christian virtues. Aristotle would not have understood this Christian virtue. Christians often confess their sins to each other and to God in the expectation of forgiveness – they therefore do not have an ideal of character which is free from sin. Hauerwas and Pinches (1997: 57) warn Christians against overusing the language of virtue. They claim that virtue cannot be defended as a thing in itself and that no person can attempt to establish their moral standing before God – this would be self-righteousness. They warn against the appropriation of pagan virtues. In the Christian life these virtues must be seen as transforming life through a dependence on God. As Hauerwas (1975: 130) argues, Christianity is concerned with something beyond the moral – it is concerned with faith. It is interested in conversion not development and seeks the attainment of a new way of life which has no completed stage. Hauerwas (1975: vii and 179) believes that human character is essentially formed by training the self to live according to the Christian story. He offers character as an alternative to the prevailing Protestant conception of the moral life in terms of command and obedience and outlines the case for Christian ethics as best understood 'as an ethics of character since the moral life is fundamentally an orientation of the self'. For Hauerwas, an ethics of character is concerned with growth over time and the unity of self. Character is closely related to virtue and human actions are seen as an expression of the character of the moral agent, with the moral quality of our actions being shaped by our ethical character.

Craig Dykstra (1981), another Protestant theologian, believes that the traditions of the Christian church together with active membership of it will in themselves be character forming. Developmental accounts of morality and character assume that there is something to be educated for. In regard to ethical behaviour and reflection, the Christian position is that it is not just a matter of judgement on moral matters. As Hauerwas and Pinches (1997: 125) say: 'These accounts are built on rationalist self-deception about the power each individual has autonomously to determine his "choices". Christian ethics are not so much concerned with decisions and choices but "with the character of a person, who is as much the choices he did not make as those he made"'. Rather than say we grow in virtue the Christian might say that we grow in grace, which is God's supernatural gift to us. Hauerwas believes that society is in need of a shared religious story and that this story should be that of Christianity, which he considers the best for cultivating a virtuous life.

Richard Bondi (1984) agrees and describes how character can be formed in and by the Christian community, for 'the proper topic of the language of character', he writes, is 'the self in relation to the world'. For him, the Christian narrative forms character through six sites of storytelling activity, which are '(a) scripture, (b) preaching, (c) the rituals, sacraments and worship of the church, (d) the lives of the saints, (e) the history, theology, creeds and social organisation of the church, and (f) the lives of the present generation of Christians, including their social and cultural setting'.

Clinton Gardner (1983) reviews the thinking of a number of other Protestant ethicists, such as H. Richard Niebuhr, James Gustafson and James Laney who, he claims, are responsible for the emergence of the theme of character in recent Protestant ethical thinking. All are concerned with and seek to check the privatization of character that they believe has occurred in the Protestant denominations. David Scott (1991), in surveying a number of evangelical English writers in the Anglican tradition, believes that Anglicanism still has something to contribute to thinking on character formation. James Wells (1998) is another evangelical Protestant who has attempted to address the question of moral formation in the evangelical Christian community, but overall Protestantism has produced few ethicists and moral philosophers. Those that exist can be divided into two groups: the neo-orthodox who lean towards separatism and isolationism in their view of character within their own Christian communities, and another liberal group who have been too open to non-Christian accounts of character. The theologians I have already considered above are more neo-orthodox than liberal.

Part of the Christian insight into character is its understanding of the Christian life as a struggle against sin. It is recognized by all Christians that there is something wrong with the human condition: we can know the good, but often end up doing wrong. The explanation for the Christian is to be found in the effects of sin. Original sin is believed to make the intellect less ready to attain what is true and the will less ready to seek what is truly good. The commission of a sin is to act against our nature – we know what to do but we do not do it. This is reflected in what St Paul said to the Romans: 'In fact, this seems to be the rule, that every single time I want to do good it is something evil that comes to hand. In my inmost self, I dearly love God's law, but I can see that my body follows a different law that battles against the law which reason dictates' (Romans 7: 21–23). A summary of the views contained in this Letter would include: *a* those who are not Christian or Jewish have the power to perceive what is right and what is wrong and the freedom to do good actions; *b* there is something in us that impels us to do the wrong thing; *c* Paul concludes that we need God's help because; *d* we have inherited this fault in our nature (original sin) from Adam and; *e* God has sent Christ to help us and given us access to his grace; *f* God has also given us the Holy Spirit who can help us to overcome our tendency to sin. In addition, the Church is established by Christ to assist Christians by guiding them through prayer and the sacraments. The formation of the Christian character depends on many complex theological concepts – ranging from different conceptions of 'natural', as opposed to 'supernatural', to views of character and how these are brought into the overall Christian view of character.

The Christian seeks to become more Christ-like: the grace that St Paul speaks of is believed to help Christians form their complete human nature. It assists them to make moral evaluations, and to act in moral ways by putting their ethical knowledge into practice. Martin Gillet (1914) deals with integrating the complex aggregate of a person's ideas, tastes, deeds, tendencies and habits into a character. We have free will to make our own decision, but sin presents obstacles to becoming virtuous. Sin is not ignorance or immaturity, it is a condition into which we are born. Yet not all sins exclude us absolutely from sharing in or preparing for the divine life. Christians, particularly Roman Catholics, make a distinction between the seriousness of the sin – not all sins remove from someone the life of grace and Christian virtue.

Neo-Aristotelian ethics in Christianity

There is currently a revival of interest, amongst both Catholics and Protestants, in the work of St Thomas Aquinas (1225–75). Aquinas was a Dominican philosopher and theologian and arguably the greatest teacher in the Middle Ages (see Peter Kreeft's (1993) excellent introduction to Aquinas's main works). Aquinas incorporated a significant part of Aristotle's moral and political theory in his great philosophic-theological synthesis. Aquinas had very advanced ideas about the psychology and pedagogy of education and set out to investigate the nature of pedagogical activity in his treatise, *On The Teacher*. For example, he taught that learning is self-activity on the part of the student who, through reason, comes to a knowledge of the unknown. Teaching is the process which draws this natural reason out of the pupil. This in itself, independent of theology, has important implications for teaching character and citizenship for it means that all genuine learning is active, not passive. Learning involves the use of the mind, not just the memory and it is a process of discovery in which the pupils, not teachers, are the main agents. Teaching is seen as an aid to learning effectively and a variety of pedagogical methods need to be employed. For Aquinas, children need to develop habits and virtues which are settled dispositions or traits of character. Teachers are not to dictate answers, rather they should suggest possible directions for character development to the child through a process of reflection. Education is not about producing rigid character types with absolutely predictable patterns of behaviour. In this, amongst other things, Aquinas follows Aristotle.

For Aquinas 'the advancement of the child to the state of specifically human excellence, that is to say, to the state of virtues' was the point of education. Aquinas found Aristotle a rich resource for his account of the virtues (see Porter 1990). There were, however, important differences. Aristotle was clear that the final end was human happiness, attainable through the possession of the virtues within political society. Aquinas believed that the possession of the virtues was important in developing a Christian life whose end was salvation in Jesus Christ. The Thomist tradition set the ancient virtues into a new context: the teachings and person of Jesus Christ. Pure Aristotelian virtues were acquired through training and education and were viewed as a personal achievement. Aquinas, on the other hand, believed that the acquisition of true virtues was not solely for us to achieve, but was dependent on God infusing us with them through the working of grace. Aquinas defines virtue as 'that which makes good he who has it and renders good his work'.

Both Aristotle and Aquinas define man not only as 'a rational animal', but also as one that is social. Human society is the natural outgrowth of human nature and is constructed upon the family, community, town, city and state. The individual achieves happiness in life through living virtuously. This, for some, presupposes that the community provides sufficient material possessions to ensure good heath and adequate leisure time. Every human being possesses an intellect and free will. The possession of knowledge of what is right is fundamental to Aquinas. Unless the morally correct position is known by the individual, how can he choose it? Morally good actions are controlled by the intellect. Aquinas believed that the will should perform what the intellect judges to be right. Failure in moral actions is either ignorance on the part of the intellect or weakness on the part of the will. Aquinas identifies two main problems in moral development: first, in ensuring that the intellect knows what is right, and second, getting the will to perform the action that is the subject of the morally correct choice once it has been identified. For Aquinas, human will, when gifted by God's grace, is (of its nature) inclined to act rightly or to do the true good, but we must be able to perceive the good in order to be attracted to do the good.

Aquinas not only accepts the virtues listed by Aristotle, but understands them in a new Christian context and adds to them. He speaks of a higher strata of virtues, not acquired by repetitive acts, but rather infused into a person by the free gift of the Creator. He calls them the 'theological virtues' and they are faith, hope and love. The Church can be the medium of these theological virtues through the sacraments, through a life of prayer and worship, and through serving others in society. The moral character of a human being is determined by living the Christian faith. We receive grace and accept it as a gift, but it also demands that we freely cooperate with it.

Aquinas does not ignore the natural intellectual virtues and teaches that amongst these wisdom is the supreme virtue, but here he believes that wisdom attaches to the highest causes, the highest of these being God. Aquinas discusses virtues at great length and lists prudence and understanding as two other crucial virtues of the intellect. He teaches that all the moral virtues are exercised under the aegis of the intellectual virtue of prudence understood as 'right reason about things to be done'.

Martin Gillet (1914: 127) makes clear that Aquinas does not have in mind here only the intelligent and he certainly does not advocate the pursuance of mechanical actions without reflection. He emphasizes again and again that virtuous actions must be the product of liberty. A person's character has eternal significance and a training in social skills alone is no education (Arthur *et al.* 2001: 33). Nevertheless, some degree of moral training is required. The papal encyclical, *The Christian Education of Youth*, issued by Pope Pius XI in 1929, refers to 'the supernatural man who thinks, judges and acts constantly and consistently in accordance with right reason illumined by the supernatural light of the example and teaching of Christ; in other words, to use the current term, the true and finished man of character'. According to Catholic teaching, all human beings have a supernatural destiny, and need to be prepared for the eternal as well as earthly life. An integrated education is needed to prepare pupils for who they must be and what they must do in order to obtain salvation. Pupils are encouraged to use the life and teachings of Christ as a model.

The development model is neo-Aristotelian – the physical, moral and intellectual are to be developed. This view was reasserted at the Second Vatican Council in the *Declaration on Christian Education*. The *Declaration* (see Abbott 1966: 641f.) placed much of the responsibility for character development on parents. It said: 'Since parents have conferred life on their children, they have a most solemn obligation to educate their offspring. Hence, parents must be acknowledged as the first and foremost educators of their children. Their role as educators is so decisive that scarcely anything can compensate for their failure.' Parents were urged to create a positive atmosphere in their homes in which 'a well rounded personal and social development will be fostered among the children'. The family should be the 'first school of those social virtues which every society needs'. The idea that parents have delegated authority from the State to act on behalf of society as a whole is rejected in Catholic teaching.

Modern-day religious interest in conceptions of character has come predominantly from inside the Catholic Church. Catholic approaches to character education have often seemed to be legalistic: post-Reformation Catholic moral theology tended to concentrate on precepts rather than on the virtues. This has had the secondary and unfortunate effect of focusing on the things we ought not to do, rather than more positively on those we should do. Aristotle and Aquinas might have put it as learning to like and dislike the things we ought to.

More recently there has been a movement in Catholic moral theology back towards a virtue ethics approach with an emphasis on the goodness of human lives. After all, the New Testament places greater importance on moral virtues and the character of a person than it does on precepts to be followed. Whilst Catholic moral theology believes – in common with developmental psychology – that character is malleable, it does not accept that it is purely cognitive. Character development is more than a cognitive process: it also involves strength of will and the redirection of desires and feelings.

Christianity has always held that psychology is important because it is sensitive to the origins of human behaviour, especially the idea of conscience, human development and the motivations and needs of human beings. However, this view of psychology contains understandings of how human beings function and provides definitions of concepts such as mind and body. These understandings and definitions are never isolated from Christianity or philosophy, as can be seen in the writings of Aquinas. The modern Catholic approach to character education could be summed up as consisting of a rational enterprise of teaching moral reasoning, together with natural law reasoning. We must add to this the promulgating teaching authority of the Church which advocates the learning of moral precepts, encourages moral decision-making and ultimately acting in a moral manner.

For Jacques Maritain (in Gallagher 1967: 75), moral education is the first aim of education, as opposed to schooling. He adopted a neo-Aristotelian approach to the education of character. Concepts such as forgiveness and the performance of penance and the effects of prayer, liturgy and ritual all influence a Christian's character. Maritain's argument is that the will of God has been revealed to all of us and we, assisted by grace, must do the will of God. He was critical of character education attempts in schools, believing that schools should not directly attempt to shape the character of children or develop moral virtues. This was more appropriate, he felt, for families and the Church. Maritain recognised that some families were not able to educate their children fully in character, but he still believed that schools should principally be concerned with the intellectual growth of the child.

Families and the Church were directly involved in the formation of the child's will, with schools making only a subsidiary contribution. Families went about this process through nurturing their children in love. The Church attempted the same task through preaching, liturgy and prayer. Maritain postulated a stage of training which was a preparation for moral education. The school acting on the child's intellect brings him to knowledge of good and evil. At first sight Maritain appears to share much with those who advocate that schools should simply provide knowledge about acting responsibly in society, but this would be a mistaken conclusion to draw.

Whilst Maritain makes the intellect and the will primary factors in moral education, he is not of the view that the formation of moral character is only concerned with the attainment of the requisite knowledge – that pupils act wrongly due to ignorance or a lack of reasoning ability. Maritain maintains that morality is not entirely a function of logical reasoning: intuition and feeling play a part. Maritain accepts the Thomist view that the will must be disciplined to follow the judgement of reason. We discover how we ought to be from a number of sources. Christians would identify not only scripture but also the accumulated moral experience of humankind as being two of these sources. Natural law and conscience are also important concepts in the Catholic view of character formation that we need briefly to consider.

Natural law and conscience

The natural law theory, as adopted by the Catholic Church, states that all human beings have potential access to moral knowledge and will be able to know what is right through the exercise of their practical reasoning. All human beings are naturally inclined towards the realization of the natural ends for which they were created. These ends are for the good. We have a natural tendency to seek this good. This expresses itself in a process of internal reflection about what is to be done in any given ethical situation. This gives us a partial understanding of moral concepts and how we should react. The Ancient Greeks believed that this universal natural law provided by providence was immutable. The ultimate source of the natural law was conceived in Christian terms as God. According to Aquinas the more we develop the theological virtues of faith, hope and love, the better we are able to obey or conform to natural law. He also believed that the first duty we have is to preserve ourselves. The well-formed person may well know what is right without much analysis. In relation to education this implies that each child has the same inherent tendencies, capacities and powers because they are human. They possess these traits in differing degrees. In this way they are unique and at the same time share in a common humanity.

Aquinas goes on to argue that human nature is not totally corrupted by sin. Human nature itself can be used to understand what our nature is to be. We can come to knowledge of the natural law from our own nature. It assists us, through our reason and reflection, to ascertain the good we should be striving to acquire. Sin interferes with this process. Human beings are also free to act contrary to the natural law even when they have discerned it.

In recent times ideas of the natural law theory have often removed the element of divinity. Some Protestant theologians reject the natural law theory as a basis for morality because they claim it overestimates the reliability of reason in the fallen condition of humanity. Nevertheless, the Catholic Church continues to promote the idea of natural law and Pope John Paul II in his encyclical *Veritatis Splendor* (1993) asserts that the way of salvation open to those who do not have biblical faith is to act in conformity with the moral requirements of the natural law – which is love of neighbour. A brief treatment of the natural law theory in Catholic teaching is given in the *Catechism of the Catholic Church* (nn. 1950–1960). The value of the natural law in relation to character formation consists in the potential of every human being to discern, through reason, what they ought to do in any given situation.

Conscience is also a central issue in contemporary moral theology. A popular understanding of the notion of conscience would have it as a sentiment which occurs after the act – as a response to some perceived misdeed. This is known as the posterior conscience. Catholic notions of the conscience also involve the conscience before or at the time of the event in question. This is known as the anterior conscience. It involves the examination of what is to be done now or in the future concerning what is right and wrong. Conscience, in Catholic tradition, is considered an abiding human characteristic which gives a general sense of value and forces one to discover the right thing through reflection, discussion and analysis. Conscience involves an awareness of moral truth and the use of reason to come to a particular judgement. Conscience needs to be informed and educated and involves a process of deliberation. Its development is essential for character education in Catholic teaching. It assists in the judgement of how to act and in deciding what to do. Conscience is concerned with the application of general moral principles to particular situations. The conscience formed according to the natural law discovered by reason and the revealed truths of the Catholic Church is known as an informed conscience.

An informed conscience will include the knowledge and wisdom we acquire combined with the ability for moral reasoning and judgement. It is an awareness of what is right and wrong based on an acquired knowledge of human nature. It has no special power or source of information beyond that which an individual actually knows. Therefore, there can be different acts of conscientious judgement by different people given exactly the same set of facts. Conscience is not an absolute, but an act performed on the basis of knowledge that may be correct or incorrect. It is necessary to acquire knowledge in order to be able to make the correct decision according to one's conscience. The Christian has a duty to do this, to 'inform' their conscience. Nevertheless, natural human limitations mean that we cannot expect greater certitude than making the honest statement: 'As far as I can determine here and now in my circumstances and with the information available to me this action is moral.'

An act of conscience is the process of knowing what to do. It does not mean the willing of it. The act is a purely cognitive event. The Christian retains a free will and must be motivated to act. Here, the virtues are essential. They include a motivational dimension: not only do we know what we should do but we are willing to do something about it. To be able to carry out the process we must be educated in the virtues. If we do this, our moral reasoning will not only result in knowing what to do, but be displayed in prudent action. It is not enough to know what is good as truth, the knowledge must influence and orientate the will to operate the good. This is the neo-Aristotelian approach described in chapter 3.

A key aim of character education in Catholic teaching must be the development of conscience. This cannot be achieved through a set of legalistic norms imposed by external authorities. The elements that make up an individual character must be freely chosen. Character, from a Catholic perspective, consists in a disciplined will and a firm adherence to moral principles within an informed conscience. Whilst the child is born with a latent conscience it is only gradually that it fully emerges with the capacity to identify its own actions, motives, intentions and aims about what is wrong or acceptable in life. The object is to bring the child to an intimate relationship with God and conformity with the natural law.

The developmental psychologists discussed in chapter 5 claim to have isolated patterns of personal growth that transcend geographical and cultural/social boundaries. These patterns are claimed to be intrinsic to human beings. Is this not a natural law theory? James Hunter (2001: 133f.) found a 'curious blending' of Christian ideals and moral psychology in many Protestant approaches to character education. In a study of evangelical materials for character education he concludes that they 'co-opt' developmental psychology for their own purposes on the basis that it 'provides tools that are, by themselves, theologically and morally neutral but useful all the same when linked to the truth of Christian faith'. This leads, Hunter claims, to a number of ambivalences and the conclusion that even evangelical Protestantism, despite its public posturing, is clearly comfortable with a therapeutic understanding of morality.

'Liberal Protestantism', which emphasizes those parts of Christianity that can be readily interpreted in fundamentally secular categories of thought, appears to be much more syncretistic with secular psychology than either Catholicism, Islam or Judaism. It is also not particularly resistant to dominant psychological tendencies in character education. It is both interesting and strange that some Protestant writers in the field are suspicious of Aristotle and not Piaget, and that they trust Kohlberg and not Aquinas.

Catholicism, Hunter notes, whilst not hermetically closed to developments in psychology, offers more resistance to it. With its traditions of personal piety, collective rituals, worship and associations and its self-understanding as community, Catholicism offers a greater barrier to wholesale psychological approaches taking root in moral education. Hunter (2001: 137f.) observes that Catholic children are often instructed in the idea of community through the biographies of great Catholic exemplars such as Mother Theresa and Maxmillian Kolbe. This approach is particular to Catholic schools. It promotes the idea of service to neighbour as well as that of the Church as a community of people who have an obligation to love others. Hunter also concludes that many of the approaches found in Catholic schools to character education are also to be found in Jewish schools – and that in much of this teaching 'psychological categories and language are conspicuous by their absence'. Catholicism also has an authoritarian structure which inhibits rapid change. It is interesting that Larry Nucci (2001: 48ff.), in studying both Catholic and Protestant children, concludes that their understandings of moral matters are independent of specific religious rules and that morality is conceptually distinct from one's apprehension of religious concepts. This is not a new claim since most moral education philosophers have asserted that there is no logical connection between morality and religion, any such connection being a contingent one. Such commentators also claim that religious morality must be an authoritarian morality. Both these claims are contestable and are indeed rejected by most Christians. Indeed, Sylvia Collins' enquiry (drawing upon a structured survey of over a thousand 13–16-year-olds in the South of England) into how young people's ethical choices are informed by their faith discovered that moral decision-making remains related to faith (see Flanagan and Jupp, 2000: 94–95, and 100).

The Christian school or the Muslim school has the potential to provide a framework and clear rationale for character education which is often lacking in State schools. They can provide a community and culture which inculcates the particular world-view and moral culture. Religious schools are particularistic institutions that share in and live out a narrative. Through the school, religious youth organizations and the local Church or mosque this moral culture is integrated and reinforced. These schools act as local communities, fostering traditional virtues and practices that seek to make for excellence of character according to the particular faith's beliefs. The respective social networks of Catholics, Jews and Muslims can be strong and priests, rabbis, imams and teachers are seen to have authority in moral matters. This provides a consistent articulation of the moral ideals and virtues which are embedded within the structure of the community. The model of moral character found in the Koran, for example, is based on the virtues of love, compassion, mercy, modesty, self-sacrifice, tolerance and peace. Catholics, Jews and Muslims would concur on a whole range of fundamental core virtues, indicating much greater agreement between them than might be expected. Through a sense of unity, shared responsibility and conviction, religious schools can be led by those who enunciate a moral character ideal. It is these interrelated characteristics which make character formation a learning function in the decision to commit to any community. The acceptance by the individual of the values and beliefs about human nature within his religion develops important aspects of his own self-understanding and self-definition. An individual's participation in the ritual and liturgical practices of his faith also acts to strengthen elements of his identity. In these ways, religion affects individuals' understanding of who and what they are. It is constitutive of character.

This is of course the ideal. It is why Catholics have pursued a policy of Catholic schools for Catholic children taught by Catholic teachers under the control of the Catholic authorities. It is also why Muslims and other faith communities are seeking the same policy. However, the erosion of this policy, at least on the Catholic side, has continued for some time, as I have shown elsewhere (Arthur 1995). David Konstant (1966: 19ff.), who was a teacher and later the bishop responsible for Catholic education in England and Wales for most of the 1980s and 1990s, appeared to encourage, whether consciously or not, a secularization of Catholic schools and education. He advocated the use of cognitive theories by Catholic teachers. This approach emphasized the subjective nature of morality, rather than the objective view traditionally found in Christianity. It promoted the notion of excessive individual autonomy rather than dependence on God and gave weight to method over Christian content.

Conclusion

Building on the previous two chapters it is clear that there has been a sustained attack on the relationship between religion and character since the Enlightenment. In the writings of David Hume and Jeremy Bentham we see how, in their view, the concept of the divine was superfluous to any thesis of morality. Education was about knowledge and was considered value-free, whilst religion was about dogma and was value-laden. These assumptions are ungrounded for they fail to examine the fundamental beliefs education rests upon. Until recently almost all modern philosophers followed this line of reasoning. This presented a serious challenge to Christianity. Elizabeth Anscombe (1981, 1958), in her well-known essay on *Modern Moral Philosophy*, contrasted Christian moral thought with contemporary moral philosophy and concluded that modern philosophy had broken with this tradition. She argued, as many prominent philosophers have since, for a return to the Judeo–Christian tradition in morality. Moral law, to Anscombe, makes no sense unless we believe in a divine lawgiver. The Christian Church has a particular view of human nature, from which follow particular ends or purposes from which may be derived certain acts. Anscombe reviewed the philosophical objection to this way of thinking in questioning the widely held philosophical dogma that an 'ought' cannot be derived from an 'is'; that how things are provides no guide to how they ought to behave. The Judeo–Christian tradition moves from a conception of what human happiness and fulfilment consist of, to how human beings ought to attain this goal: an 'ought' can be derived from an 'is'. Many moral philosophers deny any connection between these two, but if the principles of morality are not derived from any conception of human nature, then from where do they come? Christianity bases morality on human nature. However, this has proven to be difficult in a society marked by diversity and pluralism. It also makes it difficult for moral theology, which is concerned with what human behaviour should or should not be from the Christian view of things, to contribute to the debate.

Assumptions about right and wrong in society are undergoing a profound change. British culture is moving rapidly away from its Judeo–Christian foundations. In modern society few have regard for absolute values and there are no authoritative moral criteria to evaluate human action. The idea that we can derive determinate appraisals of conduct and character from an objective description of what is characteristic of human nature has been rejected. This has left us with a concept of the individual with no goals outside the confines of the self. The result is the disintegration of traditional morality. Character educators who argue that we should develop moral characters without believing in the truth of morality do so from an impoverished position. They want the forms and outcomes of traditional character education without the substance of particular sanctions.

For the Christian, character formation is not independent of religious faith. Both reason and revelation are required for ethical decisions and actions. The task of Christian ethics is to discover what God is enabling and requiring Christians to be and do. The Christian will place a high value on altruism, self-sacrifice and the common good. Christianity offers a complete world and other worldly view of morality. Character education cannot be an end in itself for the Christian. The Christian view has a teleological concept of the good life that is contained in the Christian revelation and tradition. This means that Christianity is embedded in all kinds of inclinations, feelings, attitudes, interests, habits, lifestyles, decision patterns and actions. The Christian who is concerned with moral development cannot remain long with Piaget or Kohlberg. Nevertheless, given the critical openness of Catholicism to ancient virtue, it is not surprising that it is also critically open to modern insights and attempts to integrate them into an overall Christian position. The Church provides a backdrop of images, symbols, concepts and rituals against which these virtues are internalized. As *Veritatis Splendor* (1993) says, conscience is concerned with an awareness of moral truth, of the truth that we are called to conform to so that we can be fully the beings we are meant to be. The natural law assists by helping us discern what we are to do. Each character is unique and Jesus Christ is the model for human virtues within the Christian faith community. Christianity offers a religious narrative in order to access the virtues. Catholic teaching asserts that matters of right and wrong have an objective basis and that values are not a matter of opinion – they are not relative and we can teach them to others. Christians also teach morality by using the Bible. Storytelling is a powerful way to display virtues and vices and the Bible presents numerous examples of moral success and failure.

Two approaches to character education can be discerned from Christian teaching. First, some Christians want to move deductively from scripture and/or doctrine to contemporary moral issues. Second, others wish to work inductively from contemporary empirical data back to scriptural and/or doctrinal affirmations. The realistic approach lies somewhere between these extremes. Catholic teaching holds that a synthesis of reason and Church teaching has a bearing on morality, therefore both are needed in character formation. The Catholic Church's *Code of Canon Law* (1983) states:

> Education must pay regard to the formation of the whole person, so that all may attain their eternal destiny and at the same time promote the common good of society. Children and young persons are therefore to be cared for in such a way that their physical, moral and intellectual talents may develop in a harmonious manner, so that they may attain a greater sense of responsibility and a right use of freedom, and be formed to take an active part in social life (canon 795).

An obvious weakness of the Christian approach to character is that it often seems too abstract and currently says little to teachers about the pedagogical practices or content of character formation. Nevertheless, whether it is accepted or not, the Catholic Church appears to have a clear, definite and intelligible theory of character formation which is strengthened by religious motive. In this Catholic view, a full character education is necessarily dependent on and inseparable from religion. More generally, in educating for character teachers will need to understand the beliefs and commitments of their pupils if they are to promote personal change.

5 Theories of character development

For the things we have to learn before we can do them, we learn by doing them e.g. men become builders by building and lyre-players by playing the lyre; so too we become just by just acts, temperate by doing temperate acts, brave by doing brave acts. This is confirmed by what happens in states; for legislators make the citizens good by forming habits in them .... It makes no small difference, then whether we form habits of one kind or another from our very youth; it makes a very great difference, or rather *all* the difference.

Aristotle, *Ethics*

There is a wide variety of theories concerning the acquisition of character provided by cognitive developmentalists, behaviour modificationists, theologians and philosophers. Understood from a general psychological perspective, human character often means a pattern of thinking which leads to acts that persist through time and that characterize or define a person. It indicates the persistent traits or habits of an individual. In turn, these traits relate to moral conduct, moral judgement and ultimately to attitudes and actions which identify or mark one's character. Psychology as a discipline attempts to specify the conditions that promote or impede human development. The discipline presents itself as a neutral/objective science of human nature that may be universally applied to pedagogical problems. Psychologists approach character education from a number of perspectives; moral psychologists examine questions of human responsibility whilst social psychologists attempt to explain the conduct and motivation of human beings in various types of societies. For some psychologists, moral development is not a process of imprinting rules and virtues but a process of developing and transforming cognitive structures in the child's mind. Character development, for them, is dependent on cognitive development and the stimulation of an individual by the environment. Currently, cognitive developmentalists hugely influence education and schooling, but it is an influence that is being challenged. They generally believe that moral education, like its intellectual counterpart, has its basis in applying one's intellect to moral issues. They are also developmentalists because they see the aims of moral education as being a movement through moral stages.

Each theory of human development often has its stages of maturation and its implied norms for what it is to be a full human being. In the 1900s psychologists began to realize that learning in relation to building one's character was a complicated process involving the emotions as well as cognitive elements. There was a movement to understand the content of a child's mind at various stages of growth. Whilst developmental psychology exercises an enormous influence on education, there has been little attention given to ideas of human character in the mainstream of the discipline. The main reason for this is that psychologists have often disliked working with the ethical nature of the subject matter in character and have felt more comfortable with the concept of personality. Moreover, stage theories are part of our understanding of education in general – we can see this in the way schooling and education are organized. In England there are four key stages identified in a child's education between the years of five and sixteen. At each stage we identify what a child is expected to attain in terms of understanding, skills and knowledge for each subject area in the curriculum. By the use of these stages we judge progression in a child's development. It seems that scientific theories of human development are also a means we employ for understanding moral education. It is through such theories that educators seek to make informed curricular judgements on the basis of their knowledge of a pupil's stage of development.

Some developmental theories

A distinguishing feature of those who have attempted to employ educational psychology has been to adopt approaches to character education that begin with a theory of human development which provides, it is claimed, a scientific understanding of differences among pupils. There has been widespread, and often uncritical, acceptance of many of these theories in teacher education programmes. The main issue, often overlooked, is that much of the work in psychology is not directed at teaching and learning. Many in teacher education fail to examine the original purpose of any psychological theory. They also fail to consider fully whether or not the methodologies used in psychology, together with the kinds of data collected, can be easily transferred and applied to educational questions. This chapter does not seek to address questions of psychoanalysis or behavioural psychology but focuses on some cognitive theories.

It is useful to look at six influential individuals in the fields of philosophy and psychology who have made a major contribution to how we understand the development of character education today. They are Rousseau, Dewey, Piaget, Erikson, Kohlberg and Peters. Each has produced a theory of individual development that has helped shape our understanding of how children develop character. They view the role of psychology as identifying the changes and explaining why they occur. Each built upon the work of his predecessors and offered theoretical frameworks that are still referred to in the literature today. Gordon Vessells (1998: 208ff.) provides a more comprehensive account of their ideas, together with a summary of those of a number of lesser-known developmental theorists.

Jean-Jacques Rousseau

Jean-Jacques Rousseau (1712–78) is best known for his work in political philosophy, but one of the central concerns in his writing was education. He believed
that man is born good and is corrupted by society. Education must accommodate
itself to the various stages of a child's development. In *Emile* (1762), his influential treatise on education, he outlined three developmental stages. Up to the age
of twelve is the 'Negative Period' in which there should be no verbal teaching –
the teacher simply providing opportunities for the child to discover things for
himself, with the emphasis clearly on sensory experience. The second stage
begins at twelve and is called the 'Age of Intelligence', in which the child continues to find things out for himself but with a more practical orientation.
Academic subjects are considered to be of use at this stage. The third stage is
termed the 'Education of the Sensibilities', and it is in this stage, upon reaching
the age of fifteen, that the child learns his duties towards his neighbour. In the
final stage the child must eschew evil and do good and this must become part of
his socialization. Education is now explicitly moral in intention, although
Rousseau does not recommend introducing the idea of the existence of God until
the age of eighteen.

Rousseau's position on education was extreme for his day: he dispensed with
the notion of original sin, believing in the inherent goodness of the child. The
practical recommendations he made for each of the stages were largely unrealis-
tic, exaggerated, contradictory and often shocking: he recommends that children
are left barefoot to allow freedom of movement and condemns swaddling clothes
for babies for the same reason. His attitude to women was not in the least
enlightened. In book five of *Emile* he produces *Sophie* who is designed entirely for
the use of *Emile*. His view was that women should be educated in the home with
their mothers. Despite this, and the fact that Rousseau abandoned his own children, the spirit of *Emile* was accepted by many liberal thinkers of his day. These
included Johann Pestalozzi (1746–1827) and Frederick Froebel (1782–1852),
who developed his ideas in programmes of education to promote a socially uninhibited way of life. Rousseau's ideas also influenced Robert Owen's experiment in
character formation (see chapter 2).

John Dewey

John Dewey (1859–1952) was an American philosopher/psychologist who was
deeply involved in the social issues of his day, including educational reform. He
was concerned with the question of how life should be lived and advanced a
philosophy that sought to bridge the gap between morals and science. He also
discerned a continuity between philosophy and social biological psychology. His
emphasis was on the application of the intellect in matters of morals by means
of testing, where appropriate, hypotheses created and refined from previous
experience. Dewey promulgated the practical improvement of education in
schools. He viewed children as active agents who are shaped by, but also shape

their environment. Since children acquire habits from their environment what is required is an educational structure in schools that helps the pursuit of intellectual enquiry.

Dewey was the first to state explicitly the cognitive development approach (1909, 1960). He saw the capacity for individual growth and development in both cognitive and moral domains and believed that teachers need an understanding of the order and connections of the stages in psychological development so that they can assist in this development. Dewey postulated that human development occurs through interactive adaptation to the environment, but that the final end of growth cannot be determined beforehand. His theory of human development in *The Theory of Moral Life* (1960) makes clear that the ends of human growth cannot be fixed. His influence on progressive education was widespread. For him, the criterion of a good character is not development to some higher stage. His theory of development regards human life as good so long as a person continues to develop – as he put it: 'the only goal of growth is more growth'. He allied this growth with evolving social structures within society.

The appearance of character education programmes in American schools at the beginning of the twentieth century attracted comment from Dewey. Whilst he saw education as serving social ends, he opposed most character education programmes that were introduced (see Pietig 1977) because of their faulty teaching methods. Most programmes of character education promoted particular 'virtues' that involved children in making pledges and oaths, and repeating slogans and creeds. Dewey felt that moral education was hopeless in schools. He saw a vital connection between knowledge and activity and believed that the virtues should not be emphasized at the expense of intellectual attributes. He believed that the crude methods used in character education teaching involved the overuse of extrinsic motivation. Dewey wanted schools to develop an ethos throughout the curriculum and life of the school that encouraged active service and critical social enquiry. Whilst he was concerned with ethical decision-making, he nevertheless accepted that pupils act according to habits, which they follow without much reflection. He therefore emphasized the practice of reflective deliberation grounded in the pupil's own experience. Dewey believed that education was a moral enterprise and advocated a much broader view of character education than most programmes of his day allowed for. He was also concerned not to separate knowledge from conduct, believing that learning must affect character.

Jean Piaget

Jean Piaget (1896–1980) was a Swiss biologist who formed a theory of cognitive development based on the idea that the origin of intelligence lies in sensorimotor activity. According to this theory, a child's cognitive development proceeds in a specified order based on genetically determined stages. Piaget was influenced by Dewey in developing his notion of stages and brought a more empirical approach, through interviews and direct observations of children's behaviour and thinking, to Dewey's theoretical definitions. For Piaget, it was the child's actions that were important. Some in teacher education concluded from Piaget's data that didactic teaching methods were not appropriate in education for successful learning to take place and that the sequence of teaching should exactly match the competencies of the pupil's stage of development. Piaget developed an order in which specific competencies develop. Success in school depends on this order being followed. He believed that intellectual growth is best achieved when a high priority is given to self-initiated and self-regulated discovery activities in situations that involve social interaction.

Piaget's theory of cognitive development has four stages: the sensorimotor (birth to twenty-four months); the pre-operational (two to seven years), the concrete operational (seven to twelve years); and the formal operational (twelve to adult). His basic concept is 'mental operation', which he defines as a process of logical thought. His research concluded that children in stage one are not developed enough to have structures in the mind that allow them to relate terms to one another logically. Fact and fantasy get mixed up. In stage two the child thinks intuitively and pre-rationally. At stage three the child can respond logically to concrete objects and relations. Finally, in stage four the child is capable of abstract reasoning. Piaget postulated that certain developmental tasks accompany each stage; their accomplishment enables progress from one stage to the next.

Piaget recognized that schools are not morally neutral institutions and that their atmosphere is important for imparting moral ideas (DeVries 1998). He described two types of morality. First, 'heteronomous' morality, which is when one follows rules out of obedience to authority because of the threat of coercive power. Conformity to external rules is consequently accepted and followed without question. The second type of morality is 'autonomous', which is defined as self-regulation – when a person follows rules out of a feeling of personal necessity. The individual follows an internal conviction about the necessity of showing respect for persons in relationships with others. Piaget also recognizes that 'heteronomous' morality is often appropriate and unavoidable in adult–child relationships. Nevertheless, mindless conformity is to be avoided as coercion only socializes the surface behaviour and reinforces the child's tendency to rely on regulation by others. This could result in what he describes as mindless conformity, rebellion or calculation. Calculation is when a child only performs the correct action when monitored by teachers and when not monitored refuses to follow the behaviour. Piaget sees this in terms of power – under 'heteronomous' morality the child is submissive, has low motivation and feels inferior. Under 'autonomous' morality the child is more confident, respects itself and others, is well-motivated and has a cooperative attitude towards others. He recommends that schools engage with children, ask them for their opinions and share some decision-making with them.

Eric Erikson

Eric Erikson (1902–94) was trained in Vienna as a psychoanalyst and became interested in relating psychoanalytic theory to social and cultural patterns. He is best known for his psychosocial theory of emotional development in which he proposes that each of the psychosexual stages of Freudian theory has a corresponding psychosocial modality. His work developed Freud's conceptions about character formation. Whilst Piaget addressed emotional and cognitive development, Erikson focused on emotional and social growth. His eight-stage theory together with his interpretation of the virtues needed at each stage (Erikson 1950) describe what he believes to be the primary human issues in each phase. He proposes that each person will pass through each of the stages over a life cycle that is characterized by emotional conflict. The resolution of each of these progressive conflicts depends on the development of a particular virtue. His lists these virtues in order of development: hope, will, purpose, competence, fidelity, love, care and wisdom. These virtues emerge as a consequence of the struggle experienced in each stage and they help shape the person's ethical character.

Erikson's theory recognizes that we are all personalities in the making, striving to incorporate the opposites he outlines in each stage. In confronting individuals with a crisis or dilemma, he claims, each developmental stage does not become an end point, but rather a turning point in life. Each stage builds on the past experiences for the future. In stage one he describes the basic conflict of trust *vs.* mistrust, which occurs between birth and two years old. If the child is nurtured and loved in this stage then it will develop a sense that the environment is trustworthy. If the child is not loved then its trust will become physically and psychologically disabled. If the child develops a sense of hope about moving on to the next stage, as defined by Erikson, then it has been successful. The list of virtues at each stage becomes a set of norms for evaluating the degree to which each person matures appropriately. In stage two, called autonomy *vs.* shame and doubt, Erikson (1950: 243f.) states that a basic trust in existence needs to be acquired. He explains: 'Firmness must protect [the child] against the potential anarchy of his as yet untrained sense of discrimination, his inability to hold on and to let go with discretion. As his environment encourages him to "stand on his own feet", it must protect him against meaningless and arbitrary experiences of shame and early doubt.'

The other stages include: initiative *vs.* guilt; industry *vs.* inferiority; identity *vs.* role diffusion; intimacy *vs.* isolation; generativity *vs.* stagnation; and ego identity *vs.* despair. The norms or virtues for evaluating progression through these stages are: self-control, willpower, direction and purpose in life, a sense of competence, fidelity, love, affiliation, care, generativity and wisdom. The overall vision of human growth that Erikson suggests is the development of a clear identity which encourages a creative self-giving. If the child fails to cope successfully with the conflicts in each stage then his or her development is arrested. This has some connections with programmes of character education as Erikson believed that educators should realize that each individual has their own history and identity. Character cannot be mass produced. It must involve real relationships with people. The developmental task is to form human identity.

Lawrence Kohlberg

Lawrence Kohlberg (1927–87) has been perhaps the most influential of the developmental theorists in modern times. He asserted that children who understand justice act more justly. Kohlberg posited six stages at three levels of development in moral judgement. His first stage he calls the preconventional level, at which a person responds to cultural rules and labels of good and bad, but interprets these rules in terms of the hedonistic and physical i.e. good is pleasurable and bad is painful. The second level he terms the conventional. It understands the maintenance of the expectations of the individual, family, group or nation as valuable in its own right, irrespective of consequences. Conformity to social order and loyalty are emphasized here. The third level he calls the postconventional, autonomous or principled, in which there is a clear effort by the individual to define moral values as having validity apart from the authority of the groups or persons holding them.

Kohlberg eventually considered or explored a seventh stage in which the person examines the question of why they should be moral, together with what is the meaning of life? In brief, stages one and two are almost entirely egocentric; stage three appears to be a little less egocentric; stages four and five are based on respect for socially defined norms, such as obeying laws, whilst stage six is based on abstractly and universally defined general principles. His potential stage seven could be described as a 'faith orientation'. For Kohlberg, each stage represented a qualitively different mode of moral thinking. Kohlberg accepted the Platonic idea of an ultimate unchanging good. Knowledge of the good is obtained from logical–cognitive progress through six stages. Development may stop at any one of the stages and Kohlberg did not believe that many people actually reached his stage six. For him the core of character development is the cognitive structural dimension of the human person. His stages describe a sequence of changes in the way people define and evaluate moral alternatives.

Kohlberg was criticized by Peters (1979) who found his theory defective in its dismissal of virtues as important in morality, especially his failure to recognize the role of habit in the formation of moral traits of character. Kohlberg did not recognize the benefits of the virtues tradition in education. Nevertheless, rather curiously, he proposed that there was one universal, all-inclusive ethical principle – justice. Justice is of course a virtue and the only one to be taught in Kohlberg's scheme of things. As Craig Dykstra (1981: 10) points out, justice without the virtues of wisdom, temperance, prudence, courage etc is not really possible. Kohlberg awarded Martin Luther King the status of stage six in his developmental theory. In presenting King as a moral exemplar of vision and courage he ignored his social particularities – in fact he placed King in a social, historical and cultural vacuum. King's age, social background, education and religious faith were all disregarded. Character has clear ethical and even metaphysical implications that many psychologists simply cannot reasonably explain away. As Edward Beller (1986: 70) says: 'Not only are the emotional–affective, unconscious determinants of moral growth and behaviour slighted but so are the related elements of will, self-discipline, steadfastness of purpose, or, in short, strength of character.' Kohlberg's model of moral or character development effectively turned the individual into a kind of rational, skilled judge who depended on their ability or capacity to reason at a high level. Children or adults who were less educated or for some reason lacked the capacity to reason at stage six could be viewed as less morally sound in their judgements and actions. And yet, children and adults can be actively moral without reaching stage six on the Kohlbergian scale.

A major criticism of Kohlberg's theory of development is offered by Carol Gilligan (1982). Her argument is that since Kohlberg used an all-male sample in his research he effectively ignored the potential differences that women would have revealed. Her research concluded that Kohlberg's claim to have found a universal, invariant sequence of stages in the development of moral judgement does not stand. She argues that women typically follow a different pattern of moral development to that put forward by Kohlberg and she lists the virtues of caring, nurturing and compassion which women exhibit more than men. For Gilligan, the ethic of care is more characteristic of women and an ethic of justice or rights is more implicit in the experience of men. The model of women's moral and character development Gilligan provides is a challenge to some cognitive theories. Kohlberg reduced virtue ethics to a function of social setting and structure of moral reasoning. He accepted uncritically the evidence of Hartshorne and May (1928, 1929, 1930) and believed that morality cannot be based on virtues, but rather on understanding. It was from such a basis that he criticized character education programmes and teaching methods in American schools.

Richard Stanley Peters

Richard Stanley Peters (1919–) is a British philosopher and former professor of education at the University of London who played a major part in establishing a British school of philosophy of education in the 1960s. His analytical work into the concept of education had great influence on the training of British teachers, especially his assertion that education was the initiation into 'worthwhile activities'. He was the co-founder of the British Philosophy of Education Society and the first editor of the *Journal of Philosophy of Education*. Peters was one of the first to critically appraise Kohlberg and developed his own theoretical stage theory of development. Peters believed that moral development involved more than reasoning – it must combine an understanding of moral principles with the ability to apply them in situations. To this must be added a dependable habit of good judgement and conduct. This is called the man of 'rational morality'.

Peters' stage theory consists of four stages, as explained by Tobin (1989). First is 'a-rationality', which applies up to the age of three. The child at this stage has not reached the level at which their moral thought is structured by judgement categories and therefore reactions are generally impulsive in this stage. Adults sometimes revert to this stage and in adults it is better described as 'irrationality'. Second is 'egocentricity'. Borrowing from Piaget, Peters describes this stage in terms of basic egocentric feelings and simple concepts or rules of meaning. Some qualities begin to emerge, such as determination and perseverance. In stage three, 'conventionality', people accept conventions and traditions without question.

Peters believed that most human beings remain at this stage three of development. People accept the values, priorities, and prejudices and customs of conventional morality. In stage four, called 'reasonableness', a code of moral behaviour becomes authentically the person's own. The code consists of intellectual understanding of complex moral ideas, combined with an ability to evaluate the morality of any decisions made. There is no sense of progress through the stages in Peters' model and there is the assumption that most will not proceed beyond stage three. Peters' work attempted to provide a balanced approach to debates about character education. He recognized that a rational code of behaviour was beyond the grasp of young children and that as a consequence of this fact: 'they can and must enter the palace of Reason through the courtyard of Habit and Tradition' (1963: 46ff.). Peters maintained that how this was done should not 'stultify' the development of a rational code. He called this the paradox of moral education.

There have been other influential theorists such as Peck and Havighurst (1960) who proposed four developmental periods of character formation with four corresponding character 'types': infancy – amoral; early childhood – expedient; later childhood – conforming/irrational/conscientious; and adolescence/adulthood – rational/altruistic. They emphasized the role of the family in shaping character, noting that religious affiliation is no guarantee of the successful development of character. Peck and Havighurst (1960: 8) describe the qualities of a rational altruistic type in the following terms:

> Such a person not only has a stable set of moral principles by which he judges and directs his own action; he objectively assesses the results of an act in a given situation, and approves it on the grounds of whether or not it serves others as well as himself. (He may do this either consciously or unconsciously; the issue is not the consciousness, but the quality of the judgement.) ... He is 'rational' because he assesses each new action and its effects realistically, in the light of internalized moral principles derived from social experience; and is 'altruistic', because he is ultimately interested in the welfare of others, as well as himself.

Peck and Havighurst go on to list a whole series of other qualities or virtues that make up the character of each person.

Implications for educational practice

Dewey, Piaget and Kohlberg shared the liberal Enlightenment faith that the potential growth of individuals justifies the hope that social evolution will reach a point where moral differences will no longer be perceived as a threat to the unity of society. They believed that they had discovered the key to moral development. In some respects they came to conclusions that went beyond their data, particularly for teaching and learning. Kohlberg's theory, for example, rests on the questionable claim that what makes an act moral is the reasoning motivating it. He does not adequately address or recognize that reasoning can be faulty or self-serving. It is not the case that something should be considered moral simply because an individual believes it to be so.

A number of psychologists outside education have asked interesting questions: Is what we become biased by what we are? How can we be responsible for the way we develop our character? Are we ultimately responsible for our character? In their arguments, contained in Ferdinand Schoeman's edited collection (1987), we are confronted with certain virtues that dispose us to a certain way of viewing what we might become. The developmentalists described in this chapter shared Rousseau's idea that if a child is to understand something then a method of teaching should be designed which conforms to the nature of the child's learning. In order to do this it is necessary to understand the internal development process of a child. This includes their motivations and needs. Rousseau spoke in general terms, but Piaget and his followers have since sought to clarify the process, to the extent of trying to determine what knowledge a child can actually acquire and whether it is relevant. These many theories remain for the most part unknown by teachers. One obvious reason for this is that it is sometimes difficult to apply psychological theories to the classroom. Kieran Egan (1983) argues that these theories have had no influence on teaching whatsoever and that they reduce the effectiveness of teaching, having nothing to offer curriculum design. In his *Education and Psychology* (1983) he sees no legitimate implication for educational practice of any psychological theory. Like many others, Egan asks what these theories prescribe. A student teacher, he suggests, could spend a whole year studying them and be no wiser about teaching. Egan is extreme in his criticism and does not distinguish between a theory of education as a comprehensive statement of principles produced as a guide to educational practice, and some cognitive theory intended to be used to provide insights into particular aspects of educational practice. Psychologists would not claim that educational theory should be substituted for cognitive theories of human development. Unfortunately, this is sometimes the aim, more or less, of many involved in education.

These cognitive developmental theories are perhaps no longer as important as they were in the 1960s and 1970s. James Hunter (2001: 10) describes the pedagogy based on these theories as a strategy of 'shared method' – in other words, character traits are developed by bringing them out from within the child. In this view, these traits already exist: they simply have to be released by the shared psychological method. Hunter identifies two strategies opposed to this dominant strategy and calls them a 'backlash' against the psychological approach: first, the neoclassical strategy, which is a pedagogy of cultivated 'shared virtues'; second, the communitarian strategy, which is a pedagogy of 'shared experience' in community. In practice, Hunter claims, there is not much difference between the communitarian and neoclassical strategies. Hunter's (2001: 128) main criticism is that whilst both these strategies attempt to teach traditional moral values and virtues in the classroom, they are not effective because they rework the psychological strategy within their own traditional conceptions of moral education. They present no real challenge to the dominant teaching method in schools. Hunter has a point here, since many character educators have a background in educational psychology and argue that character-based conceptions of virtue need to be embedded within a larger framework of morality as justice.

Larry Nucci, director of the Moral Development and Character Education Unit at the University of Illinois at Chicago, is one such educational psychologist who seeks to develop character in this way. His approach can be contrasted with that of Kevin Ryan, who was director of the Centre for the Advancement of Ethics and Character at Boston University and who adopts a virtue ethics approach. The difficulty with both approaches is that there is little evidence to prove the effectiveness of the character education programmes they promote, due to a lack of research.

Many developmental theorists neglect the positive role of parenting. They suggest that the parent–child relationship constrains moral development. What is meant here by 'moral development' is the rational ability to make moral choices. This tends to ignore the role that child dependency plays in moral development, especially in infancy. Infancy is a period of life in which parents help shape the future behaviour of the child. This parent–child bond is necessary for both development and survival, and character traits emerge through trial and error. Young children can read the faces of both parents and teachers – they recognize disappointment in them as well as expressions of pride and they generally adapt their behaviour accordingly. In these formative years they model their actions on others and much of their behaviour forms 'automatic patterns' as they reach adulthood. The process is described by William Gaylin and Bruce Jennings (1996: 123): 'a set of constraints and imperatives will be imposed on [their] freedom of action by an inbuilt set of values operating both consciously and unconsciously through the mediation and collaboration of their conscience, their identity, and their self-image'.

Knowles and McLean (1992: 165) believe that character is comprised of, but not equivalent to, dispositions, traits, habits, and tendencies – all of which help define a person's identity. Character is also related to behaviour in a deterministic way, either by influencing the goals an individual chooses to obtain or the actions taken to achieve these goals. Since our character controls the most profound aspects of our behaviour, it is interesting to ask in which circumstances we will sacrifice our self-interest on behalf of others. An understanding of familial influences is essential to viewing changes in children's behaviour. As every teacher will testify, the habits formed in early childhood can be stubbornly resistant to change.

We can recognize that lessons learnt in childhood persist in the unconscious perception of every adult. As William Gaylin and Bruce Jennings (1996: 123) explain, by the time a child reaches adulthood he carries within him certain values and sensibilities that will drive much of his behaviour into automatic patterns. The message is that we are not as self-determining or as autonomous as we would like to believe. Other modern psychologists, such as David Shipiro (2000: 9), detail how character can act as a 'regulating system' – it inhibits certain actions in the individual, enabling him to retain his stability as a person.

Some developmental psychologists reject the moral and social authority of the teacher, both in their professional capacity and as adults. Instead they promote the idea that child and teacher are equal and should participate on a collaborative basis through democratic methods in constructing their own moral positions. The use of coercion or punishment by parent or teacher is considered wrong. Consequently, the school itself is problematic for those who subscribe to their cognitive theories, for they believe that schools also restrain moral understanding and growth through their use of punishment. In England, within primary school education, child development has traditionally been taken to mean the natural process which occurs regardless of education. It is a spontaneous and unique happening in each child. The English system of education appears to have emphasized moral development as part of a growth process rather than being learnt through some kind of structured training.

Many cognitive psychologists also reject virtue ethics approaches because they say you cannot begin with any substantive content in moral teaching, e.g. you shall not kill. Moral content is secondary to their considerations of character development. From Rousseau through Dewey to Piaget and Kohlberg, all reject metaphysics and subordinate it to method. Process is more important than content. Neither Dewey nor Kohlberg fully appreciated the power of virtues in education, preferring to view them as historically fixed social conventions. For them moral judgement is more important, process not product is their educational concern. In the absence of any objective morality, teachers simply become facilitators of discussion and refrain from imposing any views on others, rather along the lines of the School Council Humanities Curriculum Project pedagogical recommendations (see Stenhouse 1970). The teacher does not judge anything in Kolhberg's approach, which was often portrayed to be an improvement on values clarification methods, in which the teacher could present a point of view but had to avoid any hint of 'indoctrination'.

Hunter (2001) goes much further in his criticisms of cognitive psychologists. According to him their theories take no notice of the powerful influences of the media, economics or politics. They make no sense of human commitment and appear to operate within a social vacuum. Above all they do not reveal the framework in which they operate – they talk about the importance of justice, respect and tolerance, but what is the origin of these virtues? Why are they important? These cognitive theories of character education contain nothing that might lead to the ends for which they are designed. As Hunter (2001: 191) says: 'These moral ends are conceived as extensions of an autonomous self yet these ideals are themselves subordinate to self and, often enough, its overriding moral purpose of self-actualisation and fulfilment.' He continues: 'A moral code that is, at bottom, self-generating and self-referencing undermines the existence of and adherence to a prevailing communal purpose; it precludes the possibility of any compelling collective discipline capable of regulating social life. Simply put, there is nothing to which the self is obligated to submit.' These cognitive theories do not make any clear distinction between right and wrong. Hunter is also critical of some virtue ethics approaches. He appears in general to be more positive towards virtue ethics since it, he claims, has the potential to restore some kind of 'objective morality' to moral education. However, in reference to schooling he believes that virtue ethicists simply advocate thin versions of the virtues which are really collections of virtues selectively appropriated from the general culture.

Ultimately, according to Hunter, cognitive psychologists and some virtue ethicists are not able to provide any 'normative meaning' for their approaches. Their ideas are not anchored in any 'thick conception' of the community and there is a denial of particularity. Hunter is perhaps incorrect in his total condemnation of cognitive psychologists, as it is often the application of cognitive theory as dogma by some in education rather than the theory itself that is the real issue. Graham Haydon (1995) argues that the content of morality can be thin and based on a few shared values. He asserts that children can be exposed to a limited range of values, which he considers good as long as they are reflected upon critically. Haydon presents these values as a selection from a number of 'options', but he forgets that authority, loyalty and commitment are also part of character building, for as Clark Cochran (1989) says: 'Acceptance of authority, loyalty to ideals and commitment to an historical community, though they do require sacrifice and closure of options, are the very stuff of character building.' Virtues have connotations of the past, of deference to authority and a tradition of belief and conduct that many in education would not accept. This is why it has to be admitted that there is no rational consensus on character education. The metaphysical approaches adopted by Jewish, Catholic and Muslim schools are seen as non-rational by the educational establishment. Yet they can produce particularity, 'thick conceptions of community' and clear normative meanings for moral education. According to Haydon, religious schools can focus on particular moral traditions as long as they present alternative views of the good. However, most children experience these alternative views in the general culture and so the church school does not necessarily have to teach various life options as these are already presented – for example, on talk shows on television.

The idea that the child is innately good has its origins in Rousseau. Since the 1990s there has been a greater focus on the affective domain of educational psychology and teaching. Personal well-being and the idea of 'self-esteem' have become important to the promoting of character education. The reasoning is that children must be made to feel good about themselves if they are to develop good conduct or virtuous behaviour. Levels of self-esteem, or 'emotional intelligence', are increasingly considered important for human development by some psychologists who seek to focus on the individual – it is the 'self' which has become all-important for them. Individuals have increasingly been left to themselves to decide their own standards for moral interpretation, with external points of reference including sources of traditional authority no longer available to them. It is often argued that children need to be liberated, not taught to conform to a school policy; also, that they need to develop autonomous decision-making through their own personal liberation. The standards of morality lie within the child, and the teacher simply helps draw them out so long as that child is emotionally stable. There is little evidence for this theory. Children are viewed by some psychologists as adults in the making and the method is to bring out their innate and natural moral dispositions – children are only 'developmentally delayed' if their unfolding does not occur. This view has not gone unchallenged by character educators.

James Nolan (1988: 7) speaks about the therapeutic ethos in society and in education, which has produced a 'new priestly class' of psychiatrists and psychologists who understand and decipher the emotive language coming from the 'authoritative self'. They assume, he claims, the role of the priest, of a 'secular spiritual guide' deciding not whether an action is right or wrong, good or bad, moral or immoral, but rather whether something is healthy or not. Nolan (1988: 179) details how some character education programmes in America that encourage children to help others are based not on an appeal to others or for the common good but to the self. This helps the child to enhance his or her own self-esteem and so character education is about the child's feelings, emotions and ideas. Nolan (1988: 19) concludes that the therapeutic ethos 'is both a derivative of the modern "scientific" discipline of psychology and quasi-religious in nature'. There appears to be no conception of the good character outside of the self – Stanley Hauerwas (1981: 131) calls it 'slavery to the self'. What is ignored is that true self-esteem is only possible by an individual's sense of achievement through hard work. The glamorization of psychoanalysis, psychotherapy and psychological testing in popular literature, television and films has at the very least consciously extended teachers' concerns to encompass the 'whole child' – the pupil's feelings, emotions, attitudes and beliefs.

All of the cognitive theorists mentioned in this chapter reject God or faith as a factor in their consideration. They believe that that which is measured, observed and experienced is all that matters – the endorsement of the scientific method. Whilst the models of development favoured by cognitive theorists are widely used to understand how children learn, we are perhaps less likely to see many teaching methods resulting from this understanding. Many of the methods used have been variations of the values clarification approach that advanced moral understanding in the 1960s and 1970s. Moral psychology can be useful, especially in normative reflection of the kind advocated by Owen Flannagan and Amelie Rorty (1990). This kind of moral psychology, whilst taking account of empirical psychology, is much more attentive to philosophy, history and theology. For example, whilst recent empirical psychological research indicates that shyness may be deeply rooted in our biological nature, it raises questions for the moral psychologist about whether character is chosen or self-constructed. Even if character is not chosen, Flannagan and Rorty (1990: 4) argue that we can still exercise some control over it. Nevertheless, character must be to some extent shaped by genetic factors. Otherwise how are we to explain why children born into the same family environment can have such differing temperaments? The child cannot be simply a *tabula rasa*, on which nurture engraves its mark. The *tabula rasa* theory is an inadequate concept to explain the individuation of character. More research is needed to explain the complex interaction between biology and the environment in producing character. Whether the formation of a particular type of character is a matter of chance is another interesting question discussed by moral psychologists. If character is simply about random fortune, then any idea of responsibility in respect of it becomes a nullity. Flannagan and Rorty make a clear connection between character and behaviour because if no connection existed no one would be responsible for their actions. Moral psychology, in my view, is often a more fruitful source of ideas for education, even if no statistical methods are employed and no rigorous experiment is conducted. The enthusiasm for empiricism has often obscured the real meaning of character, with many academics focusing on the scientific methods employed at great length to validate the tenuous findings of a study.

Joel Kupperman (1991) believes that empirical psychology is more appropriate for discerning what people do and not what they say. Kupperman (1991: 161) notes that no questionnaire can distinguish between what a person's character genuinely is, what a person pretends his or her character to be and what a person thinks his or her character to be. Kupperman (1991: 160) provides an example in the form of an experiment with politicians. Politicians are articulate, knowing how to use the vocabulary of moral principles in order to appear virtuous. In the right situation, with minimal risk of being exposed, even some of the most publically virtuous politicians may take a bribe. Kupperman believes this reveals something about their character. Kupperman then refers directly to Kohlberg's empirical methods for his stage theory and reflects that if different temptations had been used, and different standards of ethical sophistication, then perhaps different results would have been forthcoming. Someone who scores highly on a moral development questionnaire and who has always had good habits and patterns of behaviour may surprise the teacher when a real temptation appears. Kupperman believes that there are strong grounds for thinking that moral education based on stage theories is badly conceived. Kohlberg's theory is built upon the notion that becoming virtuous is like becoming good at mathematics, the only differences being in subject matter and progression of intellectual skills. Kupperman (1991: 174) reminds us that no major ethical philosopher has believed this. He concludes: 'To treat a student's preferences at a certain stage as basic, incorrigible data is, in effect, to regard the student as incapable of growth. Such an assumption may well promote the result it assumes.' Rigorous empirical psychology clearly requires a solid philosophical basis if it is to account adequately for character formation.

Conclusion

Different shades of meaning pertain to the term character in different psycholog-ical contexts. Cognitive psychologists place much emphasis on the development of a structure of moral reasoning that, they claim, underlies decision-making. Some claim universality for this method, claims which may go beyond that which their methodology and data can justify. The cognitive theorist also stresses the pupil's independent reasoning ability. This contrasts with the virtue ethics approach which gives first place to the internalization of virtues that change a person and their behaviour. The two approaches are in competition and (see chapter 3) are founded on very different rationales. Development theories of moral judgement do not necessarily lead to the performance of moral actions when applied to schooling. David Carr (2002) also casts doubts on the scientific basis of many of these developmental theories and questions their logical status. He rightly observes that these theories are generally employed in support of pro-gressive approaches to education with their emphasis on choice of value and lifestyle. This ignores the more traditionalist perspectives that are generally con-cerned with initiating pupils into the knowledge, values and virtues of civil society. Progressives, according to Carr, reject traditional perspectives because they do not wish to predetermine the ends and the goals of human development and because they question the worth of received knowledge and values. The dif-ficulty for most teachers is trying to understand fully the pedagogical implications of this traditional/progressive dichotomy. We need to ask what are the purposes of theories of development in education. Above all, teachers need to be careful to avoid giving uncritical acceptance and general application to any particular cognitive, emotional or behavioural theory in the classroom. These kinds of theories are not general educational theories, but are often used to pro-mote progressive teaching methods without a full consideration of their implications for teaching, positive or otherwise.

Russell Gough (1998: 10) maintains that we have the capacity to determine who we are or what we want to be or what we should be over and above what we are by nature. In summary, he offers four central points in his thesis: *a* what we are has an inseparable ethical dimension; *b* we have a innate ability to choose to be good; *c* we, in the end, determine what kind of person we ought to be; *d* we cannot blame others for who and what we are. All these points can be debated but Gough uses a powerful piece of literature in support – an extract from Anne Franks' diary dated 15 July 1944. Anne is aged 15 and it is two weeks before the Nazis would capture her. She writes: 'I have one outstanding trait in my charac-ter, which must strike anyone who knows me for any length of time, and that is my knowledge of myself.' Anne describes and examines her conscience here, par-ticularly her knowledge of right and wrong, and then continues: 'Parents can only give good advice or put them [their children] on the right path, but the final forming of a person's character lies in their own hands.' In this quotation she demonstrates both her remarkable insight and her character.

6   The politics of character

Our youth today have luxury. They have bad manners, contempt for authority, disrespect for older people. Children nowadays are tyrants. They contradict their parents, gobble their food and tyrannise their teachers.

Socrates 400BC

The worth of a state, in the long run, is the worth of the individuals composing it.

John Stuart Mill

We believe in the values of community, that by the strength of our commitment to common endeavour we can achieve the conditions in which individuals can realize their full potential. The basic principle is solidarity, that people can achieve much more by acting together than by acting alone. I think that all this is best represented by the idea of community, in which each person has the rights and duties which go with community .... Rights are not enough. You can't build a society that isn't based on duty and responsibility.

Tony Blair, *The Guardian*, 13 March 1995

Classic liberal theory, in holding that political authority should not be involved in the task of moral education, contrasts sharply with traditional understandings of politics. From Aristotle onwards the goal of politics has been to improve the character of citizens. Today, there is a debate between those who say that government should promote virtue in its citizens and those who say that the term is too pejorative to be used in a pluralist democratic society. Even so, in modern liberal society the development of a person's character is not seen as entirely a private matter for individuals or their families. It is recognized that character is intimately linked to the ethos of society itself and shaped by public forces. Public values have an influence on private life, albeit indirectly, because everything a government does is founded on the notion of it being of some benefit to the people it represents. Character is connected to the political system through the medium of schooling which modern government oversees. Character is also a major component of the making of a citizen. The decisions taken by government have a significant impact on the whole community and on individual citizens, including children. The attractiveness of character education rhetoric for politicians is evident. Character education holds out the promise of social order and stability by the creation of citizens who are satisfied with their lives. To this end, in America in the course of the last ten years, the White House has sponsored a number of character building conferences at which both those on the right and those on the left of the political spectrum have contributed ideas on improving the general character of the nation's children.

Every government therefore has an interest in the character of their citizens. Some, such as the Taliban in Afghanistan through its ministry for the suppression of vice and promotion of virtue, used extreme methods of social control. It should of course be said that it was a government which had a flawed view of what constituted virtue. Those who govern Western political democracies do not seek to use such crude methods. They rely on obtaining uncoerced public approval for their moral education programmes. The quality of political life in a democracy is largely determined by the quality and character of its people. Governments are concerned with citizens and whether the quality of their citizens' characters is improving or getting worse. It is why many politicians refer to the litany of alarm described in chapter 1. The State, as Aristotle pointed out in his *Politics*, has an interest in the education of youth, one of its functions being to bring together the competing interests of individuals and factions. The State must cultivate self-discipline among youth, partly through schooling, in order to produce good citizens. Failure in this will either lead to social and moral chaos or to draconian government intent on controlling the population by external means.

Ever since Aristotle's comments, character education has been just as much a political concern as an educational one. This concern is often expressed by left- and right-wing politicians in the form of criticism of moral education programmes in schools. Character education in America and in Britain has sought to instil a democratic spirit in individuals – witness the promotion of slogans and oaths in American schools at the start of the twentieth century. This code ethics inculcated the virtues of patriotism, loyalty to nation and respect for legitimate authorities in society. The Moral Instruction League in Britain may have used different methods, but the same virtues were listed in its syllabus. Sometimes the democratic virtues being taught were not explicitly outlined – they remained hidden and were 'caught' rather than 'taught'. In this respect, it is interesting to compare British and American attempts at character education with those in the Soviet Union – now the Russian Federation.

Political conceptions of character education

Communist authorities were absolutely explicit about their aims for moral education, particularly character training. The aim of Soviet education was no less than the creation of the Soviet Citizen – a new type of person. The primary objective of education was not to learn a range of subjects, but to develop a 'socialist morality' (Bronfenbrenner 1962). The State was viewed as having delegated authority over children to parents and teachers. The philosophical defence of the view that the State should assume direct control over the upbringing of children is provided by Plato in *The Republic*. The word used for moral education in Soviet schooling was *vositanie*, meaning 'upbringing'. It is a complex term and under Communism it involved the teaching of patriotism, love of country, knowledge of the law, respect for work and legitimate authority, and atheism. Apart from the last item there was not much difference between *vositanie* and the goals of American and British moral education between 1900 and 1950. Great emphasis was placed on physical education in Soviet schools in the belief that it helped produce determined, disciplined and courageous people. Here again there are many similarities with Western democratic ideas on the formation of character and, in particular, an echo of the English public school love of games. The Soviets sought to develop characters who would further the economic interests of the State and to this end much attention was given to the preparation for the world of work – again, the same aims exist in the current National Curriculum in England.

Every subject in the Soviet school curriculum was to contribute to forming the 'new man' who would exhibit the features of the conscientious worker, be able to work in a team, remain sober, be mindful of the war dead and develop an internationalist perspective. Extracurricular activities had the same objectives and youth leaders helped develop the collective spirit and sense of service to neighbour. Again, the voluntary youth organizations in Britain and the USA – the Boys' Brigade, Scouts and Guides – had similar intentions. The major advantage that Soviet teachers had was that the State controlled the media – nothing that pupils read or saw conflicted with what was taught in school. Robin Alexander (2001: 77) explains that although in the 1990s the Russian Federation began to give less emphasis to *vositanie* as a goal of education, the concept remains as an educational tenet in the newly democratic Russia.

Alexander (2001: 216) found that schools in 1990s Russia still gave prominence to developing personality and character traits. They still emphasized student duties and obligations and teachers were concerned with 'upbringing' in school. There still remains a commitment to comprehensive moral and character education. Since the fall of Communism in Eastern Europe, Marxist appraisals of character education have rather surprisingly given emphasis to much that traditional character educators in the West hold to be true. They have given attention to the force of 'moral exemplars'. Kit Christensen (1994: 114) argues that not only children, but adults also, require the example of morally good people as a motivational force in order that they may choose to be good. His Marxist interpretation of character education also explains that simply by being 'authoritatively informed', or 'convinced by rational argument', of what character traits or virtues should be developed is only rarely sufficient. He essentially adopts a virtue ethics approach to character formation from a Marxist position.

Many critical commentators have claimed that character education is often associated with the development of a conservative mind-set. Whilst having no empirical evidence for this accusation they point to some of the leading promoters of character education and describe how they are either politically conservative or religiously affiliated – for example, William Bennett, a leading advocate of the virtue ethics approach, who was secretary of education under President Reagan. This ignores the many liberal supporters of character education in the communitarian movement (see pages 82–83). David Purpel (1997: 140) believes that the movement espousing character education in America is ideological and political in nature and seeks to preserve the status quo in society. As he says: 'Public discussion of moral and character education has become an overtly political issue, serving as metaphor and code for those interested in pursuing the neo-conservative social and cultural agenda.' The real question for Purpel is who controls the debate about the ethical dimensions of character education. He calls upon 'liberals' to enter the debate otherwise the field will be left to those who wish to promote a 'particular and specific moral and ethical system' (1997: 144). The obvious question is would not these 'liberals' that Purpel talks about not also wish to promote a 'particular and specific moral and ethical system'? It is true that much of the recent interest in character education has been stimulated by those with a more traditional approach to morality in schools. However, simply because some may have conservative views does not invalidate their observations or critique. Robert Nash (1997: 32) describes how one of his students reacted to different character educators. He observed that the student generally showed resistance to those she suspected of holding a religious agenda. According to this line of thought, if the author is white, male, conservative and religious, then he is not worthy of attention. Nash's book is significantly weakened by the use of such arguments, for he seems to have failed to notice that one of the first lessons in political philosophy is not to judge the message by the messenger.

Another critical approach is provided by Amy Guttman (1987: 19) who, in *Democratic Education*, argues that moral education is a conscious effort shared by parents, teachers and society to help 'shape the character of less well educated people'. She believes that many educators are not interested in the process of education, merely the results. It is not the moral reasoning that matters but the moral outcomes. Guttmann labels the direct teaching methods that produce this attitude as 'conservative moralism' (1987: 57). The opposite of this she terms 'liberal moralism', in which the object is to assist children to attain moral autonomy and respect for moral principles rather than established moral authority. She polarizes the debate on morality unnecessarily in order to advance her argument. William Damon (1988) also adopts a critical position. He suggests that those who push for character education are ideologically driven conservatives seeking to make children conform, uncritically, to society's mores. He even suggests that they are a danger to democracy. He says: 'Habits without reflection is adoptive only in a totalitarian climate.' (1988: 145). His allegations are that the process of character education leads to unthinking behaviour and conduct – indoctrination by any other name.

Another example of the link between politics and character education is illustrated through attempts to understand the causes of crime. There have been many studies by criminologists who map the criminal character and conclude that character education in schools is essential for defeating crime. The political consensus in British party politics appears to be more concerned with the detention of young offenders than any concerted attempt to reform their character. Both the courts and the general public seemed to have abandoned faith in the possibility of changing a young person's antisocial or criminal character. Parents are of course critical shapers of character and there have been studies by Richard Barth (1979) and Henry Wilson (1980) that suggest that parents can also reinforce what the school teaches in moral education. However, whilst the law rightly lays down obligatory and authoritative guidance for the individual actions of members of society, it is doubtful that expanding the prison population will improve the character of young people.

Ivor Pritchard (1988: 486) raises questions about whose interests character education serves and calls for more research in the political implementation of character education policies. In Britain it could be argued that the concept of moral conviction is enjoying a temporary popularity and could fall from favour as soon as the mood changes once more. In the 1980s and early 1990s the phrase 'character education' was most often associated with a concern to defend traditional moral teachings in society, promoted by religious and political conservatives. With the election of New Labour in 1997 the phrase had become part of a more complex moral debate addressed by a range of 'liberals' as well. The shift in ownership of character and its associated issues was most apparent at the level of political culture (see Bentley 1998). New Labour is now committed to character education as a key element in school reform.

What is the role of the State in securing certain values? Does the school serve the State, the pupils or the parents? It would seem that in a liberal pluralistic democracy, the aim is to produce characters that are not exclusively committed to any particular cause. The Western idea of the State encourages individuals to remain open to all types of criticism, all choices, and to be prepared to change in a world which is itself rapidly changing. Whilst reflection and critical evaluation are emphasized, in the end every ideal, including our deepest commitments and character itself, is constantly open to change. This contrasts sharply with an Aristotelian conception of character outlined in chapter 3. We have seen how, to Aristotle, character is something abiding: that commitments are not accidental, but part of an organized and well established pattern of behaviour and that this does not change easily. Ronald Beiner (1992: 176) comments:

> The problem with the liberal commitment to individuality, diversity, pluralism, and toleration is certainly not that these are bad things, unworthy of concern, but that liberal individualism and pluralism are too often a phoney individuality and phoney pluralism. How can we know whether the individuality and diversity fostered by a society is genuine without looking at the substantive choices and forms of character cultivated by members of that society, which the liberal will regard as itself a kind of "moral intrusiveness" destructive of liberal autonomy.

Conservative politics and character education

The main principles behind the Conservative Party's education policy in government was the enhancement of individualism and freedom of choice
conceived primarily as occurring through the operation of the free market
economy. Between 1979 and 1997 successive Conservative governments
sought to reverse what they perceived to be a decline in moral standards,
encouraging more traditional 'family-orientated values'. Mrs Thatcher gave an
address to the Scottish Kirk (Church of Scotland) in 1989 in which she
expressed her belief in the relevance of Christianity to public policy. In the
address she stated that there was a 'strong practical case for ensuring that children at school are given adequate instruction in the part which
Judaic–Christian tradition played in moulding the laws, manners and institutions' of British society (McLellan 1997: 145). The Conservative Party
produced the National Curriculum in 1988, so it could be argued that they
established State control of what children should know, how they should learn
it and how it should be assessed. Section 1 of the Education Reform Act
imposes a basic duty in respect of all maintained schools to promote the 'spiritual, moral, cultural, mental and physical development of pupils at the school
and of society' and prepare such pupils 'for the opportunities, responsibilities
and experiences of adult life'. These are very wide aspirations and clearly have
a relationship to the development of character. In a speech to an Oxford education conference in 1994 the secretary of state for education, John Patten,
argued that no school was value-free and that schools should deliberately teach
their pupils regard for proper authority, self-restraint, loyalty and fidelity, and
respect for rational argument. There were other conservatives who talked
about a return to 'Victorian values'. This was part of the failed 'Back to Basics'
campaign begun by the Conservative government in October 1993, which
some thought to be an attempt to 're-moralize' society.

The Conservatives were also responsible for connecting education more
closely with employment through the merging of these two state departments.
The DfEE (as was) outlined the aims of the newly merged department in Press
Notice 210/95: 'To support economic growth and improve the nation's competitiveness and quality of life by raising standards of educational achievement and
skills and by promoting an efficient and flexible labour market.' By November
the DfEE declared that this was 'the government's principal aim for the education service at all levels and all forms of learning'. A clear subordination of the
school to the demands of the work culture seemed to have been intended.
Conservative education policy sought to promote individuality and competition.

In 1996 the Conservative government allowed the Schools Curriculum and
Assessment Authority (SCAA) to enter the public debate about morality by establishing the National Forum. This was intended not to increase children's
knowledge of morality, but to improve their behaviour (Marenbon 1996). SCAA
established a Forum for Values in Education and the Community which sought to
discover whether there were any values upon which there was common agreement

within society. Whilst this endeavour began under a Conservative government, it was continued under New Labour, with Tony Blair suggesting that a fourth 'R' should be added to education – the teaching of Responsibility (see Arthur 2000). It often seems that Conservative party policies are motivated by a negative view of modern youth and society rather than by an approach that positively asserts the development of moral reasoning and participation in democracy. Character education presented simply as a matter of what is right and what is wrong is popular with Conservative politicians, but it has very little relevance to educational practice in schools. How then did the 'left' respond to morality in schools?

Communitarian politics and character education

Communitarianism has been reflected in many of New Labour's public policies and it is often described as the 'Third Way'. The term communitarian has been popularized by a sociology professor in America, Amitai Etzioni, who has had considerable influence over the centre left in America and Britain. Concepts of community, responsibility and duty have been raised to pre-eminence within Labour's manifesto commitments (Arthur 2000: 6). Communitarians are essentially either 'theoretical' in approach or seek a communitarian perspective on legal, social and educational public policies. The second category I call 'public philosophy communitarians' and they can have either liberal or conservative political leanings. Etzioni (1993: 9) locates his own position against the background of traditional political divisions: 'Between individuals, who champion autonomy, and social conservatives, who champion social order, lies communitarianism, which characterizes a good society as one that achieves balance between social order and autonomy.' Etzioni emphasizes the importance of common values in society and particularly family values. The revival of interest in community largely stems from the work of Robert Bellah *et al.* (1985). Bellah initially raised concerns in the USA about the loss of community which he claimed had been sacrificed to individualism. He suggested an approach which emphasized shared practices in society, claiming that liberalism had overemphasized the autonomy of individuals. Nash (1997: 64) believes that: 'In educational terms, communitarians are generally conservative, even though politically many are utopians and some are even populists.' One of the dangers in communitarian thought is that children become the 'community's children' and therefore the direct concern of the school and other social welfare agencies of the State. So influential have communitarians been that President Clinton raised the question of character education as a federal concern and initiated the Character-Building White House/Congressional Conferences in the early 1990s in association with the Communitarian Network.

Etzioni speaks of the 'parenting deficit' and how schools are the 'second line of defense' after families, who he recognizes might fail. In the communitarian manifesto it is declared that: 'We hold that schools can provide essential moral education – without indoctrinating young people' (Etzioni 1993: 8). From this statement communitarians have developed an explicit policy on character education for state education based on a form of 'virtue ethics'. Character education is offered as a remedy to curb antisocial tendencies in the young so that they may become more virtuous. Etzioni (1993: 92) again says: 'schools are left with the task of making up for under-education in the family and lay the psychic foundations for character and moral conduct'. He believes many young people have underdeveloped characters and he is very critical of the influence of Piaget and Kohlberg in education. Young people, he says, should learn to internalize values: 'What is missing between character formation (the ability to commit and guide oneself) and the development of moral reasoning is the internalisation of (i.e., making part of oneself) commitments to a set of substantive values, to be achieved through moral education' (1997: 99). It is the government of the State which will develop public policies to teach these virtues to the young, as character can be deliberately formed by teachers.

However, communitarians are not united around any single concept of character education and often disagree about exactly what 'virtues' should be taught. It is also the case that when an ethics of character is grounded in political concepts of the community, it is vulnerable to rejection as arbitrary and relativistic.

New Labour and the rediscovery of character education

New Labour has added to the National Curriculum in England by articulating new aims for schooling. In its Statement of Values, Aims and Purposes of the National Curriculum for England (1999: 10f.) the following are included: the development of children's social responsibility, community involvement, the development of effective relationships, knowledge and understanding of society, participation in the affairs of society, respect for others, and the child's contribution to the building up of the common good. More specifically, the values that underpin the school curriculum are that education should reaffirm 'our commitment to the virtues of truth, justice, honesty, trust and a sense of duty'. The school curriculum should aim to 'develop principles for distinguishing between right and wrong', and pass on 'enduring values'. Whilst the document also encourages the promotion of 'self-esteem' and 'emotional well-being', the main thrust is the promotion of 'responsibility and rights'. The extent to which these statements have their origins in partisan politics is limited because they were largely compiled by committees of teachers and civil servants, but they have been endorsed as official government policy.

The Crick Report (1999) on Citizenship Education was commissioned by New Labour and recommended compulsory citizenship education, which the government has accepted. All secondary schools in England are obliged by law to provide their pupils with citizenship education, which should include a moral dimension. The report (1999: 44) provides an overview of the 'essential elements to be reached by the end of compulsory schooling' for every child in England. These include an ambitious list of character traits and virtues: pupils 'should develop the proclivity to act responsibly', they should have 'premeditation and calculation' about the effect actions have on others and 'acceptance of responsibility for unforeseen or unfortunate consequences'. Pupils are not only to understand 'tolerance', but they should be able to practise it and they should 'act by a moral code', although no code is specified in the report. Pupils are expected to act with 'courage', be committed to voluntary service, show a 'determination to act justly', and have a 'disposition to work with and for others'. The report lists the skills, understanding, attitudes, values and dispositions which pupils should develop. The Citizenship Order (1999) lists similar virtues and demands. In New Labour's first White Paper on education, *Excellence in Schools* (1997: 10) it was also stated that schools and families should take responsibility so that children 'appreciate and understand a moral code on which civilized society is based' and that these children 'need to develop the strength of character and attitudes to life and work'. Once again, no explicit definition or suggestion is given of what this moral code might or should be.

New Labour also seeks to implement a policy of 'education with character' which it claims lies at the heart of its policies on education. In the White Paper *Schools: Achieving Success* (2001: 25ff.) it is stated that 85 per cent of those who responded to the Green Paper *Schools: Building on Success* (2001) supported the provision of 'education with character' and that the government intend to press ahead with encouraging schools to provide this. There were a total of 421 responses to the Green Paper, of which 279 responses addressed the question of 'education with character'. Of these, the DfES claim that 279 (85 per cent) strongly supported or supported the policy of 'education with character' whilst 36 (13 per cent) supported some of the proposals. Only six responses (2 per cent) did not support any of the proposals. However, the overwhelming majority responded by ticking a box indicating broad support for the proposals but did not comment on the specific proposal of 'education with character'. Consequently, only a very small minority of the 279 made written responses supporting the proposal for out-of-school opportunities to be incorporated within the broader school curriculum. It is worth noting that only 69 teachers and 37 parents responded to the Green Paper and not all of these addressed the question of character.

Six organizations submitted written responses addressing the question of 'education with character' and the DfES provided me with access to these submissions. The Association of Heads of Outdoor Education Centres was particularly pleased on the value and emphasis given to outdoor education and adventure activity in the Green Paper. The Duke of Edinburgh Award also welcomed the recognition that 'all round character development, enabling active citizenship within schools and local communities can be supported by enrichment activities including sport, the arts and outdoor adventure'. This response also claimed that the personal qualities such an approach would foster would benefit the business community. The Duke of Edinburgh Award was established for the purpose of all-round character development and it has considerable experience of accrediting character building programmes. It is not surprising that it offered to work with government and schools in providing an 'award accreditation experience to every pupil aged fourteen and above'.

The Carnegie Young People Initiative submitted a response claiming that more needs to be done within schools for pupils 'to build a daily and routine habit of participation and engagement'. The Carnegie Initiative associated 'education with character' with promoting the involvement of young people in public decision-making. Save the Children also associated 'education with character' with participation in the affairs of the school and even included a limited consultation with 119 schoolchildren and young people on the Green Paper in the written submission it made. The National Union of Teachers agreed that pupils should be involved in the decision-making processes of schools, but made clear that judgement on when and how to implement such approaches should be left to teachers. The response by the National Union of Teachers also stated that: 'It is vital that the place of arts, drama, sport and music should be considered within the framework of a curriculum entitlement, and not as optional extracurricular activities.' The relationship between sport and the development of character has a long history. Some would argue that the very rationale of 'character building', including social, moral and even citizen development, is what justifies the place of physical education on the school curriculum. However, the research literature does not necessarily support the view that sport automatically builds ethical character (see Shields and Bredemeier 1995: 194 for a review of this literature). New Labour has simply accepted the nineteenth-century public-school belief in the character building efficacy of sport. Indeed, New Labour policy follows exactly the same reasoning promoted by the previous Conservative government, seen in John Major's introductory letter in the Department of National Heritage's 1995 publication *Sport: Raising the Game*.

None of the six written responses to the Green Paper attempted to define 'education with character' or comment on the ethical implications. There was simply an assumption behind these responses that various outdoor activities, together with certain school subjects that lend themselves to additional extracurricular activities, are character building. These limited responses to a national consultation are reflected in the content of the White Paper. The kind of character education outlined in the White Paper is not entirely new, nor does it reveal any new ideas. The government lists a series of well-known themes, such as encouraging the establishment of school councils and the active involvement of pupils in the life of schools, the introduction of citizenship education 'which had already been announced', placing increased emphasis on sport and competition between schools and encouraging voluntary mentoring of pupils, together with summer activities and the promotion of out-of-school activities like the Duke of Edinburgh Award and the Youth Achievement Award, as well as work experience for pupils. All these activities are viewed as 'character building' and are essentially a return to some of the educational policies that the Labour government of 1945–1951 advocated in the Ministry of Education annual reports.

In the White Paper (2001) the government recognizes that schools may not be the ideal learning environments for building character and advocates experiential learning which is about informed participation in communal affairs. In addition, Ofsted will seek the views of children about their experiences in schools during future inspections. All of this aims to build character by developing 'rounded individuals', but there is hardly anything which is new and much will depend on how schools respond. Already the Citizenship Order (1999) makes the promotion of certain values obligatory in schools. Character education is given a limited definition in the White Paper, but taken with the goals of the entire National Curriculum (see chapter 10) there is an expanding concept of character development. In this context James Hunter (2001: 225) makes the observation that:

> The problem is that character cannot develop out of values "nominated" for promotion, "consciously chosen" by a committee, negotiated by a group of diverse professionals, or enacted into law by legislators. Such values have, by their very nature, lost the quality of sacredness, their commanding character, and thus their power to inspire and to shame.

Hunter's general argument is clear: the DfES is incapable of setting moral standards which will be 'inwardly compelling' for schools, pupils or staff. He does not say it is impossible for character to be developed, but doubts whether the State can achieve this – and suggests it is better promoted by small and particular communities, or religious schools and other schools which attempt to embody a moral vision.

J. Budziszewski (1992: 51ff.) describes how secular politics have ultimate concerns, which include the moral. He details how the ultimate concern for Nazism was the triumph of a particular race whilst for Marxism–Leninism it was the dictatorship of the proletariat. Budziszewski (1992: 64) provides an excellent summary of what has happened to Western democracies:

> Rough consensus on what virtue is and how virtue should be taught has been possible in the past only because there has been some common ground among the limited number of ultimate concerns to which people in our culture have adhered. As our culture becomes more diverse – as ultimate concerns that only a few followed previously are followed by ever larger numbers, and as followers are drawn to new and previously unheard of ultimate concerns – the common ground may shrink. There are, of course, two kinds of diversity. To use acoustical metaphors, one kind is cacophony, the other symphony. The former is a thousand jarring sounds in competition, the latter is a thousand blending sounds in harmony. But the latter presupposes agreement about rhythm, theme and the laws of harmony. I mean the former.

Do New Labour mean the former also?

Ronald Dworkin (1978: 136f.), in contrasting the conservative viewpoint with the liberal, describes the former's support for the virtuous society in the following general terms:

A virtuous society has these general features. Its members share a sound conception of virtue, that is, of the qualities and dispositions people should strive to have and exhibit. They share this conception of virtue not only privately, as individuals, but publicly; they believe their community, in its social and political activity, exhibits virtues, and that they have a responsibility, as citizens, to promote these virtues. In that sense they treat the lives of other members of their community as part of their own lives.

This, he claims, is the conservative view, but Dworkin proceeds to advocate a liberal view of society in which the government should not interfere with the lives of others as long as they do no harm to others. Since this is a direct threat to the formation of community-minded individuals it is not surprising that New Labour did not endorse these ultra-liberal views.

The moral and character education policies that New Labour is seeking to promote in schools are an integral element of the current political culture – part of which it has inherited from Conservative policies and part of which it has created. It is a political rather than an educational response. The prime minister, in an interview with *The Observer* on 5 September 1999, made explicit New Labour's ethical agenda when he said: 'We need to find a new national moral purpose for the new generation.' Many newspapers interpreted this to be a call for a moral crusade against vice or a return to the failed 'Back to Basics' campaign of the previous Conservative government. In the absence of any strong national religious power in society, New Labour finds itself in the position that there is no higher authority than government authority, which increasingly has expanded into moral influence, inherent within the community discourse it uses. There appears to be a justification for character education beyond the political. It is why Hunter (2001: 228) argues that the school has no reference point other than the State: if pupils are not involved in the discourse of community politics then they are disconnected from community. He argues that the social life in which morality or character education make sense has all but disintegrated and that schools are naturally reluctant to be involved in explicit character formation. The focus should be on the culture of society and how this can be changed: schools, he argues, do not have the resources or the will to effectively develop one's character. Hunter speaks here not of religious schools but of those under the complete control of the State.

Conclusion

Liberalism encourages certain kinds of virtues which are not always openly acknowledged. New Labour is seeking to implement a state-sponsored character education initiative within a pluralist society which raises certain questions: whose virtues are they promoting? What sort of good life do they have in mind? Since the 'Great Debate' in 1976 all successive governments have shown a determination to play a greater part in setting the curriculum agenda for schools. New Labour, in particular, is setting an ethical agenda in education. Governments are not neutral about conceptions of the good life and character education is no longer wholly a matter of private choice. Teachers are expected to teach certain skills, understandings and attitudes which are tools for living, but are they teaching a method of living without a conception of what to live for? New Labour seeks to promote and define some public virtues, but it is the State that is concerned to prepare and sustain democracy and seeks to foster a public character in youth with all its attendant virtues. The educative apparatus of the State includes much more than schools. It uses a wide range of legislative programmes in welfare, medicine and employment whose aims are also educative. The ideal in a liberal democracy is that the principles of morality are integrated into human character to such an extent that external control becomes unnecessary, but we are currently a long way from this ideal. In summary, the New Labour government is not neutral about the good life, for it wants citizens of a particular type with certain capacities, habits and virtues which allow them to contribute to community, economic and institutional life in society. It has identified the school as the main institution in society with the role to foster these virtues.

7 The social foundations of character

> We say we want a renewal of character in our day but we don't really know what we ask for. To have a renewal of character is to have a renewal of a creedal order that constrains, limits, binds, obligates and compels. The price is too high for us to pay. We want character without conviction; we want strong morality but without the emotional burden of guilt or shame; we want virtue but without particular moral justifications that invariably offend; we want good without having to name evil; we want decency without the authority to insist upon it; we want moral community without any limitations to personal freedom. In short, we want what we cannot possibly have on the terms that we want it.
>
> James Davison Hunter, *The Death of Character* (2001: xv)

> The person of good character is he who does the approved thing at the right time and does not break the rules when he faces inner temptation. The process of learning these positive and negating regulations is socialisation, fitting the impulsive-ridden infant into the order of social living.
>
> Martin Loeb (1951: 58)

No explanation of character education can be complete without a consideration of its sociological aspects. Character education, concerned as it is with ethical behaviour, is pre-eminently social. In sociology the idea of character is to do with the socialization of an individual and the mores of society. It highlights the connections between social understanding and character education, and it has much in common with social psychology. Sociologists approach the formation of character by asking questions about the social structure of society and institutions, about the arrangements in schools and how these influence the acquisition of moral values and moral development. The build-up of habits is viewed as a process of socialization. Schools are seen as social organizations which transmit moral codes. The concept of virtue is understood exclusively as a social phenomenon which is acquired through teacher/pupil relations, the social organization of the school and the relationship between the school and the wider community. Character is the measure of this process of socialization. The adequately socialized child is the 'good child'. Character is relative to a particular culture and sociologists are, in the main, not concerned about any particular morality.

Consequently, there is no such thing as the 'good character', as all substantive moralities are rejected. Typically, sociologists will explain character development in terms of the fulfilment of social functions within a network of social relations. In the beginning there is society, not the individual. The structural arrangements of the school will socialize the pupils to the extent that certain patterns of action are reinforced with some degree of regularity and consistency. These are social roles into which one is socialized and which are typified by a pattern of social behaviour. Family, mothers, fathers, brothers, sisters, together with 'significant others', are all seen as providing a form of mentoring in social roles which are performed, learnt and internalized – the focus is on the social context. In this scheme of things we depend on others for our character development. Henry Johnson (1987) summarizes this view in saying that: 'Character development is a social and not an individual process, because being human is a social not an individual phenomenon.' Character develops within a social environment, which means the nature of that environment, the messages it sends out and the behaviours which it encourages or prohibits are all important factors in character formation. Barbara Duncan (1997) would say that character education is really a means of moral assimilation resulting from social interaction. Jerome Kagan (1981) has suggested that character is about socially conditioned outcomes and that nurture is the key to understanding it.

Studies in the sociology of education often treat schools as social organizations, forming part of the general socialization process for each individual. Schools will define the values and norms that pupils and teachers will share and experience through its ethos, which consists of a set of customs and rules that help shape the character of a particular community. The ethos is learnt through a system of reward and punishment to reinforce particular behaviours. The patterns of behaviour that emerge, such as learning to act like a pupil, are roles that are played out by the pupil actors. The culture of the school is internalized and there is no need to be conscious of these roles. Sociologists are concerned with examining these roles and statuses rather than with the individuals themselves. They examine the values and norms that shape the roles played out in common behaviour patterns. From this they predict patterns of behaviour. They seek to clarify ideas about what rewards are given for appropriate behaviour and what punishments handed out for the elimination of inappropriate behaviour.

A school can be deemed successful if the behaviours of its members are reasonably consistent and coherent. Sociology has also identified the class context of many virtues. For example, cleanliness was a virtue often taught in English schools up to and after the Second World War. This concept had a definite social class association. Keeping one's body clean, free from disease and adequately clothed was extremely difficult for poor children. Sociologists have rightly focused our attention on these areas, especially on the actions of governments, in an attempt to raise the standards of working-class life. Sociologists have also, rightly, made the connection between resources and the formation of character, since, they claim, poor health, sub-standard housing, inadequate education and poverty will generally not assist the development of character.

Emile Durkheim and moral character

The classic theory of moral socialization is given in Emile Durkheim's (1886) *Moral Education*. Durkheim was a teacher and a professor of education as well as being one of the founding fathers of modern sociology. *Moral Education* was originally a series of lectures given to teachers. In it Durkheim is concerned with *egoism* – excessive individualism, and *anomie* – the lack of social regulation in society and in institutions like schools. The culture in his day, he felt, was one marked out by its individualism which strengthened both *egoism* and *anomie*. Durkheim sought a secular-based morality as a basis for moral conduct, which consisted of following a system of values which carried some authority. He strongly endorsed the school's active effort to instil in the young values and rules of conduct. He postulated a functionalist theory in which morality is important in schools because it helps maintain society, thus preserving order. The school can and should impose discipline to maintain this good order. He also believed that the school could, in some cases, compensate for the deficiencies of the family and that children could be socialized through attachment to particular groups such as their classroom. Durkheim was concerned about the erosion of traditional values and norms in society and he emphasized the use of discipline, punishment and rewards in schools. As a result of this emphasis on duty, responsibility, authority and discipline, Durkheim's educational views have often been ignored by progressive sociologists who have dismissed what they believe to be his conservative tendencies. This is to misread Durkheim's intentions – he did not advocate blind obedience to rules, but rather an 'enlightened allegiance' to the rules of a group and in Geoffrey Walford and W. S. F. Pickering's (1998) collection there is something of a restoration of Durkheim's contribution to education.

Durkheim was chiefly concerned with how individual and community life was ordered and sustained in a rapidly changing society. For Durkheim all moral rules have exclusively social origins and it often appears that he effectively reduced morality to social convention determined by society. Any form of discipline derives its authority from society and the thrust of this argument is to subsume personal character development under some larger social good or value such as social improvement or social progress. Whilst Durkheim was opposed to corporal punishment he believed that unrestrained egoism was the true enemy of freedom and autonomy. Groups of people, like a school, develop their own distinctive moral norms which, he observed, are not reducible to the sum of the individuals' moral perspectives. Durkheim believed that individuals could freely develop their own potential whilst attaining a stronger sense of social cohesion. This could only be achieved if individuals respected the common values and practices of the community. He called this 'moral individualism', by which individuals seek to fulfil their own potential whilst recognizing that contributing to the fulfilment of others is an integral part of their own fulfilment. The tension in this thinking is of course between the degree of individual autonomy and the conformist pressures of what Durkheim called 'organic solidarity'. John Dewey has many points of similarity in his views on the social function of the school. Talcott Parsons (1959) took a broad

Durkheimian view of moral socialization in that he believed that schools must form responsible citizens by getting children to internalize certain values. Whilst Durkheim and Parsons emphasize that education is about self-determination and growth in autonomy, there is much in their thoughts on schooling and character development which emphasizes the inculcation of conformity to social norms together with social solidarity and mutual support in community.

Many sociologists do not locate the source of these norms or virtues in the past or through philosophy. As George Noblit and Van Dempsey (1996: 13f.), adopting a sociological perspective, say: 'we define virtue as an assignment of moral traits to individuals by others as well as by themselves'. In this sense moral character is reduced to certain adopted behaviours. Noblit and Dempsey develop their sociological perspective using the following argument: first, virtue is often discussed in a rarified way and in absolutist and universal terms. This is rejected because there is often no reference to the human authorship of these virtues. They claim that it does not help us create moral actions. Second, virtue is a social construction. People make morality when they construct narratives of virtuous people. Third, virtue is interpretative. It refers to the meaning of things and less so to the actions that virtuous people are said to have engaged in. Fourth, the constitution of virtue is contextually specific. In this scheme of things schools construct their own set of virtues and do not look to the past to reproduce past virtues. Teachers and pupils participate in moral construction with the community beyond the school. Noblit and Dempsey provide an interesting minority view, with some detailed case studies in their book to illustrate the point.

Socialization and character

Socialization inevitably serves as an automatic process of character development. Functional competence in the social domain is the first aim of the process. In the socialization process the pupil has no choice or control. The pupil participates in a series of interactions 'systematically structured in a way that preserves the functioning of society or the particular institutions within it' (Pritchard 1988). Some sociologists have suggested that schools in particular are not conducive to moral development, that in fact they inhibit the moral character of pupils or even retard them. Jan Loubster (1970) argued that since schools are dominated by cognitive concerns, they provide little experience in the exercise of moral autonomy. She says: 'By maintaining moral surveillance in *loco parentis* or on behalf of society they perpetuate the notion that moral goals can be achieved by enforcement.' Further, she believes that the school inhibits the development of moral reasoning because reasoning assumes equal authority of the participants in determining the outcome. She concludes: 'If moral involvement is a component of moral action and a requisite for moral development, the very existence of the school as a separate, isolated, protected haven for youth constitutes a social structural inhibition of such development.' Charles Bidwell (1972) supports much of this thesis and speaks of the moral socialization which takes place in schools as consisting of pupils responding to moral rules or norms. The school pupil, he argues, acquires:

... culturally grounded goals and aspirations; he comes to know (though not always well) and observe (though not always willingly, scrupulously, or regularly) the rules that will govern his conduct in situations; he develops a view of the conduct of others as revealing motivations and constraints; he learns that social relations and institutions embody values and are subject to moral regulation.

Bidwell believes that moral socialization is about fostering certain moral commitments. The use of sanctions by the school is justified to reinforce these and develop these capabilities for motivated and regulated conduct. Of course both Bidwell and Loubster are not concerned with the life of the mind, simply the social environment. For some sociologists, indoctrination is inevitable in this process of socialization.

Barry Sugarman (1973: 49) defines what the morally educated person would look like in the context of a socialization process. He says:

He or she is someone who has concern for other people such that their feelings, wants and interests count with one and are not lightly overridden for the sake of one's own goals; the MEP (morally educated person) is competent at social skills, good at knowing other people's feelings and good at knowing and expressing their own; knowledgeable about the physical and social worlds; the MEP is objective and unprejudiced in sizing up situations and unafraid to proceed with the plan of action intended; lastly the MEP, when thinking about what to do in an unfamiliar situation or in passing judgement on action already taken, thinks in terms of universalistic moral principles based on concern for the rights of other people as well as himself.

The context of Sugarman's definition is social interaction and he emphasizes a concern for others throughout. He uses the term 'character' (1973: 199f.) but appears uncomfortable with it, claiming that it is part of traditional moral education. Nevertheless, he defines character as 'moral toughness' and says that the morally educated person requires this type of character to reach a higher level of moral education. It is only with character that a person will sacrifice themselves for others or stand up for principles in the face of opposition and threats.

Contemporary sociologists recognize that individual human beings do act, think and feel. A number of earlier views have been disregarded and there is greater acceptance of the notion of individual character. In addition, a more philosophical sociology has emerged which is less deterministic in regard to the formation of moral character. Critical sociologists such as Henry Giroux and Purpel (1983) and Samuel Bowles and Herbert Gintis (1976) have challenged many of the functionalist approaches to socialization described above. Some have identified power, class, gender and the economic system as being more important than schools in influencing or forming the moral values of character. For Bowles and Gintis it is all about the repressive values of capitalist society – we simply reproduce characters for capitalism. They adopt the Marxist thesis that schools are primarily concerned with the production and reproduction of labour power. Those destined for work in subordinate positions will not be encouraged to develop great ambitions or have their autonomy of thinking extended to any significant degree. They will be taught the virtues of diligence, loyalty, and respect for authority and their social superiors.

Kit Christensen (1994: 10, 57f., 70) also adopts a Marxist perspective on character education, viewing character development as a means to radically change society. For him, character is really a unique ensemble of social relations, with human beings being social products. Character education is defined as an ideological creation of a class society formed through socialization. The characters so formed serve the dominant group in society, who maintain their control and power over others. He argues that character thus formed can do very little to change the dominant social norms. As he says:

> The 'right kind' of moral character by itself will never be sufficient to bring about human flourishing-with-others, or any radical social change for the better, as long as class society exists. In fact, given the extent to which people's objective circumstances determine both 'who' they individually are, and how the actual course of events will unfold for them independently of their intentions and desires, it must be assumed that personal character will most often constitute at best only a secondary causal factor in historical development.

Sociologists of whatever philosophy appear either to exaggerate what a school can actually achieve or downplay potential influence – they can also make weighty claims for the effect of schooling which can be hard to justify. Sociology can offer insights by explaining how the aims of character education will differ according to the social characteristics of those being educated.

A whole range of sociological and social psychological theories have arisen such as the social learning theory, later called the social cognitive theory, which examines how and what people think and how thought affects their behaviour. Patterns of behaviour are chiefly understood as a result of interactions with others. This theory is interesting since it is based on human beings observing the behaviour of others – an application to education could view the teacher as role model, but it is derived from behaviourism: a simple stimulus–response mechanism by which children copy the teacher without much thought. Social control theory argues that it is social bonding that stops us from becoming criminals and places emphasis on conformity through attachment and commitment to others. Building on socialization theories the social domain theory asserts that a child develops different forms of social knowledge, including moral knowledge and behaviour, through social experiences with adults and peers. Children have qualitatively different social interactions that lead to different types of social and moral knowledge. Thus children's actions and thinking about morality in the social world are characterized by heterogeneity. Parents play a crucial moral role by providing the foundations of a system of rules that regulate the social interactions of children. Whilst there has been a strong tradition of ethical relativism in sociology some recent works have not adhered to this tradition, as seen in some of the papers in the collection edited by Kieran Flannagan and Peter Jupp (2001), entitled *Virtue Ethics and Sociology: issues of modernity and religion*.

Family, community and character

Judith Smetna (1999) looks at the parents' role in character education and describes the emotional bonds parents have naturally with the child, as well as their parenting practices of deep concern for the child's development. She concludes that this is a major source of guidance in promoting the child's moral understanding. She claims that the teacher shares in this process. There are other sociologists such as Robert Bellah and his colleagues, together with James Coleman and Christopher Lasch, who have given greater attention to historical and philosophical considerations in their sociological research. Christopher Lasch (1998: 3), for example, takes up the theme of the family as the chief agency of socialization, which he says reproduces cultural patterns in the individual. The family profoundly shapes our character by imparting ethical norms so that as thoughts and actions become habitual we will develop unconscious predispositions to act in certain ways.

Like Smetna, Lasch stresses the importance of the family's emotional influence which he says colours all subsequent experiences. He states:

> If the reproduction of culture were simply a matter of formal instruction and discipline, it could be left to the schools. But it also requires that culture be embedded in personality. Socialization makes the individual want to do what he has to do; the family is the agency to which society entrusts this complex and delicate task (1998: 4).

Lasch appears to use 'personality' for 'character', but his main sociological insight is that there has been a separation of love and discipline within the family environment which has resulted in negative personality or character traits in individuals which are incompatible with modern democracy. This separation has allowed the government to assert an inordinate amount of social control over citizens. Lasch is critical of the role of the professions in society, which he believes have encouraged a dependency culture, and he criticizes a culture of psychotherapy which has inhibited families from resolving their own problems and from engaging in the moral discourse of their communities. In particular, Lasch concludes that this has blocked the moral character development of children. He advocates a restoration of the union between love and discipline so that the family unit accepts and practises its responsibilities for the formation of character in the young.

The connection between the family and moral development is also a central theme within communitarian thinking, with Etzioni (1993: 176) describing the family as the core of the 'moral infrastructure'. Others, such as Norton Garfinkle

(1998) and Robert Coles (1997), also view the family as the source of moral development (Arthur 2000c: 46). Elsewhere, I have argued that in considering the inculcation of values and virtues it is important that the problems of the school should be understood as shared problems with the family. The school cannot hope to substitute itself for the family, but it sometimes has to compensate for the failure of the family in the formation of character.

James Coleman (Coleman and Hoffer 1987) is an eminent sociologist, but his research conclusions, first published in 1981, that private schools are on the whole 'better' than public schools in the USA, met with great hostility from many in the educational establishment. Many attacked his personal integrity in an attempt to discredit his findings and he was denounced as an enemy of the public schools even before his research was published. His main finding was that schools do make a difference to children, including their characters. The most significant difference between public and private schools concerned the greater level of discipline and the more orderly environment found in private schools. Behaviour was better in private schools. This not only helped academic achievement, but together with the increased teacher interest shown in the pupils in private schools also helped to make this discipline acceptable to the pupils. Coleman's findings were arrived at independently of the class affiliation of the pupils, but he did not go so far as to claim that children in private schools had superior ethical characters. State school parents who have individually chosen the school for their children do not usually constitute a specific community outside the school. In contrast, value communities or functional communities such as faith schools are an outgrowth of a specific community. Coleman also contributed to a report of the National Commission on Youth in 1980 which indicated that young people were insulated from adult responsibilities. He called for 'new environments' in which young people could perform some kind of public service. He even suggested that young people should serve the community for one year as part of a National Youth Service. Many others have advocated exactly the same since, and New Labour, as we have seen in chapter 6, has advocated in its White Paper (2001) and in the Citizenship Order (1999) increased community involvement to the extent that it is now obligatory in all English secondary schools.

Community is also a theme addressed by Clark Cochran (1982: 18ff.) who claims that it is essential for full character development. Character, for him, includes two elements: the *centre* and the *masks*. The *centre* is made up of a set of moral qualities or virtues that comprise personal identity. The *masks* he describes as a complex set of social roles assumed by a person in daily life. The masks are fragments of the self that are projected in life to meet the changing interests and obligations associated with conflicting and sometimes competing social roles. When the *centre* and *masks* are integrated, which is an appropriate relationship between the self and its social roles, then character is considered harmonious. Cochran believes that responsibility is the key element of character that maintains a link between the inner life of the individual and the complex social life of the modern world. Character building is the goal of human fulfilment for Cochran and it must take place within community.

Character educators have placed great emphasis on what Robert Bellah *et al.* (1985) called 'habits of the heart' – habitual behaviours based on traditional virtues. Bellah and his team of sociologists worked extensively on the conflict they found between community and individuality. They speak of two conflicting languages. First is the language of individualism, which seeks independence and the freedom to pursue a lifestyle which does not harm others. In this they seek to be detached and autonomous, free to define themselves. Second is a language of community which responds to our innate ability to be connected to each other and to cooperate and pursue the happiness that emerges from a shared conception of our common human nature. Bellah argues that these two languages are not in equilibrium and that the language of individualism has become so powerful that it seriously threatens the language of community.

As a result character has become increasingly instrumental, competitive, insulated and self-seeking. One could easily make comparisons here with the Conservative policies of the 1980s and 1990s (see chapter 6). The paradox Bellah (1985: 23) states is that individuals are free to be left alone and therefore theoretically free from having ideas imposed on them – whilst at the same time human beings wish to belong to a community and accept some of the norms of society which give direction and meaning to their life. Bellah discusses a number of American character types (1985: 27ff.) from the past, but overall his critique of modern character is pessimistic, very much along the lines described by Alasdair McIntyre. Whilst *Habits of the Heart* follows the themes described by Lasch (1998) it is perhaps more optimistic about the future.

In contrast to the sociologists discussed above, Alan Wolfe (2001) in *Moral Freedom: The Search for Virtues in a World of Choice* explains why and how he believes morality is so 'revolutionarily' different today. He observes that Americans are generally sceptical of all forms of moral authority including families, schools, churches, civil government and business organizations. These 'forms of moral authority' are described as 'old' sources of authority that have previously strongly influenced individual decision-making on questions of right and wrong. Wolfe concludes from his various empirical studies that individuals are now thinking about right and wrong independently of these old sources, which he claims are losing their influence principally because they are no longer trusted. In their place, individuals have developed a high regard for their own conscience, their moral autonomy or what Wolfe describes as their 'moral freedom'. This moral freedom is defined as occurring when individuals are expected to determine for themselves what it means to lead a good and virtuous life. They decide what is right and wrong rather than deferring to an external authority. Wolfe claims that they do this by considering who they are, what others need and require, and what consequences follow from acting one way rather than another. He essentially describes a process of how to think through and make a moral decision and in the main provides a positive account of moral decision-making in contemporary America.

However, Wolfe notes that whilst individuals are increasingly playing a greater role in governing their moral life this does not mean the same thing as saying that there are no truths by which behaviour *ought* to be governed. He even suggests that old 'middle-class' virtues, which according to him include loyalty, self-discipline and truthfulness, often appear to be observed in practice and that these can be essential for the effective functioning of modern institutions. Wolfe concludes that these virtues are normally upheld in principle, but that in practice many individuals turn them into 'options' whose use is entirely dependent on circumstances.

Wolfe provides a number of examples to illustrate the idea of virtues as 'options'. For example, the virtue of loyalty is good in principle for most people, but not at the price of unhappiness in a bad marriage. Honesty is another virtue upheld by most, but not at the cost of inflicting unhappiness on others. The difficulty with Wolfe's argument is that if families and schools no longer serve as authoritative guides for individuals, then what moral resources do children draw on in lieu of these institutions? How is our ethical character to be formed and sustained? It cannot be simply formed through a process of thinking. Wolfe provides no answers to these questions, but does recognize that the process he describes, from his sociological observations of moral decision-making in America, is complex and can potentially have adverse consequences for society.

It is perhaps because of arguments like Wolfe's that some educational philosophers, such as David Carr (1991: 112), do not believe that sociology can offer much to the debate on character education. He reminds us (1991: 128) that social customs and conventions are themselves susceptible to moral evaluation 'in order to appreciate that concepts of morality and virtue are not at all reducible to or eliminable in favour of notions of social order'. However, James Hunter (2001: xiii) provides a powerful modern sociological interpretation of character education which argues that the social and cultural conditions that make character possible in a human being are no longer present. He begins with an alarming post-mortem: 'Character is dead. Attempts to revive it will yield little. Its time has passed.' He argues that nothing will bring it back and suggests that a number of factors have combined to destroy character, including pluralism, diversity and contemporary culture. Attempts at character education are counter-productive, he claims, as they undermine the capacity for conviction in relation to which character is formed. Hunter adopts the critique of Durkheim in asking the question: what are the terms by which life will be ordered and sustained in a rapidly changing world? In this he establishes a direct relationship between individual character and the well-being of society.

As Hunter (2000: 8) says:

> Changing ideas of the self reflect changing social structures, structures that impose different requirements upon the role and presentation of the self. The older ideas of the self surrounding the character ideal suited the personal and social needs of an older political economy; the newer ideas reflected in the concept of personality emerged because they better fit the demands of a developing consumer society.

Character formation depends on a particular set of cultural conditions, which in modern Western society are no longer prevalent. Hunter believes that schools are part of the problem. He says that they aggravate rather than ameliorate the conditions necessary for forming character. His argument is that since there is no common language in which to speak of character, due to the fragmentation of culture, there can be no character. Talk about character education is simply talk about the cultural and institutional conditions that might allow for its cultivation. The death of character is about the disintegration of cultural and institutional conditions. Hunter (2001: 15) claims that character is inseparable from the culture within which it is found and formed and that it is a function of the social order as well as a manifestation of the individual person.

Character has a social content and cannot hastily be acquired. Culture shapes individual character: it must have a degree of particularity about it and it is the general culture which provides the reasons, restraints and incentives for conducting life. Charles Glenn (1994: 101) contrasts school culture with the ethos in schools and concludes that the former is the unintentional visible and underlying qualities of school life whilst the latter is the deliberately worked at visible qualities of school life. He gives greater emphasis to school ethos as a formative influence of character development. Hunter (2001: 23) reserves his most strident criticisms for psychology. He says that character education needs to be rescued from the 'tyranny of popular psychology' and its pretensions to scientific objectivity. He claims that psychology has downplayed the obvious social aspects of character development. The weakness of his argument is that he fails to differentiate between the different branches of psychology and simply condemns it *en masse*. The strength of his argument is that in common with other sociologists before him, he argues that character is formed through socialization and cannot be understood independent of a specific cultural context. However, one immediately obvious problem with Hunter's general thesis is that if character is dead how can it be formed?

Pat Hutcheon (1999: 1), like Hunter, links character to culture. He argues that to participate in culture one must acquire a character. On the question of socialization in character he believes (1999: 45f.) that most sociologists do not know how this takes place. Hutcheon claims it is a complex 'social process of system adaptation' for 'the developing child is indeed an evolving adaptive system of responses and values – a character in the process of formation'. Character development can only be understood as a process of interaction within which there is an 'ongoing exchange' – it is not a one-way process. Hutcheon (1999: 223) advocates that we should carefully select the virtues we wish to see the child exposed to or have experience of and then model and reinforce appropriate behaviour. He lists ten suggested virtues which include compassion, responsibility, justice, courage, respect, non-violence, honesty and perseverance. These, he claims, should form the major part of the socialization process and are formed over a number of years as part of an integrated programme. He provides an interesting list of 'desired learning outcomes' for each of these virtues and guidance on what stage they should be taught. Children are social beings – they have a natural disposition to sociability. They need to learn and practise a degree of social competence in order to successfully live socially with each other and with adults. Children need to acquire a social literacy, which is the acquisition of social knowledge and understanding linked to the promotion of responsible behaviour and the development of appropriate social skills. I have argued elsewhere (Arthur 2000: 11ff.) that social virtues need to be cultivated in school. These social virtues are required by all pupils for their confident social participation in community. The development of social literacy is both a prerequisite for and an essential facet of schooling. It lays the foundations for character development.

Conclusion

Sociological analysis helps in our understanding of character education because it provides us with an insight into the process of socialization. Social virtues are not simply better awareness of social rules or even doing the right thing. The social context is not fixed and our learning and understanding of virtues may change because our judgements about them will change over time. Sociology also assists us in understanding that the selection of virtues that people make is based on the assumptions about the good life that they have. Many of Hunter's arguments have their foundation in the writings of Durkheim and McIntyre. From Durkheim he takes the notions of decline in community, the increase in excessive individualism, the lack of social regulation and the inability of schools to change much of this, together with the proposition that society needs to change or be reformed first before the culture of schooling can be changed. From McIntyre he takes the ideas of how society has fragmented, how there is no public morality discourse and how there is little hope for teachers to change much in present circumstances. Hunter then says that there is no shared culture, a dissolution of a settled habitus and a denial of particularity. He concludes that character education is generally a waste of time. This ignores the fact that schools have the potential to shape people, that their curriculum can shape character as can the teachers within particular school communities. It is remarkable that despite many decades of research in sociology to find an agreed basis for social behaviour and 'character', almost no conclusion has been reached that commands general assent.

In summary, a moral socialization perspective of character education emphasizes the social transmission of values primarily through teacher example and a school curriculum that provides for exemplary moral aspirations. John Snarey and Thomas Pavkov (1992: 37) critique this approach, particularly the idea of ethics based on conformity to the requirements of society, but they conclude that there is an emerging movement toward consensus between moral socialization and the more psychological developmental approaches discussed in chapter 5. They claim that both approaches share common ground and that consensus is crucial for the success of moral character education in schools. However, the evidence is not strong for this argument. In summary, within sociology there are a number of contested views about how character is acquired and formed which provide us with important insights on how to understand the nature and process of character education in schools. Unfortunately, contemporary sociology of education provides few practical solutions for character educators.

8   Character and the market economy

> How selfish soever man may be supposed, there are evidently some principles in his nature, which interest him in the fortune of others, and render their happiness necessary to him, though he derives nothing from it except the pleasure of seeing it.
>
> Adam Smith, *The Theory of Moral Sentiments* (1759: 1)

> Preach the moral virtues of free enterprise and the pursuit of profit.
>
> Sir Keith Joseph, Secretary of State for Education, in a speech on the role of schools to the Institute of Directors, 1982

> The market, in my view, has already gone too far: not indeed as an economic system, but as a cast of thought governing relationships and the image we have of ourselves ... The idea that human happiness can be exhaustively accounted for in terms of things we can buy, exchange and replace, is one of the great corrosive acids which eats away the girders on which societies rest; and by the time we have discovered this, it is already too late.
>
> Jonathan Sacks, *Morals and Markets* (1999: 24)

Preparation for life and the world of work is one of the primary aims of the Education Reform Act 1988 for all state schools in England and Wales. There is therefore a clear relationship between the economy and the job-preparation function of schooling. The aim more or less is that the school should teach its pupils in such a way that they grow into young workers who have the values, attitudes and personal qualities required by employers. This is not a new aim in British education for since the growth of industrialization there has been an obvious need for a workforce trained in terms of future adult work: a workforce comprising adults who could read simple instructions, understand verbal commands, give and receive information and who exhibited habits of regularity, self-discipline, obedience and trained effort which were all articulated in the Board of Education's *Elementary Code* (1904, viii). Teachers were expected to: 'implant in the children habits of industry, self-control and courageous perseverance in the face of difficulties'. New Labour is explicit about these same needs in its Green Paper *Schools: Building on Success* (2001) and in its White Paper *Schools: Achieving Success* (2001). In the section on *Education with Character* in the former it is stated that employers want new employees who have the attitudes and habits of mind which exhibit motivation, flexibility, creativity and entrepreneurship. Clearly, the formation of character, in this view, should fit with the needs of the emerging economy. However, does this mean that character is to be subordinate to the needs of industry? It does appear to be the case (see chapter 6) that the policy is to produce certain types of character endowed with certain forms of stable behaviour and habits for the world of work. So what are the specific virtues of character that are required by economic life in a democratic society? More importantly, does the economic system encourage or discourage the formation of a good character? Wealth, status and power, considered in relation to the character of a person, are qualities or values that have been problematic in education, for not everyone can have them in an entrepreneurial society.

Individuals become aware of and choose a worthwhile life within the social and political community by becoming a salesperson, teacher, civil servant, bus driver and so on. Character education can help them choose a career as part of the pursuit of material well-being, but what stance should it assume towards this seeking after wealth? Christopher Winch (2000: 71) describes how a concern with the aims of and constraints of one's chosen occupation involves the moral formation of the future worker. For example, you cannot become a farmer to seek profit for yourself without consideration for the physical environment, human health and the welfare of animals. What therefore are the virtues required for successful economic activity? What role does the school have in this preparation? How does it address questions of youth hedonism, or the competitiveness encouraged in society for scarce resources? Does vocational education in school advance a person's autonomy and self-realization? What is the role of the enterprise culture in the development of the moral consciousness of youth? These are pertinent questions, especially since government has steadily increased its involvement in setting the curriculum agenda for schools, characterized by a shift towards vocational, scientific and technological studies. This effectively began with the introduction of the Technical and Vocational Education Initiative in the 1980s, which required elements such as information technology, design technology, microelectronics and business studies to be incorporated into the secondary school curriculum. All of these are connected with the economy and preparation for the world of work.

In the National Curriculum (1999) a rationale is given for promoting financial capability, enterprise and entrepreneurial skills, and work-related learning. The National Curriculum (NC 1999: 24) states the explicit intention to prepare 'confident and knowledgeable consumers' and says:

> Enterprise can be associated with a set of attributes, skills and attitudes that enable people to create and thrive on change. Enterprise education enables pupils to develop confidence, self-reliance and willingness to embrace change. Through participation in mini-enterprises pupils can practise risk management, learning from mistakes and being innovative.

Entrepreneurial activities are viewed in terms of certain human characteristics of 'tenacity, independence, innovation, imagination, risk-taking, creativity, intuition and leadership'. The document then explains how pupils should learn 'through work', 'about work' and 'for work' to help in the 'transition of young people to adult and working life'. Preparation for participation in the capitalist system is a clear objective of schooling. Indeed, it could be said that the very selection of and emphasis given to the subjects in the National Curriculum – mathematics, communication technology, science, etc. – are clearly designed to achieve economic ends. New Labour's emphasis on the virtues of enterprise education built upon the 1990 National Curriculum Council cross-curricular document *Education for Economic and Industrial Understanding* 4 (1990: 5), which was concerned with ethical issues in economic understanding including developing in the young attitudes of 'concern for the use of scarce resources', a 'sense of responsibility for the consequences of their own economic actions' and a 'sensitivity to the effects of economic choices on the environment' together with a 'concern for human rights, as these are affected by economic decisions'.

There has been a strong preoccupation with the transition from school to work. A vocationally orientated curriculum is not the same as training for a particular occupation since in the end choices must be made by the pupil. However, how do you develop autonomy within the constraints of the need to earn a living? What is the meaning of personal development and fulfilment through learning about or through work in school? Is the preparation for work through schooling and education designed to make people more productive? Is it beneficial to character and will it improve morals and behaviour – in other words will it help build the ethical character of a pupil in an appropriate way? Jonathan (1999) argues that the economic or capitalist forces in society are both psychologically reinforcing and coercive of character. Pupils are stimulated by the desire for material well-being and are afraid of failure in life which would result in their material disadvantage and even social disapproval. This stimulation for profit, she claims, and the fear of failure induce the response of competitiveness in the young. You seek the best for yourself and do not neglect your own advantage in favour of some equitable distribution of resources. In this scheme education and schooling play a small role as it is left to the discipline of the market to create opportunities and even requirements for initiative and rewards innovation and energy. However, it also punishes those who do not conform to its requirements, whether through sloth, indecisiveness, complacency or parasitic reliance on the energy of others. In other words it is left to circumstances – autonomy, rationality and critical thinking may play little part.

David Purpel (1997: 149) has criticized character educators for not showing much concern about the cruelty of the free market economy and the growing economic inequality in society. There is obviously a gap here in the character education literature. Capitalism with its competitiveness, scarcity of resources and unequal distribution can certainly lead to a hedonistic consumerism which produces the selfish character. A character which is seen as materially 'successful' is often one, therefore, that is seen worthy of emulating. We saw this in the 1980s with opportunities for the few of high salaries and conspicuous consumption within a newly individualistic and materialistic economy. These character types were called young, upwardly mobile professionals – 'yuppies'. This economic atmosphere had an impact on character traits, even of those who were not employed. Education as a whole cannot be conceived by those interested in building character as purely instrumental to working life. Vocational education can have a valued place in the school curriculum without encouraging an excessive materialism with its cult of success and possessions. A positive vocational education will give some meaning and direction to a life rather than promoting the view of a human being as a mechanism that behaves in a deterministic way. It can do this by integrating the virtues of justice, fairness and equality into its rationale. However, excessive economic disparity between individuals inhibits the force of this kind of education. Economic changes also mean that young people will not experience stability in their career patterns and will be required by the market to change jobs several times during their working life. It is why the government is keen to promote a flexible and adaptive workforce.

Alex Molnar (1997: 163) makes the point forcefully that character educators are also largely mute on the modern culture of commercialism which Molnar believes is corrosive of character. Increasingly, he believes, 'people are defined for what they purchase and valued for what they possess'. As children watch hundreds of commercials each day on TV and are subject to a culture of overt consumerism it is difficult to see how character education in schools can make much impact on youth. Even before children arrive in school they are most definitely consumers, often defining themselves and others in relation to what they wear and what they can buy, or can get their parents to buy for them. Advertising creates needs for products and children are deliberately targeted and encouraged to make immature decisions. There have been numerous studies of how destructive advertising and the cult of violence and sex can be on the formation of character. Pat Hutcheon (1999: 237ff.) provides a depressing litany of alarm in an annotated bibliography of research on the effects of media portrayals of violence and pornography on human development. Molnar is very critical of the links that are forged between schools and the world of business. Business sponsorship of schools or the distribution of promotional materials in schools is not healthy for character development. In British schools there have been cases where children are rewarded with a voucher to buy food at McDonald's when their behaviour has improved. We see company waste bins being provided by McDonald's for the school playground and also companies providing free exercise books to schools with their advertisements on every page. As Molnar says:

> Since context and circumstance are left unaccounted for in the epistemology of contemporary character education, it is hardly surprising that character education can offer only a rudimentary and simplistic understanding of how powerful cultural phenomena influence the social boundary markers that shape and define the moral understanding and ethical behaviour

of children. In practical terms, this deficiency no doubt often results in children regarding the well-intentioned exhortations built into character education programmes as out of touch with the real world that they inhabit.

Homo Economicus

The study of economics has traditionally sought to explain human behaviour with reference to expected preference satisfaction which has assumed that the preferences each human being seeks to satisfy are self-interested or egotistical desires. Adam Smith, who we should remember was primarily a moral philosopher, occupying that Chair at the University of Glasgow, believed that as one profits, one's debt to society and one's neighbour is greater. In his *Theory of Moral Sentiments* (1759) he outlines a normative ethical theory together with a descriptive psychology to account for the origins of our patterns of moral behaviour (see Heath 1995). Smith's theory of economics was therefore more accurately ethical theory since he argued that the promotion of certain virtues in individuals, such as thrift, self-help, self-reliance, industry etc., all help make the individual ultimately happy and improve society. Smith was definitely concerned with the character development of people, especially with providing them with the moral principles by which aspiring individuals could improve themselves – both materially and morally – in a commercial society. Charles Griswold (1999) provides an excellent critique of Smith's ideas on the relationship between economic activity, morality and the character of a person. He begins by explaining that Smith was not an advocate of crude laissez-faire capitalism, that he in fact had moral reservations about the unfettered operation of the free market. In his *An Inquiry into the Nature and Causes of the Wealth of Nations*, Griswold (1999: 16f.) informs us, Smith saw the pursuit of wealth as having little to do with satisfying our basic needs, but rather feeding our fears and wants by means of our imagination. Whilst consumption was viewed by Smith as the sole purpose of production, he believed that people deceived themselves when they associated consumption with happiness. He taught that neither the pursuit nor the possession of wealth actually produces happiness, but may in fact jeopardize it. Greed, dishonesty, a willingness to exploit others, vanity and many other vices are often associated with material well-being, but Smith refers to these as the 'corruption of the moral sentiments'.

Smith clearly did not advocate a free market unconcerned about the kinds of people it produced. He largely adopted an Aristotelian ethics of virtue, with morality understood in terms of an ethics of character. He was concerned and wrote a great deal about excellence of character and the civic virtues which furthered it. For him, the cardinal virtues were self-command, prudence, benevolence and justice. Griswold (1999: 209ff.) examines these virtues in detail. For example, he takes a famous passage from Smith's *Wealth of Nations* which runs as follows: 'It is not from the benevolence of the butcher, the brewer, or the baker, that we expect our dinner, but from their regard to their own interest. We address ourselves, not to their humanity but to their self-love, and never talk of them of our own necessities but of their advantages.' Griswold asserts that this is 'not an encomium to greed or depraved selfishness but a morally acceptable statement of a fact that may hold in any instance of exchange'. We address ourselves to the prudence of the shopkeeper, not his benevolence, so the shopkeeper is acting virtuously in accordance with prudence and justice. He cannot extend his benevolence indiscriminately to all who want his goods, for he needs to use judgement, and on occasion he will owe the beggar charity. Griswold (1999: 209) summarizes Smith's intentions thus:

> The secret to long-lasting and morally defensible success therefore lies in a combination of ambitious vision, suitable moderation, religious adherence to principles of justice, and a keen awareness that individuals and their contexts ought to be beneficiaries of our efforts rather than the instruments of our ideals.

Does Smith elevate the ego of commercial man above civic virtues? Christopher Berry (1992: 76) interprets Smith as asserting that society should be based on a system of rules rather than on one that embodies the practice of virtues. He agrees that Smith approved of the virtues in general but argues that he really meant virtues for individuals in their private domain – he was not suggesting, according to Berry, that these should be seen as public virtues or commercial virtues which are more to do with justice and rule-following. Berry rightly shows how Smith understood 'selfishness' as merely everyone's desire to better their own condition. Smith proposed that the natural 'sympathy' of man acts as a counter-balance to selfishness, which he defined as fellow-feeling and which humbled the arrogance of self-love. Smith defined sympathy as the capacity for and inclination to imagine the feelings of others and he believed this was the source of human moral sentiment. It was from this idea of 'fellow-feeling' that Smith attempted to build an inborn moral sense – a natural identification with other human beings which would lead to our first moral judgements. For Smith, the moral nature of a human being is only united by the voice of conscience and it is this judgemental conscience which, he says, makes us moral beings.

In commercial society Smith believed that honesty was a central virtue for the proper conduct of business and he suggested that the 'impartial spectator' or voice of conscience would also prevent total selfishness. Smith's ethical aims were practical for a growing commercial society. Robert Bellah *et al.* (1985), sums this up as the rational self-interested individual living in conditions of competitive market in which trade and exchange would replace traditional ranks and loyalties as the coordinating mechanism of social life. However, Smith's followers did not see it quite his way. As Roy Porter (2000: 388, 396) describes: 'The new political economy thus repudiated religio-moral or statesmanly policing of wealth in favour of a "scientific" endorsement of "natural" economic forces. Christian commandments against greed were sidelined, and the pursuit of gain secularized, privatized and valorised.' As a consequence, he writes, there was 'a transition from *homo civilis* to *homo economicus*, which invoked the rationalisation of selfishness and self-interest as an enlightened ideology, the privatisation of virtue and the de-moralisation of luxury, pride, selfishness and avarice'. The freedom of the individual in commerce was paramount and divorced from traditional morality for the market assumed a morality of its own. It was Samuel Smiles (1862) in *Self-Help* who outlined the moral qualities of a person who is successful in gaining wealth and they were: hard work, integrity, perseverance, diligence, self-control, sobriety, self-denial and prudence. Smith would have agreed with his fellow Scot's list, for both sought to encourage economic success among aspiring working people.

Jennifer Morse (1997) argues that Smith's analysis of sympathy was an important complement to his analysis of self-interested individuals acting in the free market. As Smith said in *Moral Sentiments*: 'There are evidently some principles in his action, which interest him in the future of others, and render their happiness necessary to him, though he derives nothing from it except the pleasure of seeing it.' In other words, self-interest leads to a concern for the common good. Much of what Smith articulated was based on the Golden Rule. Morse believes that Smith's moral ideas were simply ignored as economics became defined exclusively as a science allocating scarce resources among competing ends. The economist generally views the person as a pure stimulus–response machine who is completely reactive and whose behaviour is predetermined. The character formed in this economic view is one who confronts the prices of various choices that present themselves, calculates which of the options maximizes their utility and then acts in accordance with the calculation they have performed. In this model of economic man, Morse believes that the person does not make a decision in any meaningful way. There is only calculation – no real choice since there is only one outcome. The person is a utility function. Human character is reduced in this view to behaviour which changes in response to cost and benefits of alternative courses of action. However, whilst Smith advocated 'self-interest', he thought of it as a virtue, but of the lowest level. There is also nothing in the *Wealth of Nations* that extols either self-love or the pursuit of selfish interests to the detriment of others. Smith never expected commerce or the rise of capitalism to become divorced from civil society and never anticipated that economic markets could function without a moral life. Indeed, it is important to consider both of Smith's books together fully to understand how he understood the moral character of a person.

Smith was genuinely concerned with moral education; for him it was a matter of formation of character through a process which included teaching and actions. This character formation began in the home and took a great deal of time – a lifetime – to complete. He believed that conscience was central to this formation and that 'self-command' had to be developed. For Smith, the virtuous person feels the right things, at the right times, in the right way. Undisciplined feelings need to be trained and Smith advocated the use of literature as a sort of applied ethics from which to learn. The use of judgement is also central in his thinking for it was not simply a question of following moral rules imposed by others. Smith would perhaps have agreed with Emile Durkheim's comment that: 'It is necessary that we never lose sight of what is the aim of public education. It is not a matter of training workers for the factory or accountants for the warehouse, but citizens for society. The teaching should therefore be essentially edifying; it should detach minds from egotistic views and material interests ....' (quoted in Walford and Pickering 1998: 20). Like Durkheim, Smith believed that morality was essentially a matter of socialization, of social interaction, which taught individuals how to identify acceptable behaviour.

Smith grew up in a society ingrained with Calvinism which did not approve of indiscriminate almsgiving – rather, the aim was to reform characters so that relief was unnecessary. The qualities of character that Smith admired were those necessary for capitalism, but it was a capitalism that generated wealth for the many, not the few. Smith advocated 'instrumental virtues' necessary for the operation of economic liberty and he fully endorsed the 'work ethic'. He would have approved of Andrew Carnegie's 'gospel of wealth' (see Riley 1992: 338ff.), which essentially taught that the wealthy have a moral obligation to distribute their surplus wealth for the benefit of the common good of society. This was more of a Christian ideal than an economic principle, and one that few have since followed. Max Weber's analysis, contained in his major work, *The Protestant Ethic and the Spirit of Capitalism* (1904), reveals the impact of a religious creed upon the formation of a type of character. His theory was that the movement to a capitalist society was primarily caused by the habits, attitudes and beliefs of the kind of Scottish Calvinism which influenced Smith, Smiles and Carnegie. The Protestant mind and character will invest and reinvest money in productive enterprises for competitive advantages. He will promote accumulation of wealth and ensure that his employees work hard, and develop a disciplined capacity to delay gratification so that they can be rewarded with material gain. Progress was above all conceived to be economic. Few would subscribe to this theory today.

Alfred Marshall (1898), who was the most authoritative exponent of Smith's economics in Britain in the early 1900s had, according to Stefan Collini (1985: 29), 'displayed a pervasive concern with the shaping and the efficacy of character under modern industrial conditions', and he had always insisted that it was a central part of the economist's professional task to identify those forces which 'will help to build up a strong and righteous character'. Marshall (1898: 1) certainly believed that a person's daily working life had a major impact on their character, as he said: 'For man's character has been moulded by his every-day work, and the material resources which he thereby procures more than by any other influence unless it be that of his religious ideals.' For Marshall, economics was not simply about a study of wealth – it also involved the study of human character that was formed by the way income was earned, not by the amount of income. Of course, this character formation could lead to a capitalist character type, but Marshall also recognized that poverty was the enemy of character formation – that it often prohibited good character formation.

There was certainly continued interest in the development of character by economists and Collini demonstrates that socialists, for example, very largely justified their economic arrangements for society on the grounds that it would produce 'a higher type of character'. Collini (1985) quotes a socialist commentator of the period:

> Today the key word ... in economics is 'character' ... [The reason] why individualist economists fear socialism is that they believe it will deteriorate character, and the reason why socialist economists seek socialism is their belief that under individualism character is deteriorating.

There appears to be a genuine concern amongst economists as to whether character could potentially determine economic circumstances, rather than the other way around. However, such interest is not as evident today, with Collard (1978) and Phelps (1975) being the notable exceptions, notwithstanding the relationship of the subject to ethics. Whilst few are willing to defend the free-market economy as a moral enterprise, Henry Acton (1971: 97) concludes that making profit need not be the sole concern of those who engage in business. He notes that failures in public spirit, particularly in moral education, are much more likely to result in people acting in a purely self-interested fashion.

Terry Cooper (1991: 152) redefines the idea of self-interest and claims that enlightened self-interest is an essential quality of character. Cooper expands on Cochran's (see chapter 7) work on the relationship between community and character to develop the link between self-interest and civic virtues. He defines civic virtues as citizens voluntarily demonstrating a willingness to forgo their self-interest for the common good. Cooper (1991: 153) argues that citizens must understand their self-interest in terms of the broader interests of the community. 'Self-interest rightly understood,' he says, means 'understanding the origins of one's self in community and accepting one's resultant obligations to it.' Whilst he argues that a level of self-interest is necessary for character development, there also needs to be constraints on self-interest. George Soros (1998: 75) echoes this argument in his discussions of capitalism when he warns:

> A transactional society undermines social values and loosens moral constraints. Social values express a concern for others. They imply that the individual belongs to a community, be it a family, a tribe, a nation, or humankind, whose interests must take precedence over the individual's self-interest. But a transactional market economy is anything but a community. Everybody must look out for his or her own interests and moral scruples can become an encumbrance in a dog-eat-dog world. In a purely transactional society, people who are not weighed down by any consideration of others can move around more easily and are likely to come out ahead ... A purely transactional society could never exist, yet we are closer to it than at any time in history.

Cooper and Soros would no doubt agree with Jonathan Sacks (1999) that the social institutions of society are important for character development and that those who operate within economic markets need to respect this.

Character, employment and schooling

The current government has approved of work experience in schools and established a Committee in 2001 to review how young peoples' (between the ages of five and nineteen) understanding of business and enterprise can be improved, under the chairmanship of Sir Howard Davis, chairman of the Financial Services Authority. His report, *Enterprise and the Economy in Education* (Davis 2002) recommends that schools should make greater efforts to train Britain's next generation of entrepreneurs. Davis recognizes that in English secondary schools business studies is already taken by many children and that most schools have compulsory work experience schemes for all of their pupils. Whilst pupils experience the world of work through placements in industry and commerce, Davis felt that only about 30 per cent of them experienced 'entrepreneurship'. Work experience no doubt influences their attitudes to work and affects their character development. For example, many children believe, irrespective of school teaching, that the measure of success of an individual is pecuniary gain derived through competition between individuals. This raises the question of whether economic competition between individuals is a good thing. It depends to some extent on whether the individual who succeeds does so for selfish reasons and whether in so doing another individual is considerably worse off. Do schools balance this by emphasis on measuring success through socially useful actions directed at the welfare of others? Davis encourages the development of 'enterprise capability' or 'enterprise learning' in schools, but he notes that 'social enterprise' and 'civic entrepreneurship' are also important. Civic entrepreneurship is defined in the Report as activity carried out for social reasons but using the sort of entrepreneurial behaviour more commonly associated with business start-ups. Social enterprise is likewise a non-profitmaking business with social aims. Citizenship education, together with other subjects in the school curriculum, is seen as the key to promoting different kinds of entrepreneurship. However, Davis says little, if anything, about the moral dimension of entrepreneurship, except some references to being responsible for the environment.

Whilst preparation for the world of work, including teaching about enterprise capability, is a legitimate aim of character education it needs to be sensitive to economic circumstances and their impact on individuals. In the 1970s and 1980s Britain experienced a deep recession which created millions of unemployed people. During this period it was common for employers and politicians to blame youth for some of this unemployment – it was often claimed that they lacked proper attitudes to work and indeed that they lacked character. From this has developed the idea that individuals are responsible for their own misfortune. Indeed, some modern economists focus increasingly on the study of individual motivation in which each individual makes rational decisions based on self-interest within a framework of the free market. This approach makes little allowance for concepts of moral character in business or for the impact of the market on individual circumstances.

What are the virtues that employers want? They range from a sense of good humour to a willingness to learn, and might include motivation, technical skills, communication and numeracy skills, an ability to respect others and to be clean and tidy, social skills and other key transferable skills. Education today is often seen to be strictly interested in utilitarian ends and concerned with competencies – product and outcomes rather than with growth and development. Training of a narrowly vocational kind is often the norm: education to produce workers and consumers, with students often seen as units of resource or clients or customers. Marxist theorists argue that schools, which are instruments of the State, teach the knowledge and skills to reproduce the social division of labour. Schools and what they teach are intimately bound up with the economy. It is why, they claim, the character education movement in the USA is intimately linked with corporate sponsorship and why it advocates stronger school partnerships with the business community. One reason for this close association is that employers are concerned by what they perceive to be a lack of character in many employees. They draw increasing attention to employees who fail to turn up on time to work; who require supervisors to oversee them because of their lack of initiative and quality in performance; who use inappropriate behaviour with customers; who use office facilities for personal use and those who do not tell the truth, accept bribes and do not admit mistakes. Certain virtues are identified as necessary for success in employment and their absence can and does lead to dismissal.

An example of this kind of employer interest in the education of character traits of future employees, in other words in school pupils, is provided by the work of the *Council on Ethics in Economics* in Ohio (www.businessethics.org). The Council sought, through groups of managers, to identify the core virtues that business seeks in future employees in various key employment sectors, both public and private. One group looked at those who work in call centres that deal with telemarketing, debt collecting and customer services. The group described this kind of work as demanding the following competences: computer keyboard proficiency, an ability to work at a fast pace, good verbal communication skills and skills of negotiation and conflict resolution. Seven virtues or character traits were identified as necessary for success in this role: self-esteem, integrity, commitment, accountability, community involvement, respect for others, and what was mysteriously called 'a servant attitude'. In terms of self-esteem, the group understood this as developing a strong confident sense of self which included a recognition of personal weaknesses and humility. This would enable the employee to accept 'constructive feedback', to adapt and change in order to increase productivity. It would also enable them to bounce back from a negative phone call and be ready for the next one.

The world of business obviously values individuals for their efficiency and productivity, but it also tends to have short-term goals that do not correspond to a genuine desire to improve character. The managers' group above translated these short-term efficiency goals into suggested teaching strategies for schoolteachers which included rewarding pupils for doing the right things. Since many staff in call centres are employed on commission basis it may well be seen as 'good' preparation for pupils to get used to the idea of being rewarded for something they have done. On the question of integrity the group concluded that staff should handle calls correctly first time and not cheat because of the pressure to succeed and again they made recommendations for teachers in schools which included strategies to stop children lying, cheating, plagiarizing or colluding. Each of the management groups agreed that character traits are established early and concluded that children should learn them from an early age through constant reinforcement so that they internalize the values being taught. There are obviously many educational questions that can be raised about this kind of business ethics approach to schooling, but with the government encouraging closer relationships with the business community these kinds of issues for schools are set to increase.

Whilst the focus on the ethical character of employees is perhaps to be expected, it is both interesting and significant that a survey in 1995 revealed that more than two-thirds of British companies admitted suffering from fraud, most of it perpetrated by management (see *The Times*, 5 June 1995). A disproportionate number of senior managers in British companies have been educated in private schools that, as noted earlier, explicitly promote the idea and rhetoric of character development. However, a private-school education will not necessarily ensure the virtues of honesty or respect. In 1980, John Rae, headmaster of Westminster School in London, revealed for the first time at the Headmasters' Conference the increase in theft among pupils in private schools (see *The Times*, 17 October 1980). This concern and need for ethical character in business is as much a matter for employers as it is for employees; it is not simply from-the-top-down authoritarian approach by a management solely interested in increased productivity. Etzioni (1988: 239) has shown that employees are motivated by a range of moral factors and that the moral dimension to economic behaviour is essential for promoting good character.

Michael Young (1994: 21) describes the bonds between children and their parents as being at the 'heart of the moral economy' which, he says, holds society together. I believe this can be extended, to some extent, to the school, for the teacher acting *in loco parentis* also develops a bond with his or her pupils. Young notes that there is always tension between the moral economy and the market economy, but what would this consist of in terms of schooling? The market economy is concerned chiefly with the fundamental human activity of making a living – production, productivity, consumption, exchange and efficiency. The moral economy of the school is chiefly concerned with the desire for community, for shared purposes, a sense of moral conviction, mutual need and support, a sense of justice, solidarity, fairness and equality. These can sit uneasily with the prime function of the market which is to produce objects for human use and consumption. The market economy operates through calculation of rational self-interest and the profit motive. People stay in relationships with each other so long as each individual realizes their own purpose in the relationship. The emphasis is on competition, choice and individual fulfilment, self-expression and self-realization. In a school each pupil is a citizen and relationships should be equal and reciprocal.

Cooperation is given an important role and each pupil is valued for what they are, not exclusively for what they can do. The motive is not what is in it for me, but rather what best promotes the common good of the school community. Ethical character development finds its best environment in such a moral economy.

Conclusion

It does seem possible to equip young people with the education and training to earn a living for themselves as well as enable them to lead good human lives. An education for living as well as for a livelihood is required. Therefore, some balance needs to be given to Tony Blair's idea, reported in *The Times* (6 July 1997), that it is about how to learn more in order to earn more. It is also about living well. We are not simply economic creatures whose sense of worth and purpose in life is defined by our capacity to secure material well-being. We are not what we do for a living or what we buy, nor are we completely driven by self-interest to maximize our own utility. This reductionist view of human nature can have a powerful and an essentially negative impact on character formation from an early age. Applied to education in schools it can result in a view that anything that does not prepare children for making a living, or becoming a consumer, is a waste of time. The government appears to have an interest in wanting to shape the development of children's characters to meet prescribed economic goals. Investment in education and particularly the justifications for character education contained in the Green and White Papers of 2001 cannot be based simply on reference to economic and material advantage, or the development of instrumental values: it must also improve the quality of human life. In fairness to government policy, it is important to consider the range of statements contained in the goals of the National Curriculum to understand that New Labour's view of character is complex and incomplete. Consequently, there is a need for greater clarification of government policy on character education, particularly how it links and connects with the many reports and statements the government has commissioned and issued on the moral economy of schooling.

We have seen how economic theory has largely attempted to predict the behaviour of human beings by describing moral character according to individual preferences and objectives for life. Mozaffar Qizilbash (1994a, 1994b) details two important respects in which the analysis of character is relevant to economics. First, 'positive' economics is concerned with predicting or explaining how people actually act. Second, 'normative' economics is concerned with how people 'ought to' or should act. He argues that whilst the distinction between the two is not entirely clear, any theoretical account of human behaviour is relative to an account of human character. Consequently, he suggests that 'normative' economics needs to take more notice of the moral character of human beings. The activities of the market economy should not be conducted in a moral vacuum.

The fear is that the power of the market might undermine character, for in an advanced consumer society like Britain the market can encourage a view of human life as a series of consumer choices. As we become richer we increasingly seek to buy the 'services' we desire, which perhaps undermines our general sense and expectation of civic duty. It often seems that unless we have entered into some contractual relationship that gives rise to legally enforceable obligations, we have no clear sense of duty in relation to others. The idea of endless consumer choices, including buying basic human services from others, is given graphic illustration by the shift in our use of the terminology from 'life' to 'lifestyle', which suggests that there is nothing of substance that defines who we are. Schooling cannot advance such a view of human nature without losing its claim to genuine education. The market economy values people more for what they can do than for what they are, particularly their ability to compete against each other. We cannot allow economics to become a quasi religion which tries to establish order by providing a priestly caste of experts who determine what share of the good life we can reasonably expect. The real task, as Adam Smith would recognize, is to restore the link between economic markets and civil society so as to create a background against which ethical character can be developed.

9　Character education

The Master said: 'Put me in the company of any two people at random – they will invariably have something to teach me. I can take their qualities as a model and their defects as a warning.'

The Analects of Confucius (7.22)

It is all a matter of tone and implication, but then so is all teaching. Education is implication. It is not the things you say which children respect; when you say things, they very commonly laugh and do the opposite. It is the things you assume that really sink into them. It is the things you forget to even to teach that they learn.

G. K. Chesterton, *Illustrated London News*, 12 January 1907

The vilest abortionist is he who attempts to mould a child's character.

Bernard Shaw (in Sadler, 1908: 7)

The contemporary approach to character education in schools has been to accord the pupil a say in their own moral education, a degree of self-direction, an approach that has been largely influenced by the cognitive development theorists. At the same time adult direction and authority has suffered a great deal of criticism. Since the 1960s progressive teaching methods have emphasized child-centred learning, learning through experience, neutrality and cooperative learning and have consistently been opposed to more traditional methods, often describing them as authoritarian and indoctrinatory. This idea of education views the teacher as an adult who should not attempt deliberately to stamp character on pupils.

Teachers will commonly argue that there is little room in the school curriculum for the education of moral character. Many will say that moral character is the responsibility of parents together with faith communities and that in any case in a multicultural society there is no agreed way to determine what is good and bad character. There also appears to be a growing 'moral correctness' mindset in education, as teachers do not say things are 'immoral' for fear of being branded discriminatory. In fact, teachers are generally non-judgemental in official language about children. However, it may be that talk of indoctrination and brainwashing often excuses the teacher from the difficult task of thinking what values they might consciously inculcate. Teachers who are increasingly 'trained' to employ practical teaching skills and methods in the classroom can easily become technicians who simply look for the techniques that work. They are less interested in themes of human development and social policy. Instead of deciding what should be taught, concern is voiced about values and controversial issues. Whilst the virtue ethics approaches have made inroads in mainstream education, few teachers have been prepared to deal with their complexity. Current teacher training courses in England have mostly abandoned disciplines such as history and philosophy of education in favour of a more technical approach, which retains many elements of behavioural psychology. Teachers are, with few exceptions, ill equipped to discuss, far less consciously adopt, a virtue ethics approach to character education.

As I have noted in previous chapters there are numerous books on character education, almost all published in America, detailing both the content and the type of teaching methods that could be adopted. Suzanne Rice (1996) has noted:

> Increasingly, schools are being held responsible for the development of good character among students, but if John Dewey is correct, this responsibility ought to be seen as belonging to all our institutions. Virtue, on his account, develops and is sustained in interaction with the whole of one's physical and social environment. The school constitutes only a part of children's environment, and the other environments in which they participate will also bear on the development of character.

British teachers are not solely responsible for the character of those they educate. We have seen in chapter 5 how the discipline of psychology contains certain assumptions about human beings including those of the innate goodness of human nature and the importance of attaining one's full personal aspiration in life. Both assumptions delegate punishment and human self-sacrifice to a lower position.

Character development

Bill Puka (1999: 131) in reviewing character education programmes identifies six teaching methods. These are: *a* instruction in basic values and virtues; *b* behavioural codes established and enforced; *c* telling stories with moral lessons; *d* modelling desirable traits and values; *e* holding up moral exemplars in history, literature, religion, and extolling their traits; *f* providing in school and community outreach opportunities (service projects) through which students can exercise good traits and pursue good values. There are a wide variety of character development strategies which include those listed by Puka. There are also certain assumptions of character educators implicitly or explicitly contained in these strategies. Whilst some subscribe to the psychological idea of moral development as developmental progression through stages, some prefer to substitute the word 'development' for 'formation'. Many character educators do not accept that moral values are relative – they generally insist that moral values can be objectively grounded in human nature and experience. They would also claim that moral action is not simply rational, but involves the affective qualities of a human being. They reject many models of moral education as inadequate on the basis that they are not comprehensive enough to capture the full complexity of human character. They also advocate a holistic approach to character education which provides, they claim, an integrative view of human nature. Some also advocate that religion can provide a support structure for moral development. Dennis Doyle (1997: 440) would not accept such a view; for him, the real crux of the problem is that: 'the issue of ... character education ... is really no more and no less than the issue of pedagogy. It is process rather than content, form rather than substance. It is "critical thinking skills" as opposed to thinking critically about content, it is "learning to learn" rather than learning something substantial.' He rejects a virtue ethics content for character education.

Kevin Ryan and Thomas Lickona (1987a: 20ff.) provide an interesting model of character development that involves three basic elements – knowing, affective and action. Lickona (1991) further developed this model. First, pupils learn moral content from our heritage. This heritage is not static but subject to change, for it can be altered and added to. The pupil learns to know the good through informed rational decision-making. Moral reasoning, decision-making and the ability to gain self-knowledge through reviewing and evaluating behaviour are all essential in this dimension of character development. Second is the affective domain, which includes feelings of sympathy, care and love for others and is considered by Lickona as an essential bridge to moral action. Lickona (1991: 58ff.) refers to this second element as feelings and adds conscience, love, empathy and humility as important aspects. The conscience, for example, is also partly cognitive in that one needs to know what is right, but it has an important function of feeling – particularly the feeling of guilt. Lickona is eager to make a distinction between destructive and constructive feelings of guilt. In destructive guilt feelings the pupil thinks they may be a 'bad person' and Lickona wishes to avoid this. He feels that constructive guilt feelings result when an individual knows what should be done but doesn't do it. Guilt in this sense helps the pupil resist temptation to do wrong. The presence or absence of this feelings element in character development determines whether a pupil practises doing what is right or not. Third, action depends on the will, competence and habit of a person. Will is meant in the sense that a pupil must will their way to overcoming their self-interest and any pride or anxiety they have in order to take what they know to be the right action.

Pupils must also develop the competence to do the 'good', which involves certain skills, and they must freely choose to repeat these good actions as a form of habit. Ryan and Lickona tell us that these three elements of action do not always work together. Their model also states that character development takes place in and through human community. This requires pupils to participate in the affairs of the community. The school community must therefore challenge and support the pupil in responsible actions and relationships.

Principles of practice

Lickona (1996) also outlines eleven principles that have been largely adopted by the Character Education Partnership in the USA as criteria for planning a character education programme and for recognizing the achievements of schools through the conferment of a national award. Whilst he does not consider these principles to be exhaustive, they are:

a   schools should be committed to core ethical values;
b   character should be comprehensively defined to include thinking, feeling and behaviour;
c   schools should be proactive and systematic in teaching character education and not simply wait for opportunities;
d   schools must develop caring atmospheres and become a microcosm of the caring community;
e   opportunities to practise moral actions should be varied and available to all;
f   academic study should be central;
g   schools need to develop ways of increasing the intrinsic motivation of pupils who should be committed to the core values;
h   schools need to work together and share norms for character education;
i   teachers and pupils should share in the moral leadership of the school;
j   parents and community should be partners in character education in the school;
k   evaluate the effectiveness of character education in both school, staff and pupils.

In contrast, David Brooks and Mark Kann (1993) list eleven elements which they claim are essential for character education. These are worth summarizing briefly. They believe that there should be some direct instruction in character education, for children need to be familiar with the virtues by name – they should hear and see the words, learn their meanings, identify appropriate behaviours and practise and apply them. For Brooks and Kann language is important. Children should be encouraged to use the language of the virtues and teachers should avoid negative language like 'Don't be late' or 'Don't forget', replacing these with 'Be on time' or 'Be prepared'. They recommend visual displays to illustrate the virtues with coloured banners with, for example, the word 'Respect' printed on them in the school corridors and they place great emphasis on a positive school climate, service programmes which serve the community of the school and neighbourhood, and involvement of parents and children in the governance of the school. They conclude: 'If the whole school community fosters the language culture, and climate of good character, the student who spends a significant portion of their time there will acquire the words, concepts, behaviours, and skills that contribute to good conduct, ethical decision-making, and a fertile learning environment.' This approach contains some simple elements, but it resonates with many of the suggestions currently being advocated for citizenship education in England.

Many of these principles and elements represent a holistic approach to character education. The holistic approach raises the question of whether there should be a separate curriculum for character education in the school timetable or whether all subjects, including the school ethos, should contribute to the formation of character. William Schubert (1997: 17) addresses this question by focusing on the area of curriculum construction. He observes that whilst some curricula are established to influence the character of pupils, every learning experience in some way influences the character of a person. In short, curriculum shapes character. When teachers 'intend' to change the curriculum in some way in order to influence the behaviour or character of the pupils, then it could be said to be a 'curriculum' of character education. However, he notes that even without overt 'intentionality' many messages are conveyed through the hidden curriculum of the school by its processes and structures. Separating character education as a subject may do little to ensure that all education is about human development. In the hands of the right teacher any subject may be made a means of influencing character. This is not an unintended aim for character education, but rather should be seen as Lori Wiley (1998: 18) says: 'intentional, conscious, planned, pro-active, organized and reflective rather than being assumed, unconscious, reactive, subliminal, or random'.

Others may argue that the aims of the school curriculum are amoral since the curriculum is only concerned with teaching facts about the way the world is – not values about the way it should be. The reality is, as we saw in chapter 6, that the government has specified aims for the National Curriculum which are clearly normative and pertain to morality. The language of these official aims is to do with what the curriculum should be. Of course, there is little in the way of substance given to these curriculum aims which is why the school atmosphere is another crucial element comprising character education.

School ethos

Almost all character educators emphasize the importance of the school ethos in advancing arguments about character education (De Vries 1998; Wynne and Walberg 1985, Grant 1982). Today it is accepted that the non-academic aspects of schooling are just as significant for the development of pupils. There is no such thing as a 'value-free' school ethos, so we can conclude that there can be a good school ethos and a bad ethos in schools. Within a good school ethos Gerald Grant (1986: 174) would say that 'intellectual and moral virtues are seen as inseparable … Teachers must have equal concern for mind and character, schools should be neither morally neutral factories for increasing cognitive output nor witless producers of obedient "well-adjusted" youngsters.' Grant (1982) points to the work of Michael Rutter *et al.* (1979) whose research, *Fifteen Thousand Hours*, indicated that teachers shape the atmosphere of a school together with a core of able pupils around whom a good ethos can be formed. Difficult children with behavioural problems can be absorbed into the school policies on behaviour only if the school has a balanced mix of children. This atmosphere consists of discipline, high academic and behavioural expectations, goals shared by staff and shared norms on fairness and consistency. All these elements of school life are associated with better outcomes and Rutter *et al.* conclude that effective schools have distinctive atmospheres which influence their pupils' behaviour.

In fact, they say that the culture or ethos of a school, the 'hidden curriculum', has a greater effect on pupil behaviour than does the academic curriculum. Since this work there have been a number of critical investigations into the hidden curriculum: notable among these has been the radical perspectives contained in Henry Giroux and David Purpel's (1983) collection of essays on moral education and the hidden curriculum. Their conclusion is that schooling, and particularly moral education, can no longer be seen as simply consisting of the courses that are provided, but rather also comprising the dynamics and ideological assumptions that constitute a school's ethos.

The research and writings of Edward Wynne (1982, 1985, 1986, 1988, especially with Ryan 1997) also indicate that the school ethos is crucial to an effective character programme. Wynne focuses on the school rather than on the individual pupil. He believes that the school could teach morality without saying a single word about it. We can see this in the fact that character or moral education is rarely formally recorded in any lesson plans or schemes of work – rather it forms part of the hidden curriculum. No primary teacher in Britain would doubt how the school often acts as a family for many pupils, replicating some of the formative influences of the family environment – warmth, acceptance, caring relationships, love and positive role models. When a school has a positive atmosphere it is bound to affect the motivation of teachers by providing them with higher satisfaction levels, which in turn are transformed into higher pupil expectations.

The emphasis on school ethos is a relatively new feature within character education. There is a greater awareness of the role of the 'hidden curriculum' on character development and some believe that the indirect methods of teaching character are perhaps more beneficial than traditional curricula-based approaches. A. L. Lockwood (1997: 24), in interviewing James Leming, found that he believed that character educators are far more informed by basic research in education and by the principles of human learning than at any previous time. In other words they appreciate the positive influence of school ethos on the formation of character. Edward Wynne (1997a 70) shows how the arts and school ceremonies have always played an important role in affecting character formation. Assemblies, art displays around the school, celebrations and music identify a community's values and these can and do contribute to character development.

Wynne established a 'For-Character Program' Awards at the University of Illinois in which schools can submit an application which documents how they enhance character education. Other universities and school districts in the USA have been inspired by Wynne's initiative and have developed their own awards. Fresno County in California is one such area which seeks to evaluate the quality of the activities in schools and decide whether they should receive the Values and Character Recognition Award. There are five requirements for this award:

nd of student it wants to develop and outlines
its approach;

nds of activities which offer evidence of char-
orate the rationale for the programmes;

iat its rules of conduct and discipline together
od by all and that all, including parents, have
i;

dents are involved in the governance of the
e to the life of the school;

ey recognize student achievements in these
and school levels.

The Character Education Partnership (CEP) also runs a national award for character education in association with the Centre for the Advancement of Ethics
and Character which Kevin Ryan founded in 1989 at the University of Boston
(see chapter 10 and the special edition of Boston University's *The Journal of
Education* (Vol. 175, no. 2, 1993) entitled 'Education and the Advancement of
Ethics and Character'). This programme is based on Thomas Lickona's eleven
principles that have been largely adopted by the CEP. These awards have been
enthusiastically taken up by many schools and give recognition to excellent programmes (see Benninga 1997: 92f.) that can be replicated in other schools.
Jacques Benninga (1997: 93) believes that the adoption of these programmes
leads to successful schools because they involve the participation of students in
their running and because the staff of the schools show concern for the well-
being of the students.

Successful implementation of these programmes ensures high expectations
within the school community and prepares the students to participate in democracy. Such programmes are characterized by providing meaningful activities for
pupil involvement outside the ordinary curriculum. Indeed, Ryan and Bohlin
(1999: 7f.) speak of the 'moral ethos' of the school and of 'building a community
of virtue'. Their virtue ethics approach to character education is based on what
they say: 'knowing the good, loving the good, and doing the good involves the
head, the heart, and the hand, in an integrated way'.

The development of character naturally takes place within communities, such
as schools, which encourage respectful relationships so that pupils and staff work
together to meet common purposes. These relationships in a school should be
caring relationships which help all to feel that they belong as full members of a
community. This means schools need to design opportunities for pupils to collaborate on a frequent basis. This can be achieved and planned for in any subject
area of the school curriculum. However, it is the implicit curriculum of the
school which is the important agency for teaching character. But first an important qualification needs to be made. Schools in a democracy are not total
institutions – the home is the primary shaper of character whilst the school is
only a secondary shaper. Schools are limited institutions in democratic societies
which are only able to support certain values and virtues of home and society

when asked to do so. There is therefore the possibility of a clash between home and school values. It would be wrong to have utopian hopes for what a school can do in the way of character development – it makes a contribution but can never in a democracy be the primary shaper of character. Nevertheless, this is an important contribution and consists of certain norms such as school discipline and rules, the example of adults in the school, the general school ethos and the educational policies pursued. All of these convey messages to children about the kinds of values and virtues that should be cultivated.

The development of character education involves the acceptance of these norms imposed by the school as binding on the pupils. The pupil belongs to a moral community and must live up to such norms of self-sacrifice, sharing and responsibility within a supportive and caring environment. Teachers are of course crucial players in this. Joseph Gould's (1993) *Hyde School* experiment in character education is one example of a method which is legitimate in a democracy. Gould's aim was to develop characters which were self-governing and able to create their own destiny. Gould's philosophy was clearly different from the mainstream education establishment's views: whilst the latter emphasized intellect, he emphasized conscience; the educational establishment emphasized academic success, he promoted an education for life; he also placed great emphasis on the role of parents. In this it is worth contrasting the similar and progressive ideas of A. S. Neill (1962).

Teachers

The good example of teachers is often emphasized as important in character education, especially their ability to be mentors for the young. This aspect of their role can raise a number of difficulties for many teachers as they are often overburdened with the expectations of parents and politicians. Some have even become unwilling to be involved with much that distracts them from success in their subject teaching, seeing this as their main role. Others are also uncomfortable with adopting an explicitly moral position. Teachers may be comfortable with exploring the values of pupils, but not with changing them, which they may consider manipulation. This is one extreme. At the other end of the spectrum is the teacher who is committed to some ideological stance which they seek to 'share' with their pupils. Are teachers to display the virtues of diligence, honesty, kindness, courage, truthfulness and thoughtfulness? Do teachers see this aspect of their role as something additional to their subject teaching and something which they can choose to do or not? Some teachers may feel that these are demands that they cannot fulfil. The real problem for teachers is to decide when to tell a child that something is wrong or right and when to let them work it out for themselves.

In practice most teachers view certain kinds of action by pupils as wrong and it is not unusual to find teachers insisting that pupils ought always to tell the truth. When they do not, teachers punish them. Whilst teachers may see this as part of their job, are they not engaged in some form of moral absolutism?

Teachers are clearly already involved in the formation of character of their pupils simply by being part of the school community. The teacher has authority over them with the intention of improving their knowledge and character. This activity is not authoritarian but the action of a mature person who guides a less mature person. Teachers know that certain behaviours are more legitimate than others and follow this in their own teaching and management of a class. Teaching is a moral activity. It involves human action in regard to other human beings and ideas of justice and fairness are always present.

Teachers must have a degree of moral maturity so that they do the right thing intuitively and immediately, so that they see what is right without much in the way of deliberation or analysis. Teachers require a moral vocabulary in which to operate and that, above all, demands a community of care – which should be their classroom. Many teachers are very critical of the uncaring values they perceive in the wider society and see themselves as protecting the young against these questionable values. John Wilson (1993: 113), no advocate of the virtue ethics approach to character development, had this to say about the moral dimension of a teacher's work:

> Moral qualities are directly relevant to any kind of classroom practice: care for the pupils, enthusiasm for the subject, conscientiousness, determination, willingness to cooperate with colleagues and a host of others. Nobody, at least on reflection, really believes that effective teaching – let alone effective education – can be reduced to a set of skills; it requires certain dispositions of character. The attempt to avoid the question of what these dispositions are by employing pseudo-practical terms like 'competence' or 'professional' must fail.

Teachers are perceived to be moral authorities by their pupils, whatever they themselves think about their teaching. Indeed, it is in questions about pedagogy that the moral dimension is often most clearly seen. Professor A. H. Halsey (1994: 11f.) argues that the teaching profession should be reshaped to achieve a greater 'parenting' role for schools. He means by this that the parental function implicit within and constitutive of the teacher *in loco parentis* has been neglected and ought to be restored. Teaching, according to Halsey, has been turned into a cognitive relation between old and younger people, with someone else responsible for the really difficult part – the development of a child's character. He believes that teachers need to take the 'parenting' role more seriously as he sees education as a process of teaching someone how to live.

Competences and standards

Ryan and Bohlin (1999: 153f.) advocate seven competences that should be taught in teacher education to enable teachers to develop as character educators. In summary, each teacher should:

a model good character even if they are not themselves a paragon of virtue, and seek to improve their own character;
b see the development of their pupils' characters as a professional responsibility;
c be able to engage their pupils in moral discussions about what is right and what is wrong in life;
d be able to articulate their own position on moral matters without being authoritarian in approach;
e be able to assist pupils to empathize with the experiences of others;
f create a positive moral ethos in their classroom;
g provide activities in and out of school to help their pupils become moral actors.

Ryan and Bohlin ask the question: what would you like to see practised among members of the school? The anticipated answer is the practice of good character. A survey of the leadership of teacher education in the USA (see Nielsen Jones, Ryan and Bohlin 1999) sought to gather information on the degree of their commitment to character education, and the philosophical approaches adopted by them. Whilst there was overwhelming support expressed for the notion of character education in practice the survey found it not to be a high priority in teacher education. It was also found that there was little consensus about the nature of character education and how it should be taught among teacher educators. In a similar survey conducted by the research and teacher education group of the National Forum on Values and the Community in 1997 it was found that few teacher education institutions had incorporated values education into their teaching programmes and yet it was also recognized as being of importance to prepare teachers for their role as form teachers and as teachers of personal, social and moral education in schools. As in the American findings, there was little real time given to the moral dimensions of teaching.

The new Standards for the Award of Qualified Teacher Status (2002) issued by the Department for Education and Skills in England make no explicit reference to character or character education. Instead, they speak of professional values and practice for teachers that no doubt are intended to cover, in a general way, some of the kinds of values associated with character education. In contrast, the programme for the preparation of teachers for character education at the International Centre for Character Education at the University of San Diego includes six Teaching Standards that are worthy of recording here since they to some extent echo those of Ryan and Bohlin:

Standard 1: New and experienced teachers need to practise and reflect on their role as character educators responsible for the character formation of all students.
Standard 2: Teachers need to understand their roles and responsibilities as value transmitters, value critics and role models, and communicate high expectations for all students regarding pro-social behaviours, character development and democratic values. They should strive, along with students, to eliminate behaviours that are antithetical to good character.

Standard 3: Teachers must help create school and classroom climates that emulate mutual respect and support the tenets of a community of learners (e.g., caring, cooperative, civil).

Standard 4: Teachers need to engage all students in ethical analysis, critical inquiry, and higher-order thinking skills as they pursue ethical dilemmas found in literature, history, media, and life.

Standard 5: Teachers need to work with colleagues, students, parents and community groups to develop character lessons that will provide positive value experiences as a part of the school's curricular and co-curricular programs.

Standard 6: Understand that parents are their children's primary character educators. Knowing that the community, peer groups, and the media have a major influence on the character development of the young, teachers need to form collaborative partnerships between home, school and the community that welcome and involve others in character development efforts.

The main criticism of these standards for teachers is that they suffer from a lack of clarity and application.

The English teaching standards have statutory force in teacher training and standards 1.1 to 1.5 indicate that newly qualified teachers must demonstrate that they can 'treat pupils with respect and consideration'. Standard 1.3 states that teachers must 'demonstrate and promote positive values, attitudes and behaviour that they expect from pupils'. In other words, they must act as role models in the classroom. Whilst there is no explicit reference to the development of character it is clear that this is what is intended by this standard. There is an implicit recognition in these teaching standards that the character of the teacher matters and that pupils will acquire the habits of good character directly from teachers, who embody the ideals of character to which they expect their pupils to aspire. In respect of the teaching methods to inculcate this character development, the standards document remains silent. How moral values are actually taught is rightly left to the discernment of teachers, but teachers are still largely influenced by some dominant methods, including values clarification approaches.

Values clarification

Sidney Simon *et al.* (1972) developed the idea of values clarification as they were opposed to all moral inculcation by authority, believing that there were no final moral authorities. Pupils were free to discover their own values through open, uninhibited discussion of hypothetical situations called 'choice exercises' or 'simulations'. If pupils follow the strategies suggested by Simon, then their final decision is not questioned as long as the process of arriving at the result is sound. Only then can the decision be called one's own – clarified values are the means. There is a great deal of moral relativity in this theory, since any value a child might choose is legitimate so long as he or she can provide reasons to support it. This is an artificial approach, but it is still relatively popular with teachers. It influenced the 'procedural neutrality' developed by the Schools Council Nuffield Humanities Curriculum Project, established in 1967 and directed by Lawrence Stenhouse (1970). The teacher became almost irrelevant and the aim was simply to elicit the pupil's awareness of moral values.

Stenhouse developed the idea of an 'impartial chairperson' in which the teacher avoids stating his or her position to the class. Instead pupils adopt procedural rules and renounce the authority of teacher as 'expert'. Evidence in the argument is respected and pupils' viewpoints, however wild, are important. The teacher avoids imparting any moral positions or beliefs; instead uninhibited free discussion is encouraged. Because a value in this scheme is seen as neutral, there is no right or wrong judgement placed upon the pupils' choice. It would seem fair to conclude that even if a pupil developed the ability to clarify their own values and those of others, they still may not have the inner strength of character to act upon them. Stenhouse recognized that there was a problem of motivation in getting pupils to discuss moral issues. He felt that there was also the danger that unreliable peer-group participation together with pupils' immaturity and their lack of knowledge about the issues might effectively disable the process.

The approach was widely used in many British schools in the 1970s and 1980s under the name of 'life skills', 'personal, social and moral education', 'critical thinking' etc. How pupils 'ought' to behave was simply not a question in these lessons as the focus was on the process not the outcome. Although the acceptance by teachers of values clarification approaches has waned in the last decade or so, its principles still hold sway in many teachers' minds. Subsequently, Stenhouse (1981: 103ff.) revisited his methods and discovered that values were found in young people irrespective of the teaching methods and that they were just as likely to be influenced by their peer group. Hyland (1986) makes it clear that learning to be moral must be based on more than value-neutral approaches. He advocates the use of evidence, or arguments fully compatible with the principles of rationality. Others emphasize freedom, but as James Wilson (1995: 2) says: 'Character is not the enemy of self-expression and personal freedom, it is their necessary precondition', whilst William Gaylin and Bruce Jennings (1996: 126) conclude that: 'Good conduct will always require emotional reinforcement whether it be via the social emotions of shame, guilt, and pride or the primitive emotions of fear.'

Education is about engaging pupils with real issues in a reasoning way within a supportive environment. But Robert Nash (1997: 30) says: 'I believe that character educators go too far in separating moral reasoning from moral conduct. The result is to foster an ethos of compliance in the schools wherein indoctrination and rote learning replace critical reflection and autonomous decision-making.' Many assumptions are made in this statement. First, that children are already operating as autonomous decision-makers and are critically reflecting on what is taught to them. Second, that character educators actually separate moral reasoning from moral conduct. Third, that indoctrination and rote learning are the result of character education programmes. None of these assumptions are proven by Nash or even convincingly argued by him.

Recently, some British philosophers of education have adopted some very positive views of the role of virtues in character education, particularly David Carr (1995, 1996) Tony Skillen (1997), Jan Steutal (1997) and Colin Wringe (1998, 2000). All four view the development of virtues in pupils as essentially educative in itself and Wringe (2000) dismisses much of the cognitive development theories in this regard when he says: 'It is no longer possible to think of ... impeccable procedures of moral reasoning which, if correctly followed, will enable us to identify incontrovertibly desirable courses of action.' For Wringe, virtues, in a loose sense, are 'simply a set of terms under which we describe an act when we wish to commend it'. Virtues are excellences, irrespective of whether they are useful or not. Steutal (1997) believes that many of the practices in British schools to do with values education have incorporated elements of the virtues approach, together with, she says, values clarification and Kohlbergian approaches.

Whilst recognizing that the justification for character education, in many ways, lacks philosophical depth, Steutal argues that it should be founded on an ethics of virtue. Skillen (1997) also advocates a virtue ethics approach, but one which implies anti-authoritarian schools, classrooms which are democratic, children who are given responsibility, a pedagogy involving discussion and group activity not simply reading, listening and writing. Building character, he says, is not achieved through 'moralistic utterances', but in 'a set of experiences'. All four of these philosophers of education give great emphasis to a supportive context for teaching virtues and experiential learning. Sounding a note of caution, Wringe (1998) warns that we cannot rely on teaching virtues alone and that those virtues we do teach should be kept under review in order to respond to the different moral situations we find ourselves in.

Edward Wynne places great emphasis on teaching about heroes in the past by reading the 'great books', and on the promotion of academic discipline in schools. He believes that children often do not know what they want and require adult guides. It is the imposition of restraint by parents and teachers that dissuades children from poor behaviour and inclines them towards the good. Wynne believes that moral reasoning programmes cannot fulfil the promise of character education. He advocates that values should be espoused, compliance rewarded and violations punished in schools. He places the focus on the acquisition of good behavioural habits, rather than on the development of complex reasoning skills. He is forthright in advocating traditional moral values or virtues in schools and says that indoctrination should cease to be a dirty word in education. He says that 'destructive peer groups must be suppressed' (Wynne and Walberg 1985). Many head teachers would no doubt agree.

William Bennet (1993, 1995) also attacks values clarification and cognitive moral development approaches to character education. He says that they emphasize reflection to the neglect of habits, remove morality from the real work context in which choices need to be made and present morality as an exercise in problem-solving and decision-making. He supports the idea of moral instruction which should permeate the whole school. William Damon (1988: 145) and a few others claim that people like Bennet and Wynne are misguided. Many of the opponents of character education put forward arguments which are extreme, more often than not based on personalities and therefore exaggerated and biased. However, it should also be noted that some of the proponents of character education use terminology which they know will inflame feeling among those in the educational establishment.

Joel Kupperman (1991: 175), who is much more cautious in his writings on character education, tentatively suggests three stages:

> The first involves students who are acquiring the rudiments of what it is to have a good and strong character, but who are not ready for any sophisticated moral reflection. The second involves students who are beginning to be ready, and who, in some cases, are beginning to adopt independent perspectives. The third involves students who are in a position to make, or to adjust, crucial decisions of who they are. Very roughly, these stages correspond to primary school, secondary school, and college, although there is bound to be some overlap between them.

In the first stage Kupperman advocates 'dogmatic instruction', but qualifies this as an instruction which is authoritative, but not authoritarian – teachers should be sensitive to the questions young children ask. Teachers must avoid being 'heavy-handed' in their relations with pupils. His first stage depends on the majority of people in the community agreeing that certain things are right or wrong and that these should be taught as norms in schools. As he says: 'If we wait for reflective consent before instilling these norms, in many cases we will wait too long.' Kupperman also suggests that early education should promote sensitivity to feelings, particularly the sufferings of others. This he believes prepares the way for reflection. Children need to learn habits and attitudes before they can reflect. In the second stage the study of literature is advocated, especially historical literature so that other people's lives can be evaluated and judged. In the third stage, which is life-long, the student should be actively constructing his character. Kupperman concludes that good education promotes character development whether it is specifically directed towards the education of character or not.

There seem to be two categories of teaching morality in schools: moral education as a means of cultural assimilation and moral education as the development of rationality. Character education appears to be positioned in the middle. The two approaches to character education are often referred to as the direct and the indirect approach and form a continuum. Feminist character educators have favoured an indirect approach (Noddings 1992) whilst a number of traditional character education proponents have favoured a direct approach (Bennet 1995, Ryan 1989, Wynne 1997a). Both approaches have moved beyond the debate about rationality, which is not ignored, simply given less emphasis. In the direct approach, role modelling, rules, discipline and traditional curriculum subjects are given emphasis as are the importance of moral stories and virtues. This is a no-nonsense approach to character education which encourages good behaviour through setting clear standards and expectations and producing a well-defined list of virtues to be adopted and taught.

The assumptions behind these approaches are that pupils seek guidance and want stricter discipline in order to give a sense of direction and order to their lives. Incentives for learning are emphasized to motivate pupils, and teachers are the authority figures who intervene. The school excludes dangerous influences from its life and promotes common and shared values irrespective of the cultural background of the pupils. Uniforms or dress codes, ceremonies and school rituals are all promoted and pupils are taught to be loyal and take pride in their school community. This is the general approach adopted by Edward Wynne and Kevin Ryan (1993) in their book *Reclaiming Our Schools.*

The indirect approach to character education gives first place to the social and cognitive aspects of school life. Character is developed through social inter-action and through rational discussion of moral dilemmas. Cooperation and democratic procedures are important in this approach and all are encouraged to participate in classroom decision-making. Lawrence Kohlberg's approach to moral development is generally accepted, but some, like Nel Noddings (1995), do not like the formal academic curriculum consisting of traditional subjects. They advocate a freer curriculum with more control over what is taught and learned. Noddings believes that the indirect approach should aim to produce 'competent, caring, loving and loveable people'. The way schools are structured, she believes, is not helpful to what should be the moral mission of the school. There are others, such as Ian Kelsey (1993: 64), who believe that the aims and content of character education ought to be universal – that there should be no local variations in philosophy or what is taught. Unfortunately, the justification for his argument is not supported by any sustained evidence.

There are few evaluations of any of these approaches and James Leming (1993b) points out that those studies that do exist contain varied and mixed findings for those who promote character education. Since character refers to that combination of rational and acquired factors which distinguishes one indi-vidual from another it is clear that certain aspects of character building are beyond the realm of measurement. Lesley (1997) thinks that character educa-tion is a doubtful project, as we are attempting to teach children what adults have not learnt. Another problem concerns the nature of the teacher – an exemplary teacher will naturally establish a good ethos in their class and will promote good behaviour with or without an explicit character education pro-gramme. Mark Freakley (1996) believes that the school needs to adopt a stance on the curriculum:

Such virtues can only be developed in students by their practising these actions, consistently and persistently, within an environment which encour-ages and rewards such actions and which provides disincentives for departures from such courses of action. Of course moral argument ought to be an important addition to training, and taken together they both can com-prise a full moral education. However, it is only through training that character of an enduring kind can be developed, and in order for this to hap-pen systems and schools must take a stand.

Philip Vincent (1999: 3) provides some helpful suggestions which he calls 'rules and procedures for character education'. He suggests that schools should identify the virtues that need to be developed to help form character traits in pupils. These, he indicates, should be transformed into rules which are the expectations for appropriate behaviour and these should in turn become procedures which are practices needed to develop the habits of following rules and developing good character. So, the virtue of respect becomes a rule to treat all human beings with respect, which becomes a set of procedures such as not interrupting others whilst they are speaking. Vincent and many others have looked at ways of translating the virtues into practical suggestions for teachers, but not always with one voice or with success.

Timothy Rusnak (1998: 3f., 45) advocates an integrated approach to character education based on a combination of '*thinking* – what is to be done or learned, *feeling* – appreciating what is learned, and *action* – experiencing through deed and not only discussion what is being learned'. From this theory he proposes six principles for a school-wide approach which is worth considering within the British education context. First, character education should not be seen as a subject or course of study: instead, it should be integrated into every subject area within the school and form part of the planned experiences for each pupil. Second, character education should be seen as 'action education' involving commitment and action on the part of teachers and pupils. Third, character education should be shaped and built by the school environment – the positive atmosphere, climate or ethos of the particular school. Fourth, character education must be part of the mission and policy statements produced by the school. Fifth, character education must be taught by teachers who are empowered and free to teach without the constraints of a centralized curriculum. Finally, character education needs to involve the whole school and the local community.

Conclusion

Because of the wide variety of approaches to character education it is difficult to evaluate them *en masse*; it is necessary to look at individual projects. The virtue ethics approaches best justifies character education because of the emphasis on role modelling, its behavioural emphasis and the importance it places on developing knowledge of a wide range of virtues. Above all, it is the virtues that help make us who we ought to be. Even radical thinkers on schooling, such as A. S. Neill (1962), who was an opponent of formal character education programmes, could not avoid influencing the character of his pupils.

Neill's experiment in informal education which began in 1921 was also an experiment in character building even when the pupils learned what they wanted, when they wanted and only when they wanted. He believed passionately that children would actually be better people if they had such an education. This sits oddly with his chief philosophy that children are innately good and need only to be nourished for a spontaneous unfolding to occur. Neill was an advocate of 'freedom from character building' and yet it is ironic that he sought to 'produce children who are at once individuals and community persons'. Neill believed in developing character, but he objected to many of the methods used in mainstream schools and he objected to the word character because of its moral overtones – Neill, of course, typifies the view of many fellow psychologists of his time. Nevertheless, whether he admitted it or not, he was engaged in character building precisely because he was engaged in the *education* of youth. As William Frankena (1956) maintains: 'Education is the process by which society makes of its members what it is desirable that they should become.'

Frankena (1965: 7ff., 1974: 139ff.), borrowing from John Stuart Mill's *System of Logic*, furthermore offers us an educational model that is calculated to result in a normative philosophy of education. This schema helps us to understand and summarize much of the discussion in previous chapters. Frankena maintains that the task of a normative philosophy of education is to list and define a set of virtues and dispositions to be fostered by parents and teachers. His model identifies five integrated elements:

a   statements of the basic ends or principles of ethics and social thought;
b   empirical and other premises about human nature, life, and the world;
c   list, with definitions, of excellences to be produced;
d   empirical or scientific knowledge about how to produce them;
e   concrete conclusions about what to do, when, how, etc;

This model moves from theory *abc* to practice *cde*, in other words from a philosophical world and life view to educational practice. Whilst Frankena says that his model can be applied to the educational thought of various philosophers of education, he chooses Aristotle to illustrate the model, particularly the *abc* pattern. The following statements about Aristotle's place in Frankena's scheme correspond to the same order in the above model:

a   Aristotle believed that the good life consisted of intrinsically excellent activities;
b   If we are to achieve the good life we must cultivate these excellent activities – the virtues;
c   We must therefore define and list these virtues and desirable traits;
d   We must use our knowledge of teaching and learning to generate practical methods for transmitting these virtues;
e   We then decide on the most effective pedagogy e.g. to assist with the formation of habits and dispositions together with the content of the curriculum.

Frankena's scheme fits well with a virtue ethics approach to character education for it draws conclusions from the premises in *a*, *b*, and *c* in order to produce concrete educational practices about how to develop character in *d* and *e*. Frankena (1965) calls this the normative part of education which

... makes recommendations, instructional or administrative, with respect to the process of educating. It proposes ends, goals, or norms for this process which teachers and administrators are to promote, and it advances the means by which these ends are to be achieved. It also seeks to justify its recommendations about ends and means, so far as this is possible, by reference to such facts as may be discovered or collected by the science of education and to such moral principles as it may borrow from ethics in general.

For Frankena, this lies at the 'heart' of a philosophy of education and is the only kind of philosophy that helps guide teaching and learning. David Carr (2002) would no doubt agree, for he also concludes that any account of education must be normative to the extent that it cannot but embody some ideal of human flourishing together with some account of the role of parents and teachers in promoting this flourishing.

10 Schooling for character

Did you ever stop to wonder about how recent historical events will be reported in elementary school history books 100 years from now? We hate to think so, but in the year 2060, say, elementary school history books will probably be exactly the way they are now. Which means they will be simply written so that children who study them can find easy answers to everything, even things that college professors and historians won't fully understand. For instance, every historical figure will be either good or bad, with nobody a little good and a little bad, the way most people really are.

William Gaines (1960: 65)

Respect and responsibility – and all the other values that derive from them – give schools the moral content they can and should teach in a democracy. But schools need more than a list of values. They need a concept of character – and a commitment to developing it in their students.

Thomas Lickona (1991: 49)

Moral character is often viewed as one's personal characteristics and civics/citizenship as one's public responsibilities. There is clearly a strong interdependence as the two can and should reinforce each other, especially when citizenship is presented as concerning participation, rights, duty and responsibilities. The Crick Report (1998: 40) viewed 'morally responsible behaviour' as an 'essential pre-condition for citizenship'. New Labour has recognized this link in the principles, values, aims and purposes it has outlined as the rationale for the new National Curriculum (NC: 1999). In seeking to implement the National Curriculum there appears to be a comprehensiveness of approach that addresses both individual character development and civic responsibilities. This clearly has its origins in Section 2 (2) of the 1988 Education Reform Act, which states that all schools should promote the 'spiritual, moral, cultural, mental and physical development of pupils', together with preparing pupils 'for the opportunities, responsibilities and experiences of adult life'. Whilst these were the expressed aims of the whole curriculum, the government of the time made no statutory provision for values or civic education within it. New Labour, in preparing the new National Curriculum 2000 for England, sought to 'recognize a broad set of common values and purposes that underpin the school curriculum and the work of schools' (NC 1999: 10). New Labour has accordingly been more forthright and explicit about the kinds of goals schools should follow by moving from guidance and discussion of school curriculum goals to a mandatory and 'official' rationale contained in the new National Curriculum. In Scotland, the school curriculum is not prescribed by law, but the same New Labour language is used in curriculum guidance to schools.

The language and terminology of this new rationale, as expressed in New Labour's declared intentions for English schools, has four bases. First is the former National Curriculum Council's guidance and discussion documents, specifically: *The Whole Curriculum: Curriculum Guidance 3* (1990), *Education for Citizenship: Curriculum Guidance 8* (1990), and *Spiritual and Moral Development – A Discussion Paper* (1993). These were non-statutory guidelines for the school curriculum, but much of what they said has been incorporated into the new statutory curriculum rationale. Second, the *Statement of Values* prepared by the National Forum for Values and the Community (1997) which is reproduced in the National Curriculum handbook so that schools can use it in planning their own curriculum. Third, the Citizenship Order (CO 1999) that was compiled after the publication of the Crick Report; both these documents influenced the rationale for the National Curriculum. Fourth, the communitarian language used by New Labour, which has resulted in words such as 'virtues' and 'the common good' being incorporated into the rationale (see Arthur *et al.* 2001). Since the publication of the National Curriculum the government has given renewed emphasis to this communitarian strand of the curriculum rationale by emphasizing 'education with character' in the White Paper (2001).

This new rationale for the curriculum is of course a statutory requirement for all schools, with character building rapidly emerging as a new policy. The non-statutory framework for personal, social and health education (PSHE) and citizenship at Key Stages 1 and 2, together with the secondary non-statutory framework for personal, social and health education, also form part of the official guidelines to schools and are contained in the primary and secondary National Curriculum handbooks. The Citizenship Order is only compulsory in secondary schools, but there is guidance issued to all primary schools on citizenship education.

These documents taken together constitute a statement of philosophy for both character and citizenship education for every child in English primary and secondary state schools. This can be illustrated by grouping these extracts from these documents relating to what pupils are expected to attain under the headings of character and civics/citizenship to construct a more holistic picture. These extracts are really formulations of what education and pupils should achieve in terms of their personal and public responsibilities.

Character

- 'Education should also reaffirm our commitment to the virtues of truth, justice, honesty, trust and a sense of duty' (NC 1999: 10).

- 'The school curriculum should contribute to the development of pupils' sense of identity ... promote ... and ... develop principles for distinguishing between right and wrong ... should pass on enduring values, develop pupils' integrity and autonomy, ... promote pupils' self-esteem and emotional well-being and help them to form and maintain worthwhile and satisfying relationships, based on respect for themselves and for others' (NC 1999: 11).

- 'Pupils' *moral development* involves pupils acquiring an understanding of the difference between right and wrong and of moral conflict, a concern for others and the will to do what is right. They are able and willing to reflect on the consequences of their actions and learn how to forgive themselves and others. They develop the knowledge, skills, understanding, qualities and attitudes they need in order to make responsible moral decisions and to act on them' (NC 1999: 19).

- ' ... *moral development*, through helping pupils develop a critical appreciation of issues of right and wrong, justice, fairness, rights, and obligations' (CO 1999: 7).

- 'Religious education makes a distinctive contribution to ... the development of values and attitudes and fundamental questions concerning the meaning and purpose of life' (NC 1999: 20).

- 'Pupils should be taught ... about the nature of friendship and how to make and keep friends ... to resist pressure to do wrong, to recognize when others need help and how to support them' (NC 1999: 190).

- 'Pupils should be taught ... to recognize the stages of emotions associated with loss and change caused by death, divorce, separation and new family members, and how to deal positively with the strength of their feelings in different situations' (NC 1999: 189).

- 'Critical though effective academic education is to children's life chances, it is not the only important part of schooling. We want schools to play their part in developing rounded individuals who are well prepared for adult life' (White Paper 2001: 7).

- 'We will encourage students' active participation in the decisions that affect them, about their learning and more widely ... we are extending opportunities for children to be involved in sport adventure, art, music and drama within and outside the school day' (White Paper 2001: 28).

- 'We will now press ahead with them, to support schools to provide this "education with character"' (White Paper 2001: 27).

Civics/citizenship

- 'The school curriculum ... should ... help them to be responsible and caring citizens capable of contributing to the development of a just society ... It should develop their ability to relate to others and work for the common good' (NC 1999: 11).

- 'Pupils' *social development* involves pupils acquiring an understanding of the responsibilities and rights of being members of families and communities (local, national and global), and an ability to relate to others and to work with others for the common good. They display a sense of belonging and an increasing willingness to participate. They develop the knowledge, skills, understanding, qualities and attitudes they need to make an active contribution to the democratic process in each of their communities' (NC 1999: 19).

- ' ... *social development*, through helping pupils acquire the understanding and skills needed to become responsible and effective members of society' (CO 1999: 7).

- 'If pupils are to work with others they must develop social skills and a growing awareness and understanding of others' needs' (NC 1999: 23).

- 'Pupils have a broad knowledge and understanding of ... the rights, responsibilities and duties of citizens; the role of the voluntary sector; forms of government; provision of public services; and the criminal and legal systems ... Pupils take part effectively in school and community-based activities, showing a willingness and commitment to evaluate such activities critically. They demonstrate personal and group responsibility in their attitudes to themselves and others' (attainment target in CO 1999).

How are these statements justified? Do these diverse extracts merely represent political preference? Has the government become a moral authority? Can they be taken as having some kind of objective validity? In deciding on this curriculum framework and goals the government must have had some view about the kind of society it thinks is desirable and particularly the kind of human character that would best build and suit such a society. The government has essentially adopted a pragmatic approach. It makes no appeal to some rationale of 'universal ethic' or to the authority claims of one particular tradition of values. Public consensus appears to be the justification. Implicit within the language of these goal statements is the notion that pupils are to be 'prepared for' their future role as adults, rather than this role being expressed as an intrinsic 'developmental' aim for their education.

There is also an instrumental goal in these statements, with their undoubted focus on pre-specified objectives and outcomes that emphasize what schooling is for rather than what it is. It can be observed that a degree of conflict and tension exists between some of the goals expressed in the National Curriculum. There is a sense in which some of these goals are not conceptually clear or integrated with each other. The aims are given as universal and apply to all schools. This ignores the fact that many of the values will undoubtedly conflict with those of the pupils and their parents. It is really for each school community within its own context to reinterpret and develop its own goals for citizenship, personal, social, moral, health and character education from those contained in the National Curriculum.

Schools will need first to agree a philosophical approach which is articulated in the school's mission statement, the policy statements and in the objectives for every subject. This philosophical approach will need to produce a set of ethical principles, which is the result of a series of questions the school community asks of itself. The following provides a list of the kinds of questions schools need to ask prior to establishing a response:

How does the school understand citizenship and character?
What are the shared ethical principles of the school?
How and where are they defined?
Are parents and the local community involved in producing these principles?
How are the pupils involved?
How are they integrated into all aspects of the school curriculum and ethos?
How does the school ensure that teachers and pupils uphold these principles?
In what way does the school publicly commit itself to these principles?
What opportunities are provided to put these principles into action?
Do staff and pupils model these principles in their daily lives?
How does the school know that it is successful in its efforts to action these principles?
How does it measure the strength and success of its ethical initiatives?
To what extent is the school becoming a strong ethical community?

In attempting to answer these questions a school community will have already begun the long process needed to address some of the social and moral problems faced by individuals and society.

This book has made the assumption that character development takes place in all British schools irrespective of whether the word 'character' appears in official school documentation. Another assumption is that schools are not alone in attempting to fulfil this aim: parents are closest to the pupil and have the longest-lasting influence over them. Since parents have an essential, but not exclusive, right morally to educate their children, the school cannot supplant this right even when it considers the character formation in the home to be weak. Instead, the school needs to enter into partnership with the parents so that they are involved in school planning for character formation. Of course, there will be parents who are apathetic and non-cooperative, but these can be carried if a critical mass of parents does engage in this project.

In addition, there will be professional issues on which the school will have the last word, but parents should be consulted, not merely informed, about such matters as character building activities and the discipline and behaviour policies adopted by the school. In this way any suggestions the school makes about how to develop ethical principles are more likely to be reinforced by parents in the home. In the light of the new National Curriculum, schools need to review their principles, policies and practices in order to develop a comprehensive strategy to implement the aims of this curriculum. The renewed attention New Labour is giving to character education has the potential to benefit schools, families and the nation. The government's assertion of principles involve policy consequences which in turn should result in certain kinds of educational practices being introduced for character education.

Principles for character

All schools are concerned about their identity and about how they wish themselves to be perceived. Mission statements have provided schools with a statement of purpose that helps to identify what is distinctive about them. If these mission statements are ineffective, little-read documents then they do not serve the school community. The leadership of the school has a duty to ensure that staff, parents and pupils are invited to participate in articulating 'what we want to become'. Mission statements, properly devised, can have an important inspirational purpose for the whole school community. The principles so agreed are more likely to be widely known by all in the school, which is essential if they are to stand a chance of being acted upon. The mission statement should be an outline of philosophy and rationale which describes the kind of human beings the school seeks to develop. It should also be explicit about the kinds of values it wishes to promote, together with the types of experiences that are offered to promote them. This should be viewed as fundamental to good teaching and learning within the school and constitutive of building a strong school ethos. These principles help to explore the general ideas that give direction to specific educational policies and practices.

Policies to strengthen character

Schools today are required to have written policies on everything from admissions and assessment to sanctions and visits abroad. In regard to the development of character many of these policies are pertinent, so it is essential that the policies devised by the school allow for the fulfilment of the principles in the mission statement. Policies on subject teaching, sex education, citizenship, health education, social and personal education should not be composed in isolation from each other or without reference to the mission statement. A holistic approach should be adopted which ensures that all policies seek to strengthen character development. No policy statements can have a clear direction without reference to the character building principles outlined in the mission statement.

Practices to shape character

Both principles and policies do not dictate educational practices but instead provide a way of thinking about them. It is for each school to determine what practices are appropriate to its individual circumstances. The following are the kinds of practices that identify a good school:

Recognition practices: Good schools recognize all kinds of achievement of excellence, whether it be in the classroom, on the sports field, in the community or in the creativity of pupils. They establish school rituals that bring together the school community (including parents) to celebrate both individual and team efforts and achievements. A good school is one in which praise and recognition are regular and ordinary parts of its daily routine.

Exemplar practices: Good schools have clear ethical expectations of both staff and pupils and encourage modelling to reinforce character traits. Pupils have opportunities to assume roles that entail moral responsibility and are encouraged to be exemplars of high ethical principles. A good school is one in which the virtues are displayed in the community's thinking, attitudes and actions.

Participation practices: Good schools offer opportunities to pupils to be involved in meeting the needs of their own school and local community. Pupils have a sense of ownership of the school ethos through actively participating in school consultations and being allowed to demonstrate initiative in building a community based on fairness and respect for others.

Service practices: Good schools offer diverse opportunities for service activities in and out of school. These experiences are meaningful and pupils know why they are involved in raising money for charity or working on a community project and have made a free choice to be involved. A good school develops an atmosphere and a set of expectations that positively support such service practices.

Teaching practices: Good schools review their teaching and learning on a regular basis so that character development is infused as an aim throughout the school's curriculum. The learning needs of pupils are met and teaching is flexible and creative. Emphasis is given to a curriculum rich in the humanities subjects and tradition and culture are not neglected.

Evaluation practices: Good schools have an ongoing practice of evaluating the education offered. Evidence of success is discussed with the whole school community and aims and expectations are reinforced after reviews of practice.

Schools of character

These practices of character education need to be distinctive, whole school initiatives that are integrated into the school culture. However, the societal context in England for the operation of these practices and the ability of the school to nurture them is not a healthy one. Schools and teachers are subjected to the most narrow accountability, with pre-specified outcomes and means–ends evaluation, together with a mechanical emphasis on competence and skills. It is difficult to see how these practices can be made to flourish in such an environment even when there is a willingness among teachers to address the issue of developing a child's character.

In the USA there has been a series of attempts to create an environment for children's character to develop and flourish in schools. There has clearly been a resurgence of character education rhetoric in American schools, but how much of this has simply been subscribing to a movement? Some schools and teachers view character education as holding out the promise to fix their problems – to assist them with pupil behaviour modification together with addressing some social ills. Consequently, they have adopted character education programmes without giving much thought to an understanding of human character or how it might change their view of education and schooling. Other schools and teachers have seriously reflected upon the meaning of character education and how it can be used as a whole school strategy to improve the quality of education and help make pupils better people. The weakest part of the present campaign for character education is that so few teachers have either the time or inclination to examine its philosophical foundations. There is also severely limited data on the impact of the variety of character education programmes on children. In reality most character education programmes in the USA are largely a hybrid of values clarification, child development and cognitive dilemma approaches. The best character education takes place in schools that have a positive ethos and set of values.

William Bennet, whilst secretary of education in the federal government in the late 1980s, instituted the Blue Ribbon Award Program for outstanding public and private elementary schools: there was already in existence a Secondary School Recognition Program. The Blue Ribbon was awarded to schools that fostered, among other indicators of success, the development of character, moral values and ethical judgement in their pupils. Modonna Murphy (1998: 199ff.) has conducted an analysis of the components of effective character education in schools through a review of the applications for the award. She concludes that schools who are effective in meeting their goals for character education can be identified as having:

a   a strong mission, commitment and determination to develop character in its pupils;
b   high levels of participation by staff, pupils and parents in the decision-making process determining the desired qualities to be nurtured in the school;
c   high standards of academic performance, excellent teaching and learning and particularly strategies that encourage cooperative learning;
d   high standards of pupil behaviour which are understood by all, and a caring school community involved in the wider community and indeed in global affairs;
e   well-planned recognition programmes which communicate, encourage and reinforce character qualities, attitudes and behaviours of the whole school community;
f   a commitment by the school to character education that is comprehensive and which uses every available opportunity to reinforce it.

Bennet's initiatives have proven popular and they have been used by the federal government to promote character education. The Blue Ribbon Award has bipartisan support, with President Clinton in the State of the Nation Address on 23 January 1996 announcing: 'I challenge all our schools to teach character education, to teach good values, and to teach good citizenship.' However, it is not the only award scheme which recognizes character education in schools. Since 1999 ten schools in the USA have been annually selected for the National Schools of Character Award organized by the Character Education Partnership in collaboration with the Centre for the Advancement of Ethics and Character at the University of Boston. Each school is invited to complete an application and provide a portfolio of character education activities. A narrative is written answering three basic questions: What are the goals of character education in your school? How are you implementing character education in your school? How do you know you are successful? In reviewing the thirty winning applicants since 1999, together with a number of other promising practices citation awards, it is possible to build a picture of the kinds of goals, activities and evaluation methods a school needs to develop in order to address the development of character education. These can be summarized as follows:

Goals

The first thing that is immediately recognizable about these winning schools is that there is no overall structure uniting the various goals each school sets itself. Each school's goals are generally constructed through a range of influences and are often responses to particular needs; for example, one school sought 'to eliminate name-calling of various nationalities and religion' through a character education initiative. Goals are also not imposed from above, but are sought through or are the product of genuine discussion and meetings between teachers, parents, and pupils.

There is a sense of ownership of the goals by the whole school community. Of course, some schools are able to articulate their particular goals better than others. One school defines its goals as forming enduring habits that establish good character through the provision of core values that assist pupils become responsible members of society. These core values are listed as integrity, respect, compassion and responsibility and they are promoted so as to help pupils examine how they intend to use the knowledge they have gained while applying sound judgement and wisdom to become better citizens of their school, community, nation and world. Each school is asked to show how they meet the eleven criteria outlined in considerable detail by the Character Education Partnership, but whilst many seek to demonstrate this throughout their application, it is clear that others work towards their own articulation of goals. This second group often achieve their articulation of goals through the use of the extensive body of literature available to schools on character education which has generally stimulated discussion and reflection on the topic.

Many schools talk about their shared vision or mission and conceive of their community in partnership with other wider communities. There is an emphasis on inclusiveness and some of the schools refer to caretakers, cleaning and catering staff as contributing to this shared vision. One school district, which won an award in 2000, described how it established a character education group of teachers and parents which read, debated and raised questions and defined terms in an attempt to increase teacher and community thinking on the subject. This particular school district sought to develop morally mature people in its schools who respected human rights, demonstrated active responsibility for the welfare of others and integrated individual interests and social responsibilities. Virtues were defined and suggestions were made for practices in the classroom which included helping pupils to avoid prejudiced actions, helping them to seek social justice and involvement with and in community life. In addition, the group sought to encourage pupils to apply moral principles when making choices and judgements so that they would think about the moral consequences of their decisions. This approach also taught seeking after peaceful resolutions to conflicts.

The majority of winning schools are at the elementary level, with only a few high schools listed over the three years of this review. At secondary level the goals stated appear to be less holistic and much more of a response to a recognized or specific problem or need arising in the school. One high school, whilst stating that its goals were multifaceted, had a limited insight into character education and focused on social skills, positive self-image and academic excellence. The school viewed character education principally in terms of conflict resolution, counselling for students and positive role models. Whilst the school was also involved in fundraising for charities and had extensive award ceremonies and pupil recognition programmes it was difficult to see how all the criteria of the Character Education Partnership had been met – although it should be stated that each winning school had been visited by a team from the University of Boston to check that the criteria for the award had been met in practice. On such visits additional evidence of meeting the criteria was often forthcoming.

Activities

The first activity that is prominent in these schools of character is found in the ordinary policies on dress, attendance, discipline, homework etc. Clear expectations in all these areas are given on a regular basis through every means available to the school: newsletters, assemblies, notices etc. A minority of schools have character education lessons on the taught curriculum whilst others focus principally on developing a positive school ethos. All winning schools have recognition award schemes for pupils which include: student of the week, personal success awards, citizenship certificates, annual service awards, attendance award pins etc. Service to the wider community is emphasized in every school whilst a few schools institute pledges or oaths of loyalty made by the pupils to the school. Codes of conduct are also compiled and there are guidelines on behaviour in the playground. Some schools have reintroduced school uniform, whilst others make great use of commendations with one school reading aloud each day the virtues of particular pupils. Storytelling features in every school – using stories to convey moral messages to the pupils is part of the literature-based programmes.

Many of the schools had weekly, monthly or quarterly character themes which could be termed either character traits or virtues. Particular character traits or virtues are identified and then promoted by means of stories, assemblies, classroom or community projects, visual displays around the school and through the personal example of both staff and pupils. One school has a virtue for each month: September, respect; October, responsibility; November, peace; December, caring; January, integrity; February, courage; March, patience; April, service; May, self-control; June, goal-setting; July, honesty; and August, cooperation. The leadership of each school is also stressed, particularly in its potential ability to motivate staff, parents and pupils. Many of the school principals appear to use teams of staff or combinations of staff and parents to address issues and they invariably emphasize the qualities of teachers in modelling ethical standards.

Perhaps the most important feature observed in reviewing these winning schools is the way they use parents or rather partner parents in promoting character education. All the schools involve parents in some important way. Parents often receive letters from principals seeking their assistance with developing positive character traits in their children. One school set specific homework on character traits and sought parental help by asking them to reflect on the traits at home with their child. Parents were viewed as having an important role in reinforcing character in partnership with the school. Another school held an annual summer school for teachers and parents to discuss character qualities and to agree a programme for the coming year. A number of schools opened their doors to parents, provided character education resources and expert advice in schools for parents who asked for it. In yet another school, meetings of the whole family were often organized to resolve a conflict that had arisen with a pupil. Parents are not simply kept informed, they are encouraged to participate, but few of the schools indicate the extent to which parents actually get involved.

Evaluation

Many of the winning schools evaluate their success through sets of tables typically illustrating a decrease in suspensions and misconduct referrals, increased academic scores on tests or increased school attendance. All these tables testify to the value of introducing character education programmes. There is no doubt that the schools which have made applications for this award are convinced of the benefit of character education on their social, moral and academic success as schools.

All the schools are eager to show and demonstrate their success, which they attribute to their character education initiatives. Almost all the schools have gathered evidence of this success and prominent amongst this evidence are press cuttings from local newspapers indicating praise for school service programmes to the local community or various types of community involvement. Teacher perceptions are also prominently displayed – not surprising since teachers compiled the evidence in the first place. However, positive parental perceptions of school improvement are often critical factors in these applications. As parent satisfaction levels rise, so too it seems do the positive comments and perceptions from the local community.

A few schools include comments from pupils about how they have seen the school improve. Unfortunately, most of the evidence produced is what is known as 'soft evidence' and much of it in the form of anecdote. There are few empirical studies that verify the many claims made by these schools, particularly the claim that there is a correlation between character education and increased academic scores. The Character Education Partnership (1999) is aware of this 'weakness' in its procedures and has produced a questionnaire as a self-assessment tool to help schools reflect and evaluate their character programmes in a more standardized way, but it is still only a start.

Character and experiential learning

Whilst the Crick Report (QCA 1998: 25f.) did not ask for the inclusion of what is variously called experiential learning, service learning or community-based learning, the government decided to make it mandatory on all schools in England for pupils at Key Stages 3 and 4. Crick was originally concerned about the fear of overburdening schools and teachers, but subsequently supported the statutory entitlement for community service outlined in the Citizenship Order. John Annette (2000: 78) finds this to be an opportunity for schools not only to encourage civic participation but to develop civic virtues and political knowledge. It surely must also be an explicit way of helping to develop character. The White Paper (2001) makes this connection and is an extension of the rationale for character education through experiential learning in the community. To what extent this kind of experiential learning has a beneficial influence on character is difficult to say because of the lack of research in the area, but Annette (2000: 80) details what little findings we have. He tentatively concludes that young people do see voluntary service in the community as a meaningful activity, focusing as it does on real problems in a real community.

Teachers in Britain have long recognized the importance of activity-based learning in and outside of the classroom, but community-based experiential learning as a structured part of the National Curriculum, except in the form of work experience placements, is a relatively new idea for schools. It is popular in many American schools but not mandatory. Communitarians have long advocated that it should be mandatory and Etzioni (1993: 113) argues that it is in fact the 'capstone of a student's educational experience'. Many communitarians believe that the identity and stability of individual character cannot be realized without the support of a community and that there needs to be a contribution from the pupil to their community. The community becomes the teacher for the pupil and character is formed through the social interaction with others. Character is partly formed through this interactive experience as the pupil shares life with others and they with him. The aim of experiential learning in the community is not only to enhance critical reflection, but to advance personal development through opportunities to practise social and moral responsibility. It is concerned with encouraging positive behaviour among the young. The hope is that experience in community will lead to the development of a virtuous character. Ideally, the purpose of this practical ethical enquiry is deepened commitment and enhanced ability to lead the good life. It is a schooling for moral commitment.

Through concrete opportunities of working together in community pupils may be able to shape and test their own character. There are many kinds of community involvement – and problems associated with them (see Arthur and Wright 2001) – but the Community Service Volunteers are building a database on agencies in the community that schools can turn to, together with examples of good practice, which it intends to circulate via the internet. There are also a number of local education authorities in England who have developed community service programmes that are worth consulting, for example Birmingham and Hampshire. Whilst community involvement is mandatory, this does not mean that experiential learning should be imposed from above. If schools are concerned with character they will recognize the need to involve pupils in the planning and execution of such programmes and allow an adequate range of choices for such involvement. Schools that expect immediate results or believe they will be easily achieved will be disappointed.

Conclusion

Many of the features of character education that I have identified in American schools are not uncommon in many British schools, even where the word character does not appear in the school's mission statement or documentation. It would not be difficult to find a successful British school that: has identified core values in teaching personal, social, moral and health education; teaches a citizenship programme with service to the community as a main element; has a positive ethos with statements and guidance on behaviour in and out of school, excellent teaching and learning, established links with the local community and active fundraising activities; has strong parental involvement and pupil participation in the life of the school; and enjoys academic success and low rates of absenteeism and exclusion. It would perhaps be more rare to find a large number of schools involving pupils and parents in the actual running of the school, but even this is on the increase. The outcomes may well be the same, the only difference being that there is an explicit commitment to character education in some American schools. Alternatively, it may be that the lack of conceptual clarity in British schools about that which constitutes good character in pupils or what represents right or wrong in reference to pupils' moral development reinforces confusion amongst teachers, pupils and parents. Only a major longitudinal research project of actual child behaviour and thought patterns in home and school could possibly begin to provide us with an adequate answer.

11 Conclusion

The grandfather had become very old. His legs wouldn't go, his eyes didn't see, his ears didn't hear, he had no teeth. And when he ate, the food dripped from his mouth.

The son and daughter-in-law stopped setting a place for him at the table and gave him supper in back of the stove. Once they brought dinner down to him in a cup. The old man wanted to move the cup and dropped and broke it. The daughter-in-law began to grumble at the old man for spoiling everything in the house and breaking the cups and said that she would now give him dinner in a dishpan. The old man only sighed and said nothing.

Once the husband and wife were staying at home and watching their small son playing on the floor with some wooden planks: he was building something. The father asked: "What is it that you are doing, Misha?" And Misha said: "Dear Father, I am making a dishpan. So that when you and dear Mother become old, you may be fed from this dishpan."

The husband and wife looked at one another and began to weep. They became ashamed of so offending the old man, and from then on seated him at the table and waited on him.

Leo Tolstoy,
The Old Grandfather and the Grandson

It is clear that an understanding of how character is formed, acquired and attained is largely dependent on the disciplinary or professional perspective from which the issue is viewed. It will depend upon one's belief in what it is to be a human being and the nature of a moral person. In my view character is ultimately experienced in action. As Robert Coles (1997: 7) writes, it is about 'how we live, what we do', but it is particularly transmitted through the witness and example of parents and teachers, especially through their storytelling or narratives. The role of literature as an applied ethics course in homes and schools cannot be overstated. The choice by parent or teacher of a good story is crucial. Such a narrative often does not need to have its 'moral' explained or emphasized – children instinctively recognize the message conveyed. This moral message influences both their thoughts and actions and can become an integral part of their conscience.

Whilst teachers are not generally specialist character educators they cannot avoid influencing the character of their pupils both by personal example and by what they teach them. 'Can virtue be taught?' is a question that Meno asks of Socrates. If virtue cannot be learnt, nor acquired by practice, Meno asks whether it comes to us by nature or in some other way? No answer is given. For Aristotle, as we have already seen, virtue is teachable, not as a course of instruction but rather by exercise – we learn by doing. Habits are nurtured or mature into virtues. The good is not something to be reflected upon, it is something to be done. Moreover, the desire for the good does not, by itself, produce the good. According to Aristotle's developmental theory of education, moral reasoning follows upon and does not precede habituation in virtuous conduct.

The virtuous character is more than one which conforms to rules and principles. It must ultimately rest on *being* a certain kind of person and not only *doing* certain kinds of things. Aristotle eschews a rationalistic account of moral education, according priority not to the giving of reasons for behaving in one way rather than another, but to the formation of character and right conduct. Another anti-rationalist element in Aristotle's account is his view that developing the ability to engage in moral reasoning presupposes the growth of appropriate affective responses. Education and schooling cannot simply be about academic outcomes. Whilst teachers might agree with R. M. Hare (1976: 12) that: 'the only solution is to teach as many people as possible to think as well as possible', they must also provide their pupils with opportunities to engage with fundamental moral problems through *practice*.

The study of human character was one of the great hallmarks of the Scottish Enlightenment in Britain. The many figures in this intellectual movement included Francis Hutcheson, Adam Smith and David Hume who, together with their followers, never lost sight of their educational mission. They argued that our fundamental character as human beings is constantly developing within a social environment over which we as individuals have limited control. They presented human character as a product of history, insisting that changes to the social environment were not arbitrary or chaotic, for they believed that there were certain principles and discernible patterns that could be identified and modified by society. It followed that human character could also be modified by changing the environment in which it developed. They argued that to develop a responsible character there are two indispensable conditions – freedom and knowledge.

Their work laid the foundations for modern approaches to character education which consist in a belief that nurture is all-important in determining human behaviour and that nature, the psycho-physical capacity or potential with which individuals are born, is a negligible factor in character formation. This thinking has tended to view the individual as a product of social environment and to view the person as less important than the group. The cultivation of virtue for character can be a form of socialization – of socializing pupils into the inherited traditions of society and local communities, principally through narratives and social rules. In recent years there has been a closer examination of the relationship between moral reasoning and moral action, which has led to a renewed understanding that moral reasoning takes place in a social framework of substantive values.

This appears to necessitate a content-based moral education curriculum that many today have rejected as too problematic. Most academic discussions of character education have been rife with controversy, with constant disputes about definitions and methods. Many teachers and academics have sought to construct a character education rationale without subscribing to any particular set of values. They find subscribing to any set of values deeply problematic in a pluralist society and so commit themselves to nothing in particular. They seem to deny the premise that education's larger purpose is to shape character. Because of this, many character educators assume a general moral decline in culture, which they insist is detrimental to character formation in both homes and schools. They point to the fact that schools are less certain about what values to transmit and even if a school has a coherent ethics to teach it may be at odds with society.

The promotion of character education does not consist simply in the way we teach or in the content of our teaching. Underlying all education we find a series of basic principles, explicit or implicit, conscious or unconscious, determining the specific type of commitment to what makes a good human being and to what constitutes a good society. The ethics of character focuses upon how individuals are formed as moral agents and this 'complex' process is more important than what rules children should necessarily follow or even how they should follow them. Despite the resurgence of interest in virtue and character, no single analysis has won general acceptance. Thus, there is no overall theory of virtue ethics for schooling in character and it is therefore not surprising that the term character education is used in the educational literature in very different, and sometimes in contrary and antagonistic ways. Nevertheless, every school contributes to the development of character in its pupils as does every teacher.

Character education is a community-wide responsibility involving families, neighbourhoods and schools. It is for teachers, parents and pupils to collaborate and devise, discuss and subscribe to a clear code of ethics. At the same time a person's character is made up of a number of traits in a delicate structure which psychology has not been able to penetrate. Psychology in education has largely focused on cognitive development and not on the inner human nature. It is why character has resisted scientific measurement by psychologists and it is also perhaps why they largely ignore the use of the concept. Plato's assumption that knowledge is virtue became the major weakness of modern cognitive psychologists who assumed that skill in moral reasoning naturally led to moral behaviour; it was for them entirely about an abstract process of decision-making rather than building character. Consequently, much of what goes under the label of 'character education' is little more than therapeutic child care or development based on an assorted combination of child-development theories, cognitive development activities and values clarification methods. I have argued that the family and school are at the heart of the moral economy for they, especially when operating together, hold out the best possibility of nurturing in the child the ability to transcend self-interest and to regard the interests of others as in some way their own. It seems that both parents and teachers are ascribed a 'parenting' role in modern schooling and they are often credited together as being the seed-bed from which all the civic virtues flow. Unfortunately, when they are in opposition to each other or when the home or school ethos is poor they can also be the fount of vice.

The location of character education has traditionally been firmly placed in the home and Church, particularly within Catholic countries. However, Protestant Anglo-Saxon cultures, like those of America and Britain, have increasingly given emphasis to character development in the school and, as the influence of the Protestant denominations has declined, schools have become even more the focus for character and moral educational initiatives.

Today, schools are often seen as co-equal with the family in terms of their responsibility for producing good character – an idea that is still alien in many countries with a distinct Catholic culture such as in France, Italy or Spain, which have no school-based character education movements. As the moral force and function of the *family* in nurturing character appears to be in decline in Britain, the idea of *home* and *Church* is being rapidly replaced with *school* and *State* as the prime movers in character building in the young. It is increasingly the State and school which have taken the lead in moral and character education. Character educators in America have sought to restore the primary role of parents in character formation and it would seem wise for teachers in Britain to do likewise. The State should seek to support the role of families in character development.

In Britain, it is the government that is currently advocating the teaching of virtues in schools and seeking policies to build the character of the young. However, it does so on a largely nebulous philosophy – a philosophy which fails to provide a substantive explanation of what the basis of this moral or character education is. There is no consensus in schools of what virtues should be taught or how they should be taught. Government policy on 'education with character' appears fragmented, but a careful reading of the range of official documents indicates the potential for a more coherent view, albeit one that side-steps any fundamental agreement.

In America character education is seen largely as a social movement and even though it cannot be defined adequately, it is a useful starting point for further positive development. In the same way, character education in England is an emerging policy which the government is attempting to make legitimate in education. The history of character education in Britain revealed that, apart from the activities of some conservative evangelicals in the nineteenth century, character education has been principally advocated by liberals and progressives in education. This can be traced from the liberal thinkers in the Scottish Enlightenment, through to the radical experiments by Robert Owen, and on to the secular humanists in the late Victorian era and thence the progressives in moral education in the early part of the twentieth century. All of them saw character development as part of a process in reforming society. The explicit Communist ideology of creating the 'socialist character' in the 1920s and beyond tarnished the name of character education, but experiments in education by the likes of A. S. Neill were no less character building. It therefore should be of little surprise that it is a Labour government at the start of the twenty-first century which has reintroduced character education on to the agenda for schools. We live in a moralist age, which New Labour exploits, but it is a morality created by the media and politics not by religion. The moral education in schools is likewise a product of non-religious humanistic education based on secular concepts of human rights, justice, openness, civics and tolerance.

Thomas Hennessey (1986) argues that character education can still look to religion, and specifically to the Judeo–Christian tradition, for moral guidance and that educators should acknowledge this as a legitimate activity. Above all, religion offers a deeper foundation for character education with the Christian sense of forgiveness, grace, love, hope, faith and humility. Religion also plays a substantial part in placing an emphasis on the dignity of human beings. It can be an important stimulus for the conscience and will to do the right thing. After all, much of the moral education taught in schools has its origins in the 'golden rule' that you must love your neighbour as yourself. Despite these obvious and com-pelling links between religion and character education, many within the field of education and schooling are, at the very best, unsympathetic to the role of reli-gion in character education, rejecting the idea of religion as a motivating force for character. Others are even more hostile, portraying Christianity in particular as antiquated and repressive of both freedom and individual character.

The relationship of character to the economic order is also critical for educa-tion and schooling. The activities of the State and market economy have expanded to such an extent that they are usurping some of the initiatives of families in forming character. Moral values are bound to come into conflict with economic values, whether it be the dilemma of the just price for something being pitted against the harsh reality of supply and demand, or whether it take the shape of self-interest, once a vice, now conceived as an economic virtue. Human beings have become utility maximizers in their daily lives, with eco-nomics, largely driving ethical principles from the marketplace, abetted by the media exploiting and manipulating public consciousness. As a consequence, there is a growing schism between character and what might be called talent, so that particular skills or competencies that are valued in the marketplace are viewed independently of moral behaviour as a citizen. Some argue that the emphasis on consumerism will be compensated by the influence of the family and school but this is unlikely. Much more likely to occur is what Robert Bellah calls 'utilitarian individualism', which is when a person maximizes their own interests, desires and choices over and above those of their neighbour and the community. Character education is often reduced to economic and technologi-cal development in the consumer mind. And yet human character is not entirely selfish and this unselfishness must, in turn, have implications for the conduct of economic activity.

It is interesting that there have been so many voices in character education in the USA advocating contradictory practices and goals in the language of both character development and virtue-ethics. This is well illustrated by Larry Nucci and Edward Wynne who were at the same institution, University of Illinois in Chicago, and worked on the same topic from radically different perspectives, one as a developmental psychologist and the other from a more philosophically and sociologically grounded perspective. One wrote of cognitive moral development and the other of virtue. It is why Emily Neilsen Jones, Kevin Ryan and Karen Bohlin (1999: 4) conclude that: 'schools of education emphasize very different approaches in teaching character education to future teachers, ranging from experimental education to religious education to moral reasoning'. It seems clear that many of the character education initiatives in America have little to do with a virtue ethics approach and are really a continuation of recent moral education courses based on values clarification and abstract moral reasoning pedagogies. There is no unity of understanding among members of the character education movement in the USA.

This work began by pointing out the lack of consensus in our society about the nature of character and consequently of character education. A review of the differing positions suggests that their wide differences will continue to prevent the production of a general consensus. On the other hand, the increasing importance of character education in a post-Christian society which feels the need to develop a 'new ethics' will ensure that the topic continues to attract increasing political and academic interest. Further research and practical application will continue to be needed because all schools are already heavily engaged in character education. The question is whether they are doing it well or not.

Bibliography

Abbott, W.M. (1966), *The Documents of Vatican II*, New York: Guild Press

Ackland, A.H.D. (1980), 'The Education of Citizens', in Reeder, D. (ed.), *Educating Our Masters*, Leicester: Leicester University Press

Acton, H.B. (1971), *The Morals of Markets: An Ethical Exploration*, London: Longman

Adler, M.J. (1990), 'This Pre-war Generation', in G. Van Doren (ed.), *Reforming Education: The Opening of the American Mind*, New York: Westview Press

Adler, M.J. (1996), *The Time of Our Lives: The Ethics of Common Sense*, New York: Fordham University Press

Alexander, R. (2001), *Culture and Pedagogy: International Comparisons in Primary Education*, Oxford: Blackwell

Anderson, D. (1992), *The Loss of Virtue: Moral Confusion and Social Disorder in Britain and America*, London: Social Affairs Unit

Annas, J. (1993), *The Morality of Happiness*, New York and Oxford: Oxford University Press

Annette, J. (2000), 'Education for Citizenship: Civic Participation and Experiential and Service Learning in the Community', in D. Lawton, J. Cairns and R. Gardner, *Education for Citizenship*, London: Continuum

Anscombe, G.E.M. (1981, 1958), 'Modern Moral Philosophy', in *Philosophy* vol. 33: 1ff.; also in *Collected Philosophical Papers* vol. III: 26ff., *Ethics, Religion and Politics*, Minneapolis: University of Minnesota Press

Archard, D. (1993), *Children: Rights and Childhood*, London: Routledge

Archer, W. (1916), *Knowledge and Character: The Straight Road in Education*, London: G. Allen & Unwin

Aristotle, *Nichomachean Ethics* trans. D. Ross (1998), Oxford: Oxford University Press

Aristotle, *Politics*, ed. T.J. Saunders (1981), Harmondsworth: Penguin

Arthur, J. (1995), *The Ebbing Tide – Policy and Principles of Catholic Education*, Leominster: Gracewing

Arthur, J. (2000), *Schools and Community: The Communitarian Agenda in Education*, London: Falmer Press

Arthur, J. and Wright, D. (2001), *Teaching Citizenship in the Secondary School*, London: David Fulton

Arthur, J., Davison, J. and Stowe, W. (2000a), *Social Literacy, Citizenship Education and the National Curriculum*, London: Falmer Press

Arthur, J., Gaine, G. and Walters, H. (2000b), *Earthen Vessels: The Thomistic Tradition in Education*, Leominster: Gracewing

Arthur, J., Davies, I., Wrenn, A., Haydn, T. and Kerr, D. (2001), *Citizenship through Secondary History*, London: Routledge

Asayesh, G. (1992), 'Creating values and character education programs', *Journal of Staff Development*, vol. 13: 4, pp. 38–41

Atherton, M. (1988), 'Virtues in moral education: objections and replies', *Educational Theory*, vol. 38:, pp. 299–310

Audi, R. (1997), *Moral Knowledge and Ethical Character*, Oxford: Oxford University Press

Avis, G. (1987), *The Making of the Soviet Citizen: Character Formation and Civic Training in Soviet Education*, London: Croom Helm

Backhouse, W.H. (1947), *Religion and Adolescent Character*, London: Lutterworth Press

Baldwin, W.H. and Robson, W. (1913), *Lessons in Character-Building*, London: T. Nelson & Sons

Bardsley, J. (1861), *The Formation of English Character*, London: YMCA

Barker, E. (1948), *National Character and the Factors in its Formation*, London: Methuen & Co

Barth, R. (1979), 'Home-based reinforcement of social behaviour: a review and analysis', *Review of Educational Research*, vol. 49:, pp. 436–458

Batho, G. (1990), 'The history of the teaching of civics and citizenship in English schools', *The Curriculum Journal*, vol. 1: 1, pp. 91–100

Beauchamp, E., Rousmaniere, K. and Dehli, K. (eds) (1997), *Discipline, Moral Regulation and Schooling: A Social History*, New York: Garling Publishing

Beiner, R. (1992), *What's the Matter with Liberalism?*, Berkeley, Cal: University of California Press

Bell, Q. (1968), *Bloomsbury*, New York: Basic Books

Bellah, R.N. *et al.* (1985), *Habits of the Heart: Individualism and Commitment in American Life*, Berkeley: University of California Press

Beller, E. (1986), 'Education for character: an alternative to values clarification and cognitive moral development curricula', *Journal of Educational Thought*, vol. 20: 2, pp. 67–76

Bennet, W.J. (1991), 'Moral literacy and the formation of character', in J. Benninga, *Moral Character and Civil Education in the Elementary School*, New York: Teachers College Press

Bennet, W.J. (1993), *The Book of Virtues: A Treasury of Great Moral Stories*, New York: Simon & Schuster

Bennet, W.J. (1995), *The Moral Compass: Stories for a Life's Journey*, New York: Simon & Schuster

Benninga, J. (ed.) (1991), *Moral Character and Civic Education in the Elementary School*, New York: Teachers College Press

Benninga, J. (1997), 'Schools, character development and citizenship', in A. Molnar (ed.), *The Construction of Children's Character*, Chicago: National Society for the Study of Education

Bentley, T. (1998), *Learning Beyond the Classroom: Education for a Changing World*, London: DEOMOS/Routledge

Berry, C.J. (1992), 'Adam Smith and the virtues of commerce', in *Virtues*, W. Chapman and W.A. Galston (eds), *Nomos*, vol. 34, pp. 69–88, New York: New York University Press

Bidwell, C.E. (1972), 'Schooling and socialisation for moral commitment', *Interchange* 3, No. 4, pp. 1–27

Blakenhorn, D. and Glendon, M.A. (1995), *Seedbeds of Virtue: Sources of Competence, Character, and Citizenship in American Society*, New York: Madison Books

Bloom, A. (1987), *The Closing of the American Mind*, New York: Simon & Schuster

Board of Education (1910) Circular 753, London: HMSO

Bondi, R. (1984), 'The elements of character', *Journal of Religious Ethics*, vol. 12: 2, pp. 201–18

Bowles, S. and Gintis, H. (1976), *Schooling in Capitalist America*, New York: Basic Books

Boyd, W. (1950), *The History of Western Education*, London: Adam & Charles Black

Boyed, N. (ed.) (1956), *Emile for Today: The Emile of Jean-Jacques Rousseau*, London: Heinemann

British Social Trends (2002), No. 32, London: HMSO

Bronfenbrenner, V. (1962), 'Soviet methods of character education: some implications for research', *Religious Education*, vol. LVII: 4, pp. 45–61

Brooks, B.D. and Kann, M.E. (1993), 'What makes character education programs work?' in *Educational Leadership*, November, pp. 19–21

Brooks, B.D. and Goble, F.G. (1997), *The Case for Character Education: The Role of the School in Teaching Values and Virtue*, Northridge, CA: Studio 4 Productions

Budziszewski, J. (1992), 'Religion and civic virtue', in *Virtues*, W. Chapman and W.A. Galston (eds), *Nomos*, vol. 34, pp. 49–68, New York: New York University Press

Budziszewski, J. (1999), *The Revenge of Conscience: Politics and the Fall of Man*, New York: Spence Publishing

Bull, N. (1969), *Moral Education*, London: Routledge & Kegan Paul

Burnyeat, M.F. (1980), 'Aristotle on learning to be good', in A.O. Rorty (ed.), *Essays on Aristotle's Ethics*, Berkeley: University of California Press

Burstyn, J.N. (1996), *Educating Tomorrow's Valuable Citizen*, New York: State University of New York Press

Campbell, V. and Bond, R. (1982), 'Evaluation of a character education curriculum', in D. McClelland (ed.), *Education for Values*, New York: Irvington Publishers

Carr, D. (1984a), 'Three approaches to moral education', *Educational Philosophy and Theory*, vol. 15: 2, pp. 39–51

Carr, D. (1984b), 'Moral philosophy and psychology in progressive and traditional educational thought', *Journal of the Philosophy of Education*, vol. 18: 1, pp. 41–53

Carr, D. (1991), *Educating the Virtues: An Essay on the Philosophical Psychology of Moral Development and Education*, London: Routledge

Carr, D. (1995), 'The primacy of virtues in ethical theory part I and II', in *Cogito*, vol. 9: 3, pp. 238–244 and vol. 10: 1, pp. 34–40

Carr, D. (1996), 'After Kohlberg: some implications of an ethics of virtue for the theory of moral education and development', *Studies in Philosophy of Education*, vol. 14: 4, pp. 353–370

Carr, D. (2002), 'Moral education and the perils of developmentalism', *Journal of Moral Education*, vol. 31: 1, pp. 5–19

Carr, D. and Steutal, J. (eds) (1999), *Virtue Ethics and Moral Education*, London: Routledge

Catachism of the Catholic Church (1994), London: Geoffrey Chapman

Character Education Partnership (1999), *Character Education Quality Standards: A Self-Assessment Tool for Schools and Districts*, Alexandria, VA: CEP

Character Education Partnership (2000), *Character Education in US Schools: The New Consensus*, Alexandria, VA: CEP

Chazan, B. (1985), *Contemporary Approaches to Moral Education: Analysis Alternative Theories*, New York: Teachers College Press

Childs, J. (1967), *Education and Morals*, New York: John Wiley

Christensen, K.R. (1994), *Politics of Character Development: A Marxist Reappraisal of the Moral Life*, New York: Greenwood

Clarendon Commission (1864), *On the Principal Public Schools*, London: HMSO

Clarke, F. (ed.) (1938), *Church, Community and State in Relation to Education*, London: George Allen & Unwin

Clifford, C. and Feezell R.M. (1997), *Coaching for Character*, Champaign, IL: Human Kinetics

Close, F.P. (1993/1994), 'The case for moral education', in *The Responsive Community*, vol. 4: 1, pp. 23–29

Cochran, C.E. (1982), *Character, Community and Politics*, Alabama: University of Alabama Press

Cochran, C.E. (1989), 'The thin theory of community: the communitarians and their critics', in *Political Studies*, vol. 37, pp. 422–435

Code of Canon Law (1983), trans. the Canon Law Society of Great Britain and Ireland, London: Collins

Cohen, P. (1995), 'The content of their character: educators find new ways to tackle values and morality', in *Curriculum Update*, Spring, pp.1–8

Cole, M. (1953), *Robert Owen of New Lanark*, London: The Batchworth Press

Coleman, J.S. and Hoffer T. (1987), *Public and Private High Schools: The Importance of Communities*, New York: Basic Books

Coles, R. (1986), *The Moral Life of Children*, Boston: Houghton Mifflin

Coles, R. (1989), *The Call of Stories: Teaching and the Moral Imagination*, Boston: Houghton Mifflin

Coles, R. (1997), *The Moral Intelligence of Children*, New York: Random House

Collard, D. (1978), *Altruism and Economy: A Study in Non-Selfish Economics*, Oxford: Martin Robertson

Collini, S. (1985), 'The idea of character in Victorian political thought', in *Transactions of the Royal Historical Society*, vol. 35, pp. 29–54

Collins, M. (1990), *Marva Collins Way*, New York: Putnan

Comte-Sponville, A. (2002), *A Short History Treatise on the Great Virtues: The Uses of Philosophy in Everyday Life*, London: Heinemann

Cook, S.W. (ed.) (1962), 'Review of recent research in religion and character formation', *Religious Education*, vol. LVII: 4

Cooper, T.L. (1991), *An Ethic of Citizenship for Public Administration*, Englewood Cliffs, New Jersey: Prentice Hall

Copleston, F.C. (1965), *Aquinas*, Middlesex: Penguin

Cordner, C. (1994), 'Aristotelian virtue and its limitations', in *Philosophy*, vol. 69, pp. 291–316

Crittenden, B. (1988), *Parents, the State and the Right to Educate*, Melborne: Melborne University Press

Crittenden, P. (1990), *Learning to be Moral*, New Jersey: Humanities Press

Damon, W. (1988), *The Moral Child*, New York: Free Press

Damon, W. (1996), *Greater Expectations: Overcoming the Culture of Indulgence in America's Homes and Schools*, New York: Free Press

Dancy, J. (1963), *The Public School and the Future*, London: Faber & Faber

Darling-Smith, B. (1993), 'Can virtue be taught?', in *Boston University Studies in Philosophy and Religion*, vol. 14, Notre Dame, Ind: Notre Dame University Press

Davis Report Enterprise and the Economy in Education (2002), HM Treasury/Department of Trade and Industry/Department for Education and Skills, London: HMSO

Department for Education and Employment Excellence in Schools (1997), London: The Stationary Office

Department for Education and Employment National Curriculum for England (1999), London: The Stationary Office

Department for Education and Employment (2001), *Schools: Building on Success*, London: The Stationary Office

Department for Education and Skills (2001), *Schools: Achieving Success*, London: The Stationary Office

DeRoche, E.F. and Williams M.M. (2001), *Educating Hearts and Minds: A Comprehensive Character Education Framework*, Thousand Oaks, CA: Corwin Press Inc

DeVries, R. (1998), 'Implications of Piaget's constructivist theory for character education', in *Action in Teacher Education*, vol. 20: 4, pp. 39–47

Dewey, J. (1909), *Moral Principles in Education*, Boston: Houghton Mifflin

Dewey, J. (1916), *Democracy and Education*, New York: Macmillan

Dewey, J. (1934), *A Common Faith*, New Haven, CT: Yale University Press

Dewey, J. (1960), *The Theory of Moral Life*, New York: Holt, Rinehart & Winston

Donlan, T.C. (1952), *Theology and Education*, Dubuque, Iowa: Brown

Downey, M. and Kelly A.V. (1978), *Moral Education: Theory and Practice*, London: Harper & Row

Doyle, D.P. (1997), 'Education and character: a conservative view', in *Phi Delta Kappen*, vol. 78, pp. 440–443

Duncan, B.J. (1997), 'Character education: reclaiming the social', in *Educational Theory*, vol. 47: 1, pp. 119–130

Durkheim. E. (1886), *Moral Education: A Study in the Theory and Application of the Sociology of Education*, New York: The Free Press

Dworkin, R. (1978), 'Liberalism', in S. Hampshire (ed.), *Public and Private Morality*, New York: Cambridge University Press

Dykstra, C.R. (1981), *Vision and Character: A Character Educator's Alternative to Kohlberg*, New York: Paulist Press

Eberly, D.E. (1995), *The Content of America's Character*, Lenham, New York: Madison Books

Edwards, C.P. (1986), *Promoting Social and Moral Development in Young Children*, New York: Teachers College Press

Egan, K. (1983), *Education and Psychology*, London: Methuen

Elias, J.L. (1989), *Moral Education: Secular and Religious*, Malabar, Florida: R. E. Krieger Publishing

Ellis, F.H. (1907), *Character-forming in Schools*, London: Longmans

Entwistle, D. (1994), 'Sunday-school book prizes for children: rewards and socialisation', in D. Wood (ed.), *The Church and Childhood*, Oxford: Blackwells

Erikson, E.H. (1950), *Childhood and Society: Eight Ages of Man*, 2nd edn., Middlesex: Penguin

Etzioni, A. (1988), *The Moral Dimension: Toward a New Economics*, New York: Free Press

Etzioni, A. (1993), *The Spirit of Community: Rights, Responsibilities and the Communitarian Agenda*, New York: Crown Publishers

Etzioni, A. (2000), *The New Golden Rule Community and Morality in a Democratic Society*, New York: Basic Books

Flannagan, K., and Jupp, P. (eds) (2001), *Virtue Ethics and Sociology: issues of modernity and religion*, Basingstoke: Palgrave

Flannagan, O. and Rorty, A.O. (eds) (1990), *Identity, Character, and Morality: Essays in Moral Psychology*, Cambridge, MA: The MIT Press

Foot, P. (1981), *Virtues and Vices*, Berkeley: University of California Press

Fowler, J. (1981), *Stages of Faith: The Psychology of Human Development and the Quest for Meaning*, San Francisco: Harper & Row

Frankena, W.K. (1956), 'Toward a philosophy of the philosophy of education', *Harvard Educational Review*, vol. 26: 2, pp. 94–98

Frankena, W.K. (1965), *Philosophy of Education*, New York: Macmillan

Frankena, W.K. (1973), *Ethics*, Englewood Cliffs, New Jersey: Prentice-Hall

Frankena, W.K. (1974), 'A model for analysing a philosophy of education', in J. Park, *Selected Readings in the Philosophy of Education*, New York: Macmillan

Freakley, M. (1996), 'The values opt-out and the case for character development in moral education', in *Educational Practice and Theory*, vol. 18: 2, pp. 22–37

Freeman, M.D.A. (1983), *The Rights and Wrongs of Children*, London: Francis Pinter

French, P., Vehling, T. and Wettstein, H. (1988), *Midwest Studies in Philosophy: Ethical Theory: Character and Virtue*, Notre Dame, Ind: Notre Dame University Press

Frymier, J. *et al.* (1995), 'Values on which we agree', in *Phi Delta Kappa*, Bloomington, Ind

Gaines, W. (1960), *Self-Made Man*, New York: New American Library

Gallagher, D. and I. (eds) (1967), *The Education of Man: The Educational Philosophy of Jacques Maritain*, Notre Dame, Ind: University of Notre Dame Press

Gardner, E.C. (1983), 'Character, virtue and responsibility in theological ethics', in *Encounter*, vol. 44: 4, pp. 315–339

Garfinkle, N. (1998), *Moral Character Formation in the First Three Years*, Washington DC: Institute for Communitarian Policy Studies

Garrod, A. (ed.) (1992), *Learning for Life: Moral Education Theory and Practice*, Westport, Conn: Praeger

Gauld, J. (1993), *Character First: The Hyde School Difference*, San Francisco: ICS Press

Gay, G. (1997), 'Connections between character education and multicultural education', in A. Molnar (ed.), *The Construction of Children's Character*, Chicago: National Society for the Study of Education

Gaylin, W. and Jennings, B. (1996), *The Perversion of Autonomy*, New York: The Free Press

Geach, P. (1977), *The Virtues*, Cambridge: Cambridge University Press

Gillet, M.S. (1914), *The Education of Character*, London: Washborne

Gilligan, C. (1982), *In a Different Voice: Psychological Theory and Women's Development*, Cambridge, MA: Harvard University Press

Giroux, H.A. and Purpel, D. (1983), *Hidden Curriculum and Moral Education: Deception of Discovery*, Berkeley, CA: McCutchan

Glenn, C.L. (1994), 'School distinctiveness', in *Journal of Education*, vol. 176: 2, pp. 73–103

Goldman, L. (1996), 'Mind, character and the deferral of gratification', in *The Educational Forum*, vol. 60: 2, pp. 135–140

Gough, R.W. (1998), *Character is Destiny*, Rocklin, CA: Forum

Gould, F.J. (1929), *Moral Education: A Chapter from the Story of Schools in England and Wales 1895–1925*, London: Watts & Co

Grant, G. (1982), 'The character of education and the education of character', in *American Education*, vol. 18: 1, pp. 37–46

Grant. G. (1986), *The World We Created at Hamilton High*, Cambridge, MA: Harvard University Press

Green, A. (1990), *Education and State Formation*, London: Macmillan

Grech, P. (1960), *Educating Christians*, London: Herder Publications

Griffin, R.S. and Nash, R.J. (1990), 'Individualism, community and education: an exchange of views', in *Educational Theory*, vol. 40: 1, pp. 1–18

Griffiths, V.L. (1953), *Character and its Psychology*, in the Good Citizens series, London: Longman

Grisez, G. (1983), 'The Way of the Lord Jesus', in *Christian Moral Principles*, vol. 1, Chicago: Franciscan Herald Press

Griswold, C.L. (1999), *Adam Smith and the Virtues of the Enlightenment*, Cambridge: Cambridge University Press

Guttman, A. (1987), *Democratic Education*, Princeton, NJ: Princeton University Press

Hadfield, J.A. (1924), *Psychology and Morals: An Analysis of Character*, London: Methuen

Halsey, A.H. (1994), 'The transformation of society', in National Commission on Education *Insights into Education and Training*, London: Heinemann

Halstead, J.M. and McLaughlin, T.H. (eds) (1999a), *Education and Morality*, London: Routledge

Halstead, J.M. and Taylor, M.J. (1999b), *Values in Education and Education in Values*, London: Falmer Press

Hare, R.M. (1976), 'Value education in a pluralistic society', in *Proceedings of the Philosophy of Education Society of Great Britain*, July

Hare, W. (1973), 'Education and character development', in *Journal of Moral Education*, vol. 2: 2, pp. 115–120

Hargreaves, D.H. (1980), 'A sociological critique of individualism in education', in *British Journal of Educational Studies*, vol. 28: 3, pp. 187–198

Harman, G. (1999), 'Moral philosophy meets social psychology', in *Proceedings of the Aristotelian Society*, vol. 99, pp. 315–331

Hartshorne, H. and May, M. (1928), 'Studies in deceit', in *Studies in the Nature of Character*, vol. 1, New York: Macmillan

Hartshorne, H. and May, M. (1929), 'Studies in self-control', in *Studies in the Nature of Character*, vol. 2, New York: Macmillan

Hartshorne, H., May, M. and Shuttleworth, F. (1930), in 'Studies in the organization of character', *Studies in the Nature of Character*, vol. 3, New York: Macmillan

Hauerwas, S. (1975), *Character and the Christian Life: A Study in Theological Ethics*, San Antonio, TX: Trinity University Press

Hauerwas, S. (1981), *Visions and Virtues*, Notre Dame, Ind: Notre Dame University Press

Hauerwas, S. and Pinches, C. (1997), *Christians among the Virtues*, Notre Dame, Ind: Notre Dame University Press

Haydon, G. (1995), 'Thick or thin? The cognitive content of moral education in a plural democracy', in *Journal of Moral Education*, vol. 24: 1, pp. 53–64

Haydon, G. (1997), *Teaching about Values: A New Approach*, London: Cassell

Havighurst, J.R. and Taba, H. (1949), *Adolescent Character and Personality*, New York: John Wiley

Heath, D.H. (1994), *Schools of Hope: Developing Mind and Character in Today's Youth*, San Francisco: The Jossey-Bass Education Series

Heath, E. (1995), 'The commerce of sympathy: Adam Smith on the emergence of morals, in *Journal of the History of Philosophy*, vol. 33, pp. 447–66

Hennessey, T.C. (1986), 'The role of religion in character development', in *Content, Character and Choice in Schooling, Public Policy and Research Implications*, proceedings of a symposium of the National Council of Educational Research, 24 April, USA

Hersh, R., Paolitto, D. and Reimer, J. (1977), *Promoting Moral Growth: From Piaget to Kohlberg*, New York: Longman

Heston, K.L. (1933), *The Character Emphasis on Education*, Chicago: Chicago University Press

Hilliard, F.H. (1961), 'The Moral Instruction League 1897–1919', in *Durham Research Review*, vol. 12: 3, pp. 53–63

Himmelfarb, G. (1995), *The Demoralization of Society: From Victorian Virtues to Modern Values*, New York: Alfred A. Knopf

Hirst, P.H. (1974), *Moral Education in a Secular Society*, London: Hodder & Stoughton

Hogan, R. (1973), 'Moral conduct and moral character: a psychological perspective', in *Psychological Bulletin*, vol. 79, pp. 217–232

Hughes, G.J. (2001), *Aristotle on Ethics*, London: Routledge

Hughes, T. (1957 edn.), *Tom Brown's Schooldays*, London: Murray Abbey Classics

Hunt, J. (1976), *Education in Evolution*, London: Hart Davis

Hunt, L.H. (1997), *Character and Culture*, New York: Rowman & Littlefield

Hunter, J.D. (2001), *The Death of Character: Moral Education in an Age without Good or Evil*, New York: Basic Books

Hutcheon, P.D. (1999), *Building Character and Culture*, London: Praeger Press

Hutchins, R.M. (1938), 'The university and character', in *Commonwealth* 27 (22 April)

Hutchison, H. (1976), 'An eighteenth-century insight into religious and moral education', in *British Journal of Educational Studies*, vol. 24, pp. 233–241

Hyland, J.T. (1986), 'Instruction, rationality and learning to be moral', in *Journal of Moral Education*, vol. 15: 2, pp. 127–138

Isaacs, D. (1984), *Character Building: A Guide for Parents and Teachers*, Blackrock, Ireland: Four Courts Press

Jackson, P.W., Boostrom, R.E. and Hansen, D.T. (1993), *The Moral Life of Schools*, San Francisco: Jossey Bass

Johnson, H.C. (1987), 'Society, culture and character development', in K. Ryan and G.F. McLean (eds), *Character Development in Schools and Beyond*, New York: Praeger

Jonathan, R. (1999), 'Agency and contingency in moral development and education', in J.M. Halstead and T.H. McLaughlin (eds), *Education and Morality*, London: Routledge

Jones, M.J. (1952), *Hannah More*, Cambridge: Cambridge University Press

Kagan, J. (1981), 'The moral function of the school', in *Daedalus*, vol. 110: 3, pp. 151–165

Kaplan, J.A. (1995), 'Conversing about character: new foundations for general education, in *Educational Theory*, vol. 45: 3, pp. 359–378

Kelsey, I.B. (1993), *Universal Character Education*, Edinburgh: Pentland Press.

Kessler, G.R. and Ibrahim F.A. (1986), 'Character development in adolescents', in *Adolescence*, vol. 21: 81, pp. 1–9

Kilpatrick, W. (1992), *Why Johnny Can't Tell Right From Wrong: Moral Literacy and the Case for Character Education*, New York: Simon & Schuster

Knowles, R.T. and McLean, G.F. (eds) (1992), *Psychological Foundations of Moral Education and Character Development: An Integrated Theory of Moral Development*, Washington DC: Council for Research in Values and Philosophy

Kofodimos, J. (1990), 'Using biographical methods to understand managerial style and character', *Journal of Applied Behavioral Science*, vol. 26: 4, Special Issue: Character and leadership, pp. 433–459

Kohlberg, L. (1976), 'The cognitive–developmental approach to moral education', in T. Lickona (ed.), *Moral Development and Behaviour: Theory, Research and Social Issues*, New York: Holt, Rinehart & Winston

Kohlberg, L. (1981), *Essays on Moral Development: The Philosophy of Moral Development*, vol. I, San Francisco: Harper & Row

Kohlberg, L. (1984), *Essays on Moral Development: The Psychology of Moral Development*, vol. II, San Francisco: Harper & Row

Kohn, A. (1997), 'The trouble with character education', in A. Molnar (ed.), *The Construction of Children's Character*, Chicago: National Society for the Study of Education

Konstant, D. (1966), *A Syllabus of Religious Instruction for Catholic Primary Schools*, London: Burns & Oates/Macmillan

Kreeft, P. (1993), *A Shorter Summa, the essential philosophical passages of Saint Thomas Aquinas' Summa Theologica*, San Francisco: St Ignatius Press

Kupperman, J. (1988), 'Character and ethical theory', in *Midwest Studies in Philosophy*, vol. 13, pp. 115–125

Kupperman, J. (1991), *Character*, New York: Oxford University Press

Kupperman, J. (2001), 'The indispensability of character', in *Philosophy*, vol. 76: 297

Kruschwitz, R.B. and Roberts, R.C. (1987), *The Virtues: Contemporary Essays on Moral Character*, Belmont, CA: Wadsworth Publishing

Lasch, C. (1998), *Haven in a Heartless World: The Family Besieged*, New York: W.W. Norton

Lauwerys, J.A. and Hans, N. (eds) (1951), *The Yearbook of Education*, London: University of London Institute of Education and Evans Publishing

Leck, G.M. (1986), 'Theories of moral development', *Educational Studies*, vol. 17: 1, pp. 74–80

Leming, J.S. (1987), 'Curricular effectiveness in character education: what works, what doesn't, what might, and what we still need to know', U.S. Department of Education, working conference on 'Moral Education and Character'

Leming, J.S. (1993a), *Character Education: Lessons From the Past, Models for the Future*, Camden, ME: The Institute for Global Ethics

Leming, J.S. (1993b), 'In search of effective character education', *Educational Leadership*, November issue, pp. 63–71

Leming, J.S. (1994), 'Character education and the creation of community', *The Responsive Community*, vol. 4: 4, pp. 49–57

Leming, J.S. (1997), 'Research and practice in character education: a historical perspective', in A. Molnar (ed.), *The Construction of Children's Character*, Chicago: National Society for the Study of Education

Leming, J.S. (2000), 'Tell me a story: an evaluation of a literature-based character education programme, *Journal of Moral Education*, vol. 29: 4, pp. 413–427

Lesley, T.J. (1997), 'The missing ingredient in character education', *Phi Delta Kappan*, vol. 78: 8, pp. 654–655

Lewis, C.A. (1987), 'A word about character', *Phi Delta Kappan*, vol. 68: 10, pp. 724–725

Lewis, C.S. (1965), *The Abolition of Man*, New York: Macmillan

Likhanchev, V.T. (1970), 'Socio-educational variables and their role in the process of character education', *Soviet Education*, vol. 7: 6–7, pp. 82–101

Lickona, T. (ed.) (1976), *Moral Development and Behaviour: Theory, Research and Social Issues*, New York: Holt, Rinehart & Winston

Lickona, T. (1985), *Raising Good Children From Birth Through the Teenage Years*, Toronto: Bantam

Lickona, T. (1988a), 'Educating the moral child', in *Principal*, vol. 68: 2, pp. 6–10

Lickona, T. (1988b), 'Four strategies for fostering character development and academics in children', *Phi Delta Kappan*, vol. 69: 6, pp. 419–423

Lickona, T. (1991), *Educating for Character: How Our Schools Can Teach Respect and Responsibility*, New York: Bantam

Lickona, T. (1993), 'The return of character education', *Educational Leadership*, November issue, pp. 6–11

Lickona, T. (1996), 'Eleven principles of effective character education', *Journal of Moral Education*, vol. 25: 1, pp. 93–100

Livingstone, R. (1954), *Thoughts on the Education of Character*, lecture at Doncaster Grammar School

Lockwood, A.L. (1975), 'A critical view of values clarification', *Teachers College Record*, vol. 77: 1, pp. 35–50

Lockwood, A.L. (1997), 'What is character education', in A. Molnar (ed.), *The Construction of Children's Character*, Chicago: National Society for the Study of Education

Lockwood, A.T. (1997), *Character Education: Controversy and Consensus*, London: Corwin Press/Sage

Loeb, M.B. (1951), 'Social relationships and the development of character', in J.A. Lauwerys and N. Hans (eds), *The Yearbook of Education*, London: University of London Institute of Education and Evans Publishing

London, P. (1987), 'Character education and clinical intervention: a paradigm shift for US schools', *Phi Delta Kappan*, vol. 68: 9, pp. 667–673

Lord, F. (1926), *Man and His Character*, London: Kingsgate Press

Loubster, J.J. (1970), 'The contribution of schools to moral development: a working paper in the theory of action', *Interchange*, 1: 1, pp. 99–117

Louder, R.B. (1987), 'On some vices of virtue ethics', in R.B. Kruschwitz and R.C. Roberts, *The Virtues: Contemporary Essays on Moral Character*, Belmont, CA: Wadsworth Publishing

Lucci, L. (2001), *Education in the Moral Domain*, Cambridge: Cambridge University Press

McClelland, B.E. (1992), *Schools and the Shaping of Character: Moral Education in America 1607–Present*, Clearing House for Social Studies: Indiana University

McClelland, V.A. (1979), *The Liberal Education of England's Youth*, inaugural lecture, University of Hull, 4 December 1978

MacCunn, J. (1919), *The Making of Character: Some educational aspects of ethics*, Cambridge: Cambridge University Press

McIntyre, A. (1967), *A Short History of Ethics*, London: Routledge

McIntyre, A. (1985) 2nd edn., *After Virtue: A Study in Moral Theory*, London: Duckworth

McIntyre, A. (1987), 'The idea of an educated public', *Education and Values: The Richard Peters Lecture*, London: Institute of Education

McIntyre, A. (1999), 'How to seem virtuous without actually being so', in J.M. Halstead and T.H. McLaughlin (eds), *Education and Morality*, London: Routledge

McKeon, R. (1968), 'Character and the arts and disciplines', *Ethics*, vol. 78: 2, pp. 111–112

McKinnon, C. (1999), *Character, Virtue Theories and the Vices*, Ontario: Broadview Press

McKown, H.C. (1935), *Character Education*, New York and London: McGraw-Hill Book Co

McLaughlin, T.H. and Halstead, J.M. (1999), 'Education in character and virtue', in J.M Halstead and T.H. McLaughlin (eds) (1999), *Education and Morality*, London: Routledge

McLean, G.F. *et al.*, 'Character development in schools and beyond', in *Cultural Heritage and Contemporary Change*, Series IV, *Foundations of Moral Education*, vol. 3

McLean, G.L. (1986), *Act and Agent: Philosophical Foundations for Moral Education and Character Development*, Lantham, MD: University Press of America

McLellan, D. (1997), *Political Christianity: A Reader*, London: SPCK

MacLester, A. (1931), *The Development of Character Traits in Young Children*, London: C. Scribner & Sons, printed in USA

Marenbon, J. (1996), *A Moral Maze: Government Values in Education*, London: Politeia

Maritain, J. (1943), *Education at the Crossroads*, New York: Yale University Press

Marshall, A. (1898), *Principles of Economics*, London: Macmillan

Mason, C.M.S. (1906), *Some Studies in the Formation of Character*, London: Kegan Paul, Trench, Trubner & Co

Meyer, S.S. (1993), *Aristotle on Moral Responsibility: Character and Cause*, Oxford: Blackwell

Miller, P. and Kim, K. (1988), 'Human nature and the development of character: the clash of descriptive and normative elements in John Stuart Mills educational theory', *Journal of Educational Thought*, vol. 22: 2, pp. 133–144

Miller, R.F. and Jarman, B.O. (1988), 'Moral and ethical character development – views from past leaders', *Journal of Physical Education, Recreation and Dance*, vol. 59: 6, pp. 72–78

Ministry of Education (1947), *School and Life: A First Enquiry into the Transition from School to Independent Life*, report of the Central Advisory Council for Education, London: HMSO

Ministry of Education (1949), *Citizens Growing Up: At Home, In School and After*, London: HM Stationary Office

Mitchell, B. (1980), *Morality: Religious and Secular*, Oxford: Clarendon Press

Molnar, A. (ed.) (1997), *The Construction of Children's Character: The Ninety-Sixth Yearbook of the National Society for the Study of Education*, Chicago: University of Chicago Press

Monro, E. (1849), 'Education: its true province the formation of individual character', a letter to William Gladstone, Oxford

Morgan, M. (1994), *Manners, Morals and Class in England 1774–1858*, London: St Martin's Press

Morse, J.R. (1997), 'Who is rational economic man?', *Social Philosophy and Policy*, vol. 14: 1, pp. 179–206

Mountford, E.A. (1933), *The Education of Character*, London: Lincoln Williams

Murphy, M.M. (1998), *Character Education in America's Blue Ribbon Schools: Best Practices for Meeting the Challenge*, Lancaster, PA: Technomic Pub. Co. Inc.

Musgrave, P.W. (1978), *The Moral Curriculum: A Sociological Analysis*, London: Methuen

Nash, J.B. (ed.) (1932), *Character Education through Physical Education*, New York: Barnes

Nash, R.J. (1997), *Answering the Virtuecrats: A Moral Conversation on Character Education*, New York: Teachers College Press

National Commission on Youth (USA 1980), *The Transition of Youth to Adulthood: A Bridge Too Long*, Boulder, Colo: Westview

National Education Association of the USA (1932), *Tenth Year Book on Character Education*, Washington DC

Neall, B.S. (1983), *Concepts of Character in the Apocalypse with Implications for Character Education*, Washington DC: University of America Press

Neill, A.S. (1962), *Summerhill: A Radical Approach to Education*, London: Victor Gallancz

Neumann, H. (1932), *Lives in the Making. Aims and Ways of Character Education*, New York and London: D. Appleton & Co

Newsom Report *Half Our Future* (1963), DES, London: HMSO

Newsome, D. (1961), *Godliness and Good Learning*, London: John Murray

Neilsen Jones, E., Ryan, K. and Bohlin, K.E. (1999), *Teachers as Educators of Character: Are the Nation's Schools of Education Coming Up Short?*, Washington DC: Character Education Partnership

Noblit, G. and Dempsey, V.O. (1996), *The Social Construction of Virtue: the moral life of schools*, Albany: State University of New York Press

Noddings, N. (1987), 'So we really want to produce good people', *Journal of Moral Education*, vol. 16: 3, pp. 177–188

Noddings, N. (1992), *The Challenge to Care in Schools: An Alternative Approach to Education*, New York: Teachers College Press

Noddings, N. (1995), 'A morally defensible mission for schools in the 21st century', *Phi Delta Kappan*, vol. 76: 5, pp. 365–368

Noddings, N. (1997), 'Character education and community', in A. Molnar (ed.), *The Construction of Children's Character*, Chicago: National Society for the Study of Education

Nolan, J.L. (1988), *The Therapeutic State*, New York: New York University Press

Nucci, L. (1989), *Moral Development and Character Education: A Dialogue*, Berkeley, CA: McCutchan

Nucci, L. (2001), *Education in the Moral Domain*, New York: Cambridge University Press

Oakshott, M. (1975), *On Human Conduct*, New York: Oxford University Press

O'Hear, A. (1981), *Education, Society and Human Nature: An Introduction to the Philosophy of Education*, London: Routledge & Kegan Paul

O'Leary, P. (1983), 'Moral education, character traits, and reasons for action', *Canadian Journal of Education*, vol. 8: 3, pp. 217–231

Owen, R. (1813), *Essays on the Formation of Character*, reprinted in Owen, R. (1967), *The Life of Robert Owen*, London: Frank Cass

Owen, R. (1916), Address delivered on opening the institution for the formation of character, at New Lanark, on 1 January 1915, reprinted in Owen, R. (1972), *Robert Owen at New Lanark: Two Books and One Pamphlet*, New York: Anno Press

Owen, R.D. (1824), *An Outline of the Education System at New Lanark*, Glasgow: Wardlaw & Cunninghame, reprinted in Owen, R. (1972), Robert Owen at New Lanark: Two Books and One Pamphlet, New York: Anno Press

Parsons, B. (1998), 'Values education as character education: creating a successful programme', *Journal of Values Education*, vol. 3: June, pp. 10–13

Parsons, T. (1970), *Social Structure and Personality*, London: Free Press

Pear, T.H. (1951), 'The training of character in some English schools', in J.A. Lauwerys and N. Hans (eds), *The Yearbook of Education*, London: University of London Institute of Education and Evans Publishing

Peck, R.F. and Havighurst R.J. (1960), *The Psychology of Character Development*, New York: John Wiley

Peters, R.S. (1960), 'Symposium: the development of moral values in children', *British Journal of Educational Psychology*, pp. 250–265

Peters, R.S. (1962), 'Moral education and the psychology of character', *Philosophy*, vol. 37: 139, January

Peters, R.S. (1963), 'Reason and habit: the paradox of moral education', in W.R. Niblet (ed.), *Moral Education in a Changing Society*, London: Faber & Faber

Peters, R.S. (ed.) (1969), *Perspectives on Plowden*, London: Routledge & Kegan Paul

Peters, R.S. (1974), *Psychology and Ethical Development*, London: George Allen & Unwin

Peters, R.S. (1979), 'Virtues and habits in moral education', in D.B. Cochrane, C.M. Hamm and A.C. Kazepidos (eds), *The Domain of Moral Education*, New York: Paulist Press

Peters, R.S. (1986), Ethics and Education, George Allen & Unwin

Peterson, M.L. (1986), *Philosophy of Education: Issues and Options*, Leicester: Inter-Varsity Press

Phelps, E.S. (1975), *Altruism, Morality and Economic Theory*, London: Russell Sage Foundation

Piaget, J. (1965), *The Moral Judgment of the Child*, New York: The Free Press

Pietig, J. (1977), 'John Dewey and character education', *Journal of Moral Education*, vol. 6: 3, pp. 170–180

Plato, *The Republic*, (ed. T. Irwin, 1993, London: Everyman)

Plowden Report (1969), *Children and their Primary Schools*, DES Central Advisory Council for Education (England), London: HMSO

Porter, J. (1990), *The Recovery of Virtue*, Louseville: Westminster/John Know Press

Porter, R. (2000), *Enlightenment: Britain and the Creation of the Modern World*, London: Penguin

Prelinger, E. and Zimet, C.N. (1964), *An Ego-Psychological Approach to Character Assessment*, London: The Free Press/Collier-Macmillan

Pring, R. (2001), 'Education as a moral practice', *Journal of Moral Education*, vol. 30: 2, pp. 101–112

Pritchard, I. (1987), 'Moral education and character', a summary of the working conference held in Washington DC: US Department of Education

Pritchard, I. (1988), 'Character education: research prospects and problems', *American Journal of Education*, vol. 96: 4, pp. 469–495

Pritchard, M.S. (1996), *On Becoming Responsible*, Lawrence, KS: University Press of Kansas

Puka, B. (1999), 'Inclusive moral education: a critique and integration of competing approaches', in Leicester, M., Modgil, C. and Modgil, S. *Moral Education and Pluralism*, London: Falmer Press

Purpel, D.E. (1997), 'The politics of character education', in A. Molnar (ed.), *The Construction of Children's Character*, Chicago: National Society for the Study of Education

Qualifications and Curriculum Authority (1998), *Education for Citizenship and the Teaching of Democracy in Schools: Final Report of the Advisory Group on Citizenship*, London: Qualifications and Curriculum Authority

Qizilbash, M. (1994a), *Decisions and Moral Character*, University of Southampton Department of Economics

Qizilbash, M. (1994b), *Corruption, Temptation and Guilt: Moral Character and Economic Theory*, University of Southampton Department of Economics

Rawls, J. (1971), *A Theory of Justice*, Cambridge, MA: Harvard University Press

Reddie, C. (1901), *John Bull: His Origin and Character and the Present Condition of his Big Property; and Two other Papers on Education*, London: George Allen

Reed, T.M. (1987), 'Developmental moral theory', *Ethics*, vol. 97, January, pp. 441–456

Reid, J. (1906), *Manual of Moral Instruction*, London

Reimer, J., Paolitto, D.R. and Hersh, R.H. (1983), *Promoting Moral Growth: From Piaget to Kohlberg*, New York: Longman

Rice, S. (1996), 'Dewey's conception of virtue and its implications for moral education', *Educational Theory*, vol. 46: 3, pp. 276–277

Riley, J. (1992), 'Liberal philanthropy', in W. Chapman and W.A. Galston (eds), *Virtues, in Nomos*, vol. 34, pp. 338–385, New York: New York University Press

Roberts, K., White, G.E. and Parker, H.J. (1974), *The Character-Training Industry: Adventure-Training Schemes in Britain*, Newton Abbot: David & Charles

Robinson, J. (1963), *Honest to God*, London: SCM

Rodney, W.O. (1922), *Character Education in the Elementary School*, New York: Macmillan

Rothblatt, S. (1976), *Tradition and Change in English Liberal Education*, London: Faber & Faber

Rusnak, T. (ed.) (1998), *An Integrated Approach to Character Education*, London: Corwin Press

Rutter, M., Mortimer, P. and Maughan, B. (1979), *Fifteen Thousand Hours: Secondary Schools and their Effects on Children*, London: Open Books

Ryan, K. and Lickona, T. (1987a), 'Character education: the challenge and the model', in K. Ryan and G.F. McLean (eds), *Character Development in Schools and Beyond*, New York: Praeger

Ryan, K., and McLean. G.F. (eds) (1987), *Character Development in Schools and Beyond*, New York: Praeger

Ryan, K. (1989), 'In defence of character education', in L. Nucci, *Moral development and character education*: a dialogue, pp. 3–17, Berkley, CA: McCutchan

Ryan, K. and Bohlin. K.E. (1999), *Building Character in Schools*, San Francisco: Jossey-Bass Publishers

Ryle. G. (1975), 'Can virtue be taught?', in R.F. Dearden, P.H. Hirst and R.S. Peters (eds), *Education and the Development of Reason*, London: Routledge & Kegan Paul

Sacks, J. (1999), *Morals and Markets*, London: Institute of Economic Affairs

Sadler, M.E. (1908), *Moral Instruction and Training in Schools: Report of an International Inquiry*, 2 vols, London: Longmans, Green & Co

Sandin, R.T. (1992), *The Rehabilitation of Virtue*, New York: Praeger

Shields, D.L.L. and Bredemeier, B.J.L. (1995), *Character Development and Physical Activity*, Champaign, Il: Human Kinetics

Schoeman, F. (1987), *Responsibility, Character and the Emotions*, Cambridge: Cambridge University Press

Schools Curriculum and Assessment Authority (1996–1997), *National Forum for Values in Education and the Curriculum*, London: SCAA

Schubert, W.H. (1997), 'Character education from four perspectives on curriculum', in A. Molnar (ed.), *The Construction of Children's Character*, Chicago: National Society for the Study of Education

Schulman, M. and Mekler, E. (1994), *Bringing Up a Moral Child: A New Approach for Teaching Your Child to Be Kind, Just, and Responsible*, New York: Doubleday

Scott, D.A. (1991), *Christian Character: Jeremy Taylor and Christian Ethics Today*, Oxford: Latimer Studies No. 38

Scottish Office (1950), *Young Citizens at School*, Edinburgh: HM Stationary Office

Sherman, N. (1989), *The Fabric of Character: Aristotle's Theory of Virtue*, Oxford: Clarendon Press

Shipiro, D. (2000), *Dynamics of Character*, New York: Basic Books

Sichel, B. (1988), *Moral Education: Character, Community, and Ideals*, Philadelphia: Temple University Press

Simon, S., Howe L. and Kirschenbaum, H. (1972), *Values Clarification: A Handbook of Practical Strategies for Teachers and Students*, New York: Hart

Simpson, P. (1992), 'Virtue ethics and Aristotle', *Review of Metaphysics*, vol. 45: 3, pp. 503–524

Sisson, E.O. (1910), *The Essentials of Character: A Practical Study of the Aims of Moral Education*, New York: Macmillan

Skillen, T. (1997), 'Can virtue be taught – especially these days?', *Journal of Philosophy of Education*, vol. 31: 3, pp. 375–393

Slote, M. (1992), *From Morality to Virtue*, Oxford: Oxford University Press

Smetna, J.G. (1999), 'The role of parents in moral development: a social domain analysis', *Journal of Moral Education*, vol. 28: 3, pp. 311–321

Smiles, S. (1862), *Self-Help: With Illustrations of Character and Conduct*, London: Murray

Smith, A. (1759), *Theory of Moral Sentiments* (ed. D.D. Raphael and A. L. Macfie, 1976), Oxford: Clarendon Press

Smith, A. (1776), *An Inquiry into the Nature and Causes of the Wealth of Nations* (1993 selected edition, intro. K. Sutherland), Oxford: Oxford University Press

Smith, M. (1977), *Practical Guide to Values Clarification*, Oceanside, Cal: University Associates

Smith, R. (1997), 'Judgement day', in R. Smith and P. Standish (eds), *Teaching Right and Wrong: Moral Education in the Balance*, Stoke-on-Trent: Trentham Books

Snarey, J. and Pavkov, T. (1992), 'Moral character education in the United States: beyond socialisation versus development', in A. Garrod (ed.), *Learning for Life: Moral Education Theory and Practice*, Westport, Conn: Praeger

Sockett, H. (1993), *The Moral Base for Teacher Professionalism*, New York: Teachers College Press

Sockett, H. (1997), 'Chemistry or character?', in A. Molnar (ed.), *The Construction of Children's Character*, Chicago: National Society for the Study of Education

Soros, G. (1998), *The Crisis of Global Capitalism*, London: Little, Brown & Co

Spangler, M.M. (1983), *Principles of Education: A Study of Aristotelian Thomism Contrasted with Other Philosophies*, Lantham, MD: University of America Press

Spens Report (1938), Ministry of Education, *Report on Secondary Education*, London: HMSO

Starratt, R.J. (1994), *Building an Ethical School: A Practical Response to the Moral Crisis in Schools*, London: Falmer Press

Stenhouse, L. (1970), *The Humanities Curriculum Project*, London: Heinemann

Stenhouse, L. and Verma, G.K. (1981), 'Educational procedures and attitudinal objectives: a paradox', *Journal of Curriculum Studies*, vol. 13, pp. 329–337

Steutal, J. (1997), 'The virtue approach to moral education: some conceptual clarifications', *Journal of Philosophy of Education*, vol. 31: 3, pp. 395–407

Stewart, W.A.C. and McCann, W.P. (1967), *The Educational Innovators 1750–1880*, London: Macmillan

Straughan, R. (1982), *Can We Teach Children to Be Good?: Basic Issues in Moral, Personal and Social Education*, London: Allen & Unwin

Straughan, R. (1999), 'Weakness, wants and the will', in J.M. Halstead and T.H. McLaughlin (eds), *Education and Morality*, London: Routledge

Strike, K.A. (1982), *Educational Policy and the Just Society*, Urbana: University of Illinois Press

Strike, K.A. and Ternasky, P.L. (eds) (1993), *Ethics for Professionals in Education: Perspectives for Preparation and Practice*, New York: Teachers College Press

Sugarman, B. (1973), *The School and Moral Development*, London: Croom Helm

Sullivan, E.V., Beck, C., Joy, M. and Pagliuso, S. (1975), *Moral Learning*, Paramus: Paulist Press

Sullivan, E.V. (1977), 'A study of Kohlberg's structural theory of moral development: a critique of liberal social science ideology', *Human Development*, vol. 20, pp. 352–376

Tam, H. (ed.) (1996), *Punishment, Excuses and Moral Development*, Aldershot: Avebury

Tam, H. (1998), *Communitarianism: A New Agenda for Politics and Citizenship*, London: Macmillan

Tate, N. (1996), 'The role of the school in promoting moral, spiritual and cultural values', *Education Review*, vol. 10: 1, pp. 66–70

Taunton Commission (1868), *Schools Enquiry Commission*, London: HMSO

Thatcher, M. (1989), Address to the Scottish Kirk, in Rabin, J., *God, Man and Mrs Thatcher*, London: Chatto & Windus

Thomas, L. (1989), *Living Morally: A Psychology of Moral Character*, Philadelphia: Temple University Press

Tobin, B.M. (1989), 'Richard Peters' theory of moral development', *Journal of Philosophy of Education*, vol. 23: 1, pp. 15–27

Verbeke, G. (1990), *Moral Education in Aristotle*, Washington DC: Catholic University of America Press

Veritatis Splendor (1993), Encyclical of John Paul II, London: Catholic Truth Society

Vessells, G.G. (1998), *Character and Community Development*, Westpoint, Connecticut: Praeger

Vincent, P.F. (1996), *Promising Practices in Character Education: Nine Success Stories From Around the Country*, Chapel Hill, NC: Character Development Group

Vincent, P.F. (1999), *Rules and Procedures for Character Education*, Chapel Hill, NC: Character Development Publishing

Walberg, H. and Wynne, E. (1989), 'Character education: toward a preliminary consensus', in Nucci, L. *Moral development and character education: A dialogue*, pp. 19–36, Berkley, CA: McCutchan

Walford, G. and Pickering, W.S.F. (1998), *Durkheim and Modern Education*, London: Routledge

Walker, A.D.M. (1989), 'Virtue and character', *Philosophy*, vol. 64, pp. 349–362

Warnock, M. (1977), *Schools of Thought*, London: Faber

Watkinson, W.L. (1904), *The Education of the Heart: Brief Essays on Influences that Make for Character*, London: Charles H. Kelly

Webb, E. (1915), *Character and Intelligence, An Attempt at an Exact Study of Character*, Cambridge: Cambridge University Press

Wells, J. (1998), *Losing Our Virtue: The Way the Church Must Recover Its Moral Vision*, New York: Eerdmans

Wenham, J.G. (1892), *The School Manager*, London: St Anselm's Press

White, J. (1989), 'The aims of personal and social education', in P. White (ed.), *Personal and Social Education: Philosophical Perspectives*, The Bedford Way Series, London: Kogan Page

White, J. (1990), *Education and the Good Life: Beyond the National Curriculum*, London: Kogan Page

White, P. (1996), *Civic Virtues and Public Schooling: Educating Citizens for a Democratic Society*, London: Teachers College Press

Wicksteed, J.H. (1913), *Conduct and Character*, London: Nelson

Wilcox, B. (1997), 'Schooling, school improvement and the relevance of Alastair McIntyre', *Cambridge Journal of Education*, vol. 27: 2, pp. 241–260

Wiley, L.S. (1998), *Comprehensive Character-building Classroom: A Handbook for Teachers*. Manchester, NH: Character Development Foundation.

Wiley, L.S. (1998), *Comprehensive Character-Building Classroom*, Longwood, Florida: De Barry Publishing

Williams, M. and DeRoche, E. (1998), *Educating Hearts and Minds: A Comprehensive Character Education Framework*, USA: Corwin Press

Wilson, H. (1980), 'Parents can cut the crime rate', *New Society*, 4 December

Wilson, H.E. (1938), *Education for Citizenship*, New York and London: McGraw-Hill Book Co

Wilson, J. (1993), *Reflection and Practice: Teacher Education and the Teaching Profession*, University of Western Ontario: Althouse Press

Wilson, J.Q. (1985), 'The discovery of character: private virtue and public policy', *Public Interest*, vol. 81, pp. 3–16

Wilson, J.Q. (1993), *The Moral Sense*, New York: Free Press

Wilson, J.Q. (1995), *On Character: Essays by James Q. Wilson*, Washington DC: The AEI Press

Winch, C. (2000), *Education, Work and Social Capital*, London: Routledge

Wolfe, A. (2001), *Moral Freedom: The Search for Virtues in a World of Choice*, New York: W.W. Norton

Wolterstorff, N. (1980), *Educating for Responsible Action*, Grand Rapids, Mich: Eerdmans

Wright, D. (1971), *The Psychology of Moral Behaviour*, London: Penguin

Wringe, C. (1998), 'Reason, rules and virtues in moral education', *Journal of Philosophy of Education*, vol. 32: 2, pp. 225–237

Wringe, C. (2000), 'The diversity of moral education', *Journal of Philosophy of Education*, vol. 34: 4, pp. 659–672

Wynne, E. (1982), *Character Policy: An Emerging Issue*, Lantham, MD: University Press of America

Wynne, E. and Walberg, H. (1985), 'The complementary goals of character development and academic excellence', *Educational Leadership*, vol. 43: 4, pp. 15–18

Wynne, E. (1985/1986), 'The great traditions in education: transmitting moral values', *Educational Leadership*, vol. 45: 5, pp. 4–9

Wynne, E. (1986), 'Character development: renewing an old commitment', *Principal*, vol. 65: 3, pp. 28–31

Wynne, E. (1988), 'Balancing character development and academics in the elementary school'. *Phi Delta Kappan*, vol. 69: 6, pp. 424–426

Wynne, E. and Ryan, K. (1993), *Reclaiming Our Schools*, New York: Macmillan

Wynne, E. (1997a), 'For-character education', in A. Molnar (ed.), *The Construction of Children's Character*, Chicago: National Society for the Study of Education

Wynne, E. and Ryan, K. (1997b), *Reclaiming Our Schools: A Handbook on Teaching Character, Academics and Discipline*, New York: Merrill

Young, M. (1994), 'Change, British society and the family', in *Insights into Education and Training*, National Commission on Education, London: Heinemann

Index

Lightning Source UK Ltd.
Milton Keynes UK
UKHW02f0836140918
328870UK00008B/65/P